Amintaphil: The Philosophical Foundations of Law and Justice

Volume 11

Series Editors

Mortimer Sellers, University of Baltimore, Baltimore, MD, USA

Ann E. Cudd, Boston University, Boston, MA, USA

The *AMINTAPHIL book series* considers the philosophical foundations of law and justice from the perspectives of academic philosophy, practical political science and applied legal studies. The American Section of the International Association for the Philosophy of Law and Social Philosophy ("AMINTAPHIL") supervises the series, which dedicates each volume to the most pressing contemporary problems in legal theory and social justice. AMINTAPHIL holds biennial meetings of leading scholars in philosophy, law, and politics to discuss the philosophical basis of vital questions. The AMINTAPHIL volumes present the ultimate results of these discussions.

Joan McGregor • Mark C. Navin
Editors

Education, Inclusion, and Justice

 Springer

AMINTAPHIL

Editors
Joan McGregor
School of Historical, Philosophical, and
Religious Studies
Arizona State University
Tempe, AZ, USA

Mark C. Navin
Department of Philosophy
Oakland University
Rochester, MI, USA

ISSN 1873-877X   ISSN 2351-9851   (electronic)
Amintaphil: The Philosophical Foundations of Law and Justice
ISBN 978-3-031-04012-2   ISBN 978-3-031-04013-9   (eBook)
https://doi.org/10.1007/978-3-031-04013-9

This Springer imprint is published by the registered company Springer Nature Switzerland AG
The registered company address is: Gewerbestrasse 11, 6330 Cham, Switzerland

Contents

Introduction: Education, Inclusion, and Justice

Joan McGregor and Mark C. Navin

Abstract Education is a centrally important human good because it fosters the development of intellectual, moral and civic virtues necessary for a robust liberal democracy. Moreover, education is critical because it cultivates the development of valuable skills for work and for life. Accordingly, debates about justice, democracy, equality, and inclusion often focus on questions about the kinds of education people should receive, how scarce educational goods should be distributed, and the role of education in responding to historical and ongoing injustices. The 16 essays in this volume explore these kinds of pressing ethical, political, and legal issues from a range of interdisciplinary perspectives, including law, philosophy, and political science. They engage broadly with both core concepts and contemporary issues on topics including education justice, inclusive education, free speech, affirmative action, democratic citizenship, equal opportunity, and civility.

This volume is organized into six parts, and each part focuses on a different set of themes related to education, inclusion, and justice. The essays of Part I address the notion of inclusion in education. The essays of Part II focus on the grounding and basis for the universal right to education. The essays of Part III address what justice in education requires. The essays of Part IV focus on how universities and other educational institutions in society should respond to the history of institutional racism. The essays of Part V address the nature and desirability of civility, including its role in university education. Finally, the essays of Part VI focus on questions about the role of individual merit in university admission decisions.

J. McGregor (✉)
Arizona State University, School of Historical, Philosophical, and Religious Studies, Tempe, AZ, USA
e-mail: j.mcgregor@asu.edu

M. C. Navin
Oakland University, Department of Philosophy, Rochester, MI, USA
e-mail: navin@oakland.edu

1   Part I

The essays of Part I address the notion of inclusion in education. The central question is how to ensure that differently-abled students and students from a diversity of backgrounds, religions, and cultures can be included in the educational endeavor, so that they can become equal citizens in democratic societies. Professor Deen Chatterjee's "Tagore on Human Flourishing" discusses the important role that education can play in the promotion of human flourishing, especially in pluralistic societies. It focuses on the ideals and experiences of the great Indian polymath, Rabindranath Tagore (1861–1941), in the development of the experimental school he founded for girls and boys in rural Bengal, India, at the beginning of the twentieth century. Professor Chatterjee argues for the importance of local educational projects such as Tagore's for the cultivation of an egalitarian and cosmopolitan ethics. The example of Tagore's school illustrates how pedagogies based in reason and common interests can promote creative self-expression and thereby enhance human experience in diverse cultures. Such a model of education can prepare students to respect human rights and respond to human needs, in their own communities and beyond.

In "The 'Rights' Road to Inclusion: Disability Rights, Care, and Normalcy," Rachel Levit Ades identifies how primary and secondary schools socialize children to attitudes and behaviors about disability. Levit Ades argues that schools should focus their educational efforts around disability on the rights of disabled persons, rather than on their dependency or normalization. According to Levit Ades, many schools orient their education about disability around the idea that disabled people require care, or else schools fail to address disability at all, and make it invisible. This is wrong. Schools should focus neither on "caring for" the disabled nor on "normalizing" disability, but should instead prioritize the rights disabled people have to be fully included as equal participants in our shared social and political worlds. That is the kind of education about disability that a true commitment to democratic society requires.

2   Part II

The essays of Part II focus on the grounding and basis for the universal right to education, including how and whether democratic societies should fund private schooling. Professor Wade Robison argues, in "The Constitutional Right to an Education," that the right to education is implicit in the US Constitution, not as a consequence of any particular provision of that document, but based on the idea of democratic governance that the Constitution expresses. Professor Robison objects to attempts to defend a constitutional right to education as a consequence of other particular rights that the Constitution stipulates. For example, while the Constitution identifies a right to petition the government, and while people may need to be able to read and write in order to exercise this right, Professor Robison argues that the

Constitution actually defends a broader right to *education* than to *mere literacy*. Professor Robison argues that the way to argue for this right is not by piecemeal appeal to particular parts of the Constitution, but by a 'transcendental' argument that identifies a robustly educated population as a necessary condition for effective democratic government.

In "Pluralism, Diversity, and Choice: Problems with School Vouchers," Professor Emily Gill criticizes the expansion of 'school voucher' programs in many US states. A school voucher is a taxpayer-funded coupon that the government provides to parents to allow them to pay tuition and other fees at a school other than the public school that the student could have attended for free. Professor Gill argues that recent court cases, like *Espinoza v. Montana Department of Revenue*, which have upheld expansive school voucher programs, have troubling implications for state neutrality about religion. Professor Gill acknowledges that public schools cannot be neutral among all competing conceptions of the good, but she rejects the claim that school vouchers somehow correct for the sectarian values that public schools promote. Instead, she argues that school voucher programs promote a different and more troubling kind of nonneutrality than the one that public schools promote. However, Professor Gill concludes that, if US states are going to continue to endorse expansive school voucher programs, the private schools that receive voucher monies should be more accountable.

3 Part III

The essays of Part III address what justice in education requires, specifically for the inclusion of diverse groups in society and for ensuring equality of educational opportunity. Professor Columbus Ogbujah argues, in "Interculturality, Justice and Inclusion: Key Educational Values for a Pluralistic Society," that the strength of a nation depends on the educational standards it imposes in its schools. Whether a society grows or collapses depends on its schools, colleges, and universities because these are the social institutions that cultivate the skills and values of productive citizenship. Professor Ogbujah uses a case study of Nigeria to argue that many contemporary social and political problems have their origins in educational systems that are not oriented towards the public welfare, but which tolerate or encourage greed, unhealthy rivalries, and oppositional social relations. Professor Ogbujah argues that these kinds of failures in a country's educational system can contribute to broader forms of social injustice and that they encourage forms of cultural homogenization. Instead, countries should insist that their educational institutions promote intercultural dialogue, justice, and inclusion, which can promote the flourishing of pluralistic societies.

In "The Concept of Opportunity and the Ideal of Equality of Educational Opportunity," Professor Alistair MacLeod discusses the concept of opportunity and the contexts in which it makes sense to apply it. In doing so, Professor MacLeod lays the foundation for identifying an account of the diverse kinds of educational opportunities that societies may have good reasons to provide their members. Professor MacLeod attends, in particular, to a distinction between two different ideals of equal opportunity in education, one that affords the same opportunities to all, and one that applies only to sub-classes of the members of a society.

4 Part IV

The essays of Part IV focus on how universities and other educational institutions in society should respond to the history of institutional racism. These articles focus on efforts to *transition* towards greater educational justice. Regents' Professor Rebecca Tsosie describes what "institutional racism" means within public institutions of higher education. Many universities have adopted the framework of "diversity, equity and inclusion." realizing that framework is required for transformative change in higher education. Exactly how that is achieved is contested, however. The current debate about banning the teaching of "critical race theory" in educational institutions illustrates the contested nature of justice as regards to racial history. Professor Tsosie explores the need for recognition of the rights and experiences of distinctive groups as well as the epistemic forms of injustice that have been experienced by specific groups, including indigenous, Black, and Latinx peoples within nstitutions of higher education.

Professor Eric Smaw's chapter "Janus-Faced Affirmative Action: Restorative Justice and the Transition to a Just Society," reminds us of the deeply racist history of many of our most revered intellectuals and the role that racist views played in our history of education and employment. He argues for backward-looking and forward-looking affirmative action policies in education and employment. Professor Smaw engages the criticism of affirmative action programs offered by Richard Herrnstein and Charles Murray, Nicholas Capaldi, and Carl Cohen. Finding those objections without merit, and since there has continued to be state-based discrimination against African Americans, he argues that affirmative action is warranted as a redress to those injustices. Furthermore, in order to move to a just society, we need to rectify for those past injustices. He calls this conception of affirmative action Janus-faced because it is backward-looking and forward-looking simultaneously.

The final paper in this section by Professor Laurence Houlgate is "Three Responses to Racism and Systemic Racism: Therapy, Punishment, and Education." In this chapter Professor Houlgate asks what roles the responses of therapy, punishment, and education to racism should play in a pluralistic democracy that has a long history of bigotry, racism, and systemic (institutional) racism. In other words, what does justice require of any public response to racism and systemic racism? He considers these three responses to both racism and systemic racism. First, Professor Houlgate considers whether therapy which has been viewed favorable in recent years is an appropriate response to racism. Hundreds of legislators, governors, and mayors, under the banner, "Systemic racism is a public health crisis," have advocated for this approach. Professor Houlgate's analysis of the concept of therapy shows that it has implications that are unacceptable in a liberal-democratic society. Racism is not a disease, nor is it a symptom of a disease. It does not make racists candidates for cures created and administered by public health therapists. Secondly, he considers punishment as a response to racism and find it wanting as well. The concept of punishment implies the existence of a transgressor who violates the law. But racist thoughts and expressions do not violate valid laws in constitutional democracies. It is not a crime to be a racist unless the racist behavior is harmful to others. At the same time, Houlgate acknowledges that punishment is a justifiable response to *systemic* racism because such institutional systems can and often do violate contemporary valid laws. Finally, he considers the concept of education as a response to racism and finds that education as a response to racism avoids the unacceptable implications of therapy and punishment. Education does not assume that racism is a symptom of a disease, nor does it assume that racism violates valid laws. An analysis of the concept of education shows it to be a voluntary relationship between students and teachers in which students are at liberty to retain or give up their prejudicial opinions. If responsive education succeeds in an effort to eliminate or mitigate racism, then this might eventually have the side effect of abolishing all systemic racism.

5 Part V

The essays of Part V address the nature and desirability of civility, including the role of civility—and of *educating* for civility—in university education. Professor Robert Boatright in "Three Arguments for Incivility" argues that the idea that we should be civil to each other is being challenged in the current American political climate, and in particular in higher education. Are calls of civility, as suggested by some, a means of stifling dissent? Others contend, according to Professor Boatright, that uncivil acts by political leaders necessitate an uncivil response not civility. In this chapter, he argues that much of the contemporary debate over civility rests on a disagreement about what civility is. Boatright supports his argument by drawing upon Michael Oakeshott's *On Human Conduct,* where Oakeshott defines civil association as a state of voluntary equality within a particular group or society. This theory holds that civility is not a moral condition or imperative—that is, it is not something we "should" be. Instead, it is something that we are under certain circumstances. Incivility, on this account, is a denial that we are engaged in any sort of shared enterprise or have a shared set of facts or reference points. Civility is best achieved not when we call for it, but when we refer to community or to other values.

In Professor Joan McGregor's "Moral Capital, Civic Grace, and the Role of Education" she explores the notion of 'moral capital' and its role in well-functioning society. In the current society, even before the andemic of 2020–21 and racial reckoning in America, we found ourselves in a place where social norms are flaunted by our leaders, by television and radio personalities, on social media, and generally deteriorating throughout the society. This chapter explores the notion of moral capital, as that set of shared values, virtue, norms and practices, and the role it plays in flourishing societies. McGregor argues that there has been a deterioration of our nation's moral capital, which includes disregarding social practices that make a democracy work—e. g., tolerance of differences of opinions, open rational discussion and debate, reliance on empirical data—is exhibited in the behavior of both the right and the left. And finally, McGregor argues for the important role that higher education plays in supporting moral capital through cultivating the virtues of civility, civic grace, and the epistemic virtues.

6 Part VI

The essays of Part VI focus on questions about the role of individual merit in university admission decisions. Professor Ann Cudd in "'Merit' in University Admissions" challenges the preeminence of merit in university admissions, and she argues that there are reasons to doubt that individual merit is the best way to achieve the social goals of higher education. The mission of universities, according to Cudd, is primarily to create new knowledge, educate individuals, and serve society through related activities and products. Most universities are highly subsidized by their state and national governments. Higher education confers great benefits on students, especially those who attain credentials through the completion of degree and certificate programs. Beyond the intrinsic rewards of education, attaining a degree from an accredited university unlocks economic opportunity and enhances social status. Universities themselves are highly stratified by their status and quality, and the more elite the institution, she argues, the greater the social benefits that are conferred with its degree, both to society and to individuals. Given the lifelong benefits that are conferred upon those who receive a college degree for elite institutions and the governmental support of those institutions, Cudd argues against the traditional merit-based admission standards which favor some groups at the exclusion of others.

This section also includes a set of critical commentaries on Cudd's contribution, as well as a rejoinder from Cudd. In Richard Barron Parker's "An Alternative to "Merit" in University Admissions: A Comment on the paper of Ann E. Cudd" he agrees with Cudd's argument that "access inequality" to higher education in America is so severe that higher education itself "is a source of inequality in America." Moreover, he worries that the United States is in danger of going the way of Japan, England, and France where admission to the University of Tokyo, Oxford or Cambridge, or the École nationale d'administration is a prerequisite for holding high political office. Furthermore, Professor Parker agrees that any individual merit standard for university admission cannot be the basis for a fair and just system of university admissions. Cudd suggests instead a system which emphasizes diversity and looks at what the applicant can contribute to the group rather than whether or not the applicant's individual talents merit admission. Parker points to a problem with Cudd's proposal is that the ability to contribute to the group is just another sort of individual "merit." Sorting out the individuals who have the ability to "improve the excellence of the group as a whole" would require the same huge cast of admissions officers and consequent expense that now burden universities. It is easy to foresee disputes about how to determine which applicants deserve "diversity bonuses" similar to disputes over which tests should be used to determine individual "merit" under the old systems.

Another challenge to Cudd's proposal comes for Richard De George in "Collective Merit in University Admissions." In his paper, he argues that Cudd's proposal for a new system of admission goes far beyond the issue of fairness in admissions, and her model proposes a purpose of the university different from the traditional one and a radical change in the nature of the university in order to achieve more inclusive diversity. Access equality is to be achieved by building inclusive diversity into the outcome of the admissions process, according to De George. Whereas Cudd's model makes equal results replace equal access, and the change, De George argues, leads to a very different, vague and questionable notion of excellence from the one of individual merit.

In Leslie and John Francis' commentary on Cudd's paper they raise concerns about her positive account of "merit" as a group-based characteristic. In "'Merit' in University Admissions," Cudd explores the interface between inequality of access to higher education and "merit" as a criterion for admission. Her aim is to reconceptualize merit in a way that preserves selectivity while addressing inequality. Reconceptualizing "merit" as "collective" merit, she thinks, can justify differential admissions standards in light of the goals of higher education. Professors Leslie and John Francis agree with Cudd that there are many problems with how "merit" is understood in current admissions priorities and the measurements used to try to implement these priorities. Nevertheless, they raise concerns about her positive account of "merit" as a group-based characteristic. Their argument is that her claims about the relationship between diversity and merit are conceptual and rooted in ideal theory, rather than in the functioning of actual universities in the not-very-just circumstances of the United States today.

In the final commentary, Professor Alistair M. Macleod, though he finds her arguments about the merit system persuasive, he suggests that Cudd's argument have a *number* of puzzling features. They are, according to MacLeod (1) How Cudd's claim that "unequal access" to institutions of "higher education" is an ineliminable feature of defensible admissions policies to be squared with her recognition that the social goals universities must pursue include the provision of the kinds of general education needed—and needed equally—by all the members of a society? (2) Why does Cudd think that cultivation of (what she calls) a "growth mindset" in all the members of a society would be desirable? (3) What is the rationale for Cudd's attempt to link a university's pursuit of the goal of "inclusive diversity" with endorsement of (a collective version of) a merit-based admissions policy?

And finally, Professor Cudd responds to the commentaries to "Merit in University Admissions." Cudd acknowledges that the commentaries raise several important objections to the notion of collective merit and how it could be used in university admissions processes. This rejoinder provides her with the opportunity to clarify her critique of the way individual merit is currently used in university admissions and her idea of collective merit.

Part I
Inclusion, Justice, and Education

Education, Inclusion, and Identity

Tagore on Human Flourishing

Deen Chatterjee

Abstract This essay explores the role of education for human flourishing in a pluralistic society. It illustrates how local projects with global vision, when founded on reason and common interests and put into practice for promoting creative self-expression, can enhance the human experience across cultures and respond well to broader human needs and rights. I will focus on the innovative educational experiment initiated by the great educational reformer Rabindranath Tagore (1861–1941) at his school for girls and boys in rural Bengal, India, at the beginning of the twentieth century.

1 Introduction

This essay explores the role of education for human flourishing in a pluralistic society. It illustrates how local projects with global vision, when founded on reason and common interests and put into practice for promoting creative self-expression, can enhance the human experience across cultures and respond well to broader human needs and rights. I will focus on the innovative educational experiment initiated by the great educational reformer Rabindranath Tagore (1861–1941) at his school for girls and boys in rural Bengal, India, at the beginning of the twentieth century.

Amartya Sen, who had his early education at the school, writes:

The essay is based on an international conference on Tagore's Philosophy of Education that I co-directed with Martha Nussbaum on March 29–30, 2006 (https://app.box.com/s/ya70siyift0 7nm00rdde).
Amartya Sen and Kathleen O'Connell were two of the participants. In the essay I draw on Sen's, O'Connell's, and Nussbaum's writings on issues that were featured in the conference. I thank Uma Das Gupta, also a participant in the conference, for her help with historical and biographical references.

D. Chatterjee (✉)
University of Utah, Salt Lake City, UT, USA
e-mail: deen.chatterjee@law.utah.edu

© The Author(s), under exclusive license to Springer Nature Switzerland AG 2022   11
J. McGregor, M. C. Navin (eds.), *Education, Inclusion, and Justice*, Amintaphil:
The Philosophical Foundations of Law and Justice 11,
https://doi.org/10.1007/978-3-031-04013-9_2

Most of [Tagore's] work was written at Santiniketan (Abode of Peace), the small town that grew around the school he founded in Bengal in 1901. He not only conceived there an imaginative and innovative system of education ... but, through his writings and his influence on students and teachers, he was able to use the school as a base from which he could take a major part in India's social, political, and cultural movements.[1]

Martha Nussbaum—a great admirer of Tagore—writes:

Santiniketan was only one school in one region. It became world-famous, inspiring imitators in many countries, and attracting pupils from all over India [and the world].[2]

Tagore's vision was similar to John Dewey's idea that democracy, education, and good citizenship are inextricably intertwined and that there is an organic connection between education and personal experience. But Tagore's project went beyond Dewey's in its global vision, which features a far-reaching social justice and human rights arc. What was remarkable about Tagore was that as patriotic as he was in his quest to liberate India from the British subjugation, he was not a nationalist nor did he consider the Brits as his (or India's) enemies. Being a global-humanist and being ever mindful of the fluidity and contestability of cultures and identity, he went beyond the confinements of national borders as he embraced the universal mandate of broader humanity in responding to people's needs and interests at the grassroots level.

All these values featured centrally in Tagore's innovative take on liberal education that he implemented in his school for girls and boys well over a century ago. These ideas have profound implications for contemporary education in responding to the imperatives of justice, inclusion, and human flourishing in a liberal democracy.

2 Tagore's School

A global network of pioneering educators such as Jean-Jacques Rousseau, Jean Piaget, Johan Pestalozzi, Maria Montessori, and John Dewey has been influential in shaping the modern foundation of liberal education. But it was Rabindranath Tagore—the great Indian poet, novelist, educator, composer, painter, social reformer, and Nobel Laureate—who offered the most innovative vision of how best to educate the whole child. For Tagore, the cultivation of the artistic and the imaginative side of a child's personality should be given as much attention as the intellect in a child's education. Accordingly, in Tagore's school, music, art, dance, drama, and nature studies were an integral part of the curriculum for fostering a sense of empathy, wonder, and interconnectedness with the surrounding world. Set on an idyllic campus in rural Bengal, classes in the school were held outdoors under trees

---

[1] Sen (2005), pp. 90–91.
[2] Nussbaum (2013), p. 99.

for better communion with nature (except during rain or when using a laboratory).[3] It is through this playful engagement with the arts and nature, along with the basics in the sciences and the humanities, that a child can joyously develop his or her highest potential.

In exploring Tagore's contribution to education, Kathleen M. O'Connell writes:

> One...characteristic which sets Rabindranath's educational theory apart is his approach to education as a poet. He states in his essay, "A Poet's School," that in starting his school, he hoped to create a poem "in a medium other than words.".... It was this poetic vision which enabled him to fashion a scheme of education which was all inclusive, and to devise a unique program for education in nature and creative self-expression in a learning climate which was congenial to global cultural exchange.[4]

This is holistic education at its best, put into practice in a most creative way to synchronize the diverse aspirations of human personality. For Tagore, academic quest was not a narrow and one-dimensional pursuit detached from the rest of one's life—it was a living, multi-dimensional adventure meant to enrich all aspects of one's life. A rebel at heart and a non-conformist even as a young boy, Tagore persuaded his elders to take him out of formal schooling at the age of 13 because he felt it was too narrow and dry for him, set within the stifling confines of four walls. He did not graduate from any school or college. The co-educational school he founded was his own vision of education put into practice.

In Tagore's school, it was important that the teacher not only make lessons relevant to the lives of the students, but that the teacher should help students develop curiosity, imagination, empathy, and critical thinking—attributes that Tagore believed were essential for the flourishing of a student's mind.[5] For Tagore, these and similar traits were to be cultivated early in a student's life in primary and secondary education so that the student can be adequately prepared not only for college but for responsible citizenship in a global world. With an emphasis on education's local roots and global outreach, Tagore's project went a step beyond Dewey's educational vision of a healthy democracy as an engaged community of empowered individuals.

Tagore's philosophy of education has much broader implications than just education for children. Effective implementation of Tagore's ideals would call for reform of the primary and secondary school curriculum as well as a radical re-thinking of the goals of institutions of higher learning.[6] Along that line, what started as a small school in 1901 evolved into an international university by 1921. Tagore's chosen name of the university, *Visva-Bharati* (India and the World), with a

---

[3] Often during rain, students would join their teachers to hike in the countryside. Far from being viewed as disruptions, these breaks gave the students yet another outlet for a joyous celebration of their presence in nature.

[4] O'Connell (2002), p. 261. See also Tagore's essay, "My School," in Tagore (1917).

[5] O'Connell notes: "In fact, these are the same essentials that are being emphasized by some of today's most innovative thinkers." O'Connell (2003), p. 81.

[6] Professor Alistair MacLeod highlighted this point in commenting on an earlier draft of my essay.

motto of *Yatra Visvam Bhavatyeka Nidam* (Where the World Finds Its Nest),
indicates a focus on promoting a creative synthesis among the various cultures of
the world. Tagore himself put it this way in 1927: "...I have formed the nucleus of
an International University in India, as one of the best means of promoting mutual
understanding between the East and the West."[7]

Tagore's global vision behind his educational philosophy was equally matched
by his attempt to motivate the marginalized rural and tribal communities around the
university to economic self-sufficiency. For that, he set up a nearby Institute for
Rural Reconstruction in 1922 as a wing of his Visva-Bharati International University
for promoting agricultural economy and rural upliftment.[8] The Institute also helped
broaden the school curriculum by offering students on-site lessons on handicrafts
such as carpentry and pottery.

As much as Tagore admired the Western Enlightenment ideas, he saw that the
Eurocentric education in colonial India was not suited to proper human flourishing
for the students.[9] For a broad, diverse, and well-rounded education, he made efforts
to see that students' education was firmly rooted in Indian history and culture as well
as in the Asian heritage, while simultaneously pursuing relevant knowledge and
wisdom gathered from all corners of the world. This led to "the creation of a school
and university that became world-famous exemplars of arts-oriented democratic
education."[10] Over the years they produced some of the world's best-known thought
leaders and democratic stalwarts, as well as preeminent talents in arts, the social
sciences, and literature.

After Tagore's passing in 1941 and soon after India's independence from the
British rule, the university was given the status of a central research university in
1951 by an act of the Indian Parliament, with the provision of the prime minister of
India as its ex officio chancellor.

3   Reason and Imagination

There are many interwoven threads in Tagore's philosophy of education, but for this
essay I am focusing on those that are especially relevant for the imperatives of
inclusion, identity, and diversity in a liberal democracy.

The idea of inclusion in a liberal democracy requires a proper understanding of
the relationship between relativism and pluralism, especially value pluralism.
Rejecting relativism is not inconsistent with endorsing pluralism. Value pluralism
rejects the outright endorsement of anything and everything of value in the name of

---

[7] Tagore (1927), p. 202.

[8] For more on this, see Das Gupta (2021).

[9] Tagore's school is often heralded as one of the early experiments in decolonization. For that to
succeed, as Tagore saw it, students needed to decolonize their own thinking first.

[10] Nussbaum (2013), p. 87.

cultural practices, and likewise, it is skeptical of denigration of cultural practices per se.[11] Sorting out the right balance is not easy. It requires a delicate blend of reason and imagination that takes time to cultivate and must be started at an early stage in one's life.

In Tagore's school, critical thinking was a prized value in a student's education, and independence of mind and questioning of conventions were strongly encouraged. Amartya Sen notes: "Rabindranath insisted on open debate on every issue, and distrusted conclusions based on a mechanical formula . . . It is in the sovereignty of reasoning—fearless reasoning in freedom— that we can find Rabindranath Tagore's lasting voice."[12] But at the same time, Tagore's educational philosophy was rooted in the belief that a flourishing life is one that has room for play, exuberance, and imagination, which take us beyond mere acceptance of difference in favor of a joyous celebration of diversity, as well as beyond the static comfort of our daily routines to the boundless wonder of the great unknown. Satyajit Ray—the celebrated film director who got his art degree from Tagore's university—has noted that even in Tagore's paintings, "the mood evoked. . .is one of a joyous freedom."[13] This blend between "fearless reasoning" and "joyous freedom" was Tagore's recipe for a flourishing life for his students at the school.

Tagore showed us that we can nurture a global vision of shared humanity while being responsive to cultural complexities and differences. A leading critic of culture, Tagore was also a passionate global citizen who embraced the best in all cultures. This delicate balancing act is still a prized challenge in today's liberal democracy,[14] but it is truly remarkable that Tagore not only imbibed it himself but effectively put the idea in practice in his school over a century ago in a remote corner of Bengal, India! Far from being a democracy, India at that time was under colonial subjugation in the heyday of the British empire.

Tagore was deeply committed to the ideal that boundaries and differences that create barriers to our common humanity are to be transcended in favor of a joyous engagement with the global world. Turning tolerance of difference into celebration of diversity was Tagore's message of multiculturalism where cultural differences are not viewed as divides. Tagore's educational experiment reflected this ideal.

Tagore's call for unity and engagement was not a plea for uniformity. In the introduction of his book *Creative Unity*, he wrote:

---

[11] For more on this, see Chatterjee (2012).

[12] Sen (2005), pp. 119–120.

[13] Ray (1989), quoted in Sen (2005), p. 98.

[14] Here is an example of how a leading liberal democracy can still find it a challenge to pursue this balancing act. In 2011, the then British Prime Minister David Cameron announced in a speech to the annual Munich Security Conference of world leaders that multiculturalism had failed in his country. "Frankly, we need a lot less of the passive tolerance of recent years and much more active, muscular liberalism." (*The Times*, London, February 5, 2011, p. 15) Tagore's advice to Cameron would have been that we need to go beyond both the "passive tolerance" of benign neglect and the "muscular liberalism" of confronting the illiberal other. A viable project of multiculturalism must adequately articulate its professed claims of pluralism and inclusion.

> It is some untold mystery of unity in me, that has the simplicity of the infinite and reduces the immense mass of multitude to a single point. This One in me knows the universe of the many. ...This One in me is creative. Its creations are a pastime, through which it gives expression to an ideal unity in its endless show of variety.

> ... This One in me not only seeks unity in knowledge...; it also seeks union in love for its fulfilment. It seeks itself in others. ... To give perfect expression to the One, the Infinite, through the harmony of the many ... is the object alike of our individual life and our society.[15]

This poetic and mystical vision of unity in diversity lies at the core of Tagore's philosophy of education that he implemented at the school and that finds its expression in his message of pluralism and inclusion. Along with an emphasis on reasoning and critical discourse, the values of empathy, imagination, and wonder were ingrained in the school curriculum and exemplified by the remarkable teachers, scholars, and thought-leaders who were drawn to Tagore and his school from all over the world.[16]

4   Culture and Diversity

Tagore's promotion of cross-cultural understanding has important implications for rights and justice in a liberal democracy. The liberal tradition has often been challenged for being insensitive to claims of culture as well as for providing the rationale for imperialism rooted in the liberal assumptions about reason and historical progress. In other words, the tradition that supposedly champions diversity has been critiqued for displaying an uneasy commitment to pluralism.[17] Central to this tension between liberalism and pluralism are the competing rights of the individual and the group or culture to which the individual belongs, as enshrined respectively in Articles 3 and 22 of the Universal Declaration of Human Rights (UDHR). Individual and group rights are in a dynamic tension, leading to the dilemma of conflicting equalities for liberalism.

Although Tagore was not a vocal defender of group rights per se, he was sensitive to the cultural issues and has drawn attention to the complexity of group allegiance. The focus on artistic instruction at the school promoted cross-cultural experience and understanding, along with giving education a global perspective, since "works of art

---

[15]Tagore (1922), pp. v–vi.

[16]The university also drew a steady stream of distinguished foreign dignitaries. For instance, the famed Chinese Studies Institute at the university attracted General Chiang Kai-sheck and Premier Chou En-lai. Tagore's ideals of human dignity and shared humanity brought Eleanor Roosevelt to the university soon after her leadership role in the adoption of the landmark Universal Declaration of Human Rights at the United Nations in 1948.

[17]For more on this, see Chatterjee (2013).

are frequently an invaluable way of beginning to understand the achievements and sufferings of a culture or group different from one's own."[18]

Tagore took pride in his cultural heritage, yet he cautioned people not to use the rigid identities of culture and religion as a wedge in their common pursuit of justice and human dignity. Fragility of categories tells us that issues are more fluid and complex than we are prone to acknowledge. Accordingly, Tagore would like us to focus on the substantive issues of interdependence confronting our common humanity, regardless of groups and cultures, while at the same time he embraced the best in all cultures.

We find a nod to this idea in Amartya Sen's Nobel biography. Sen, a fellow Nobel Laureate from Tagore's native Bengal, writes:

> I remember being quite struck by Rabindranath Tagore's approach to cultural diversity in the world (well reflected in our curriculum), which he had expressed in a letter to a friend: "Whatever we understand and enjoy in human products instantly becomes ours, wherever they might have their origin . . . . Let me feel with unalloyed gladness that all the great glories of man are mine." ("Amartya Sen—biography," Nobelprize.org)[19]

Culture and religion are intertwined in a complex web of myth and reality. To adequately understand culture, one must discern religion. Without a proper understanding of each, no social, economic, or political empowerment of individuals or groups can take place. Tagore, who was a great admirer of Buddha's deep and abiding humanism, had a radical take on religion. Being a global humanist who was wary of misleading categories that demonize the so-called other, Tagore did not engage in the divisive rhetoric of the sacred and the profane that is at the heart of some major religions, especially those in the Abrahamic tradition. Drawing instead from the more inclusive Indian tradition, he championed the idea of the *secular as sacred* in his educational experiments and social activism. Rising above religious sectarianism, this holistic vision played a central role in the school's educational experiment of fostering a spirit of inclusion and acceptance. Martha Nussbaum calls this vision "humanism of the future,"[20] well reflected in "Tagore's development of a universalistic 'religion of man'."[21]

---

[18] Nussbaum (2009), p. 58.

[19] In his 2021 book Home in the World: A Memoir, Sen has aptly called Tagore's school "School Without Walls," which indicates not only that the classes were held outdoors, but that the school stood for transcending divides and boundaries (Sen 2021).

[20] Nussbaum (2013), p. 87.

[21] Nussbaum (2009), p. 56. See also Tagore (1931b).

5 Inclusion, Identity, and Democracy

Ingrained in Tagore's global vison is the universal mandate of a broader humanity that makes room for multifaceted and overlapping identities of individuals and groups. In recent days Amartya Sen has shown us how the exclusivity of any singular identity can lead to confrontation and violence.[22] Like Tagore, Sen is well-known for drawing attention to the multiple identities of human beings across the world, and he, like Tagore, sees no reason why national, group, or cultural divisions should have any automatic, hence undue, priority over other categorizations. Both for Tagore and Sen, the narrow conundrum of conflicting loyalties need not be an irreconcilable dilemma because cultural or political divides should not be viewed as conflicting loyalties but rather as nested multiple loyalties. Claims of culture or allegiance to specific political communities may sometimes compete with wider objects of loyalty such as human solidarity, but nested multiple loyalties, like our plurality of identities, is a challenge that we negotiate all the time.[23]

Tagore's vision and Sen's take on it have an important bearing on today's identity politics in a liberal democracy. The prime source of conflict between the proponents of multiculturalism and nativist populism on issues of identity revolves around the cherished liberal idea, articulated by John Rawls (among others), that an impartial liberal theory of justice need not be incompatible with distinct principles of affirmative equality with regard to minority groups, within reason, of course. This idea helps liberals justify minority accommodation in a pluralistic liberal democracy. But this leaves both sides—the multiculturalists and the populists—unhappy, with complaint of tokenism on one side and that of over-catering to the minorities on the other, leading to simmering anger rooted in experience of powerlessness on both sides.[24] This distrust creates a barrier to dialogue and deliberation as a means of negotiating claims of culture and identity both within and among groups. It makes pluralism—the hallmark of liberal democracy—an elusive goal.

To make democracy truly pluralistic and participatory, we need community engagement and collective action. We need to reach out to real people in real terms in all groups to help them out of their "boxed" identities and connect them with larger movements, causes, and concerns. We need to show them that our identities are not "fixed"—we are bearers of multiple and overlapping identities. This is empowerment via solidarity by reaching out and joining hands. This is community action at its best. It emboldens democracy by making it truly participatory.

Tagore himself was a great icon of community empowerment through his writings and the imaginative educational philosophy put in practice at his school. A leading figure in India's social, cultural, and political movements, Tagore was called

---

[22] Sen (2006).

[23] For more on the idea of nested multiple loyalties and how it relates to various strands of nationalism, see Oldenquist (2008).

[24] Cf. Fukuyama (2018), Nussbaum (2018).

India's guru (Gurudev) by Mahatma Gandhi. Tagore, along with Gandhi and others, was a leading visionary in the founding of modern independent India, though Tagore died a few years before India's independence in 1947.[25] By reaching out to all groups across the myriad divides of wealth, power, religion, caste, and creed, their collective community action emboldened the masses and united people in their quest for freedom from social oppression at home and colonial subjugation from abroad.

The India that emerged at independence and that carried Tagore and Gandhi's legacy for the next 50 years was a leading exemplar of a secular, liberal, and pluralistic democracy in the world—an astonishing feat for a country struggling to establish itself from the ruined ashes of the centuries-long colonial exploitation. This is what historian E.P. Thomson wrote about post-independence India:

> All the convergent influences of the world run through this society: Hindu, Moslem, Christian, secular; Stalinist, liberal, Maoist, democratic socialist, Gandhian. There is not a thought that is being thought in the West or East that is not active in some Indian mind.[26]

If Tagore were alive today, he would have been appalled to see how the current trend in India's national politics has taken his vision of a democratic India from liberal pluralism to illiberal (Hindu) majoritarianism. This populist surge leading to the disfiguring of modern liberal democracies is happening all around the world today, making the need for a revival of Tagore's vision all the more urgent.

6 Women's Empowerment

Tagore's educational experiment was especially mindful of empowerment of girls and women.

Martha Nussbaum writes:

> Tagore gave his pupils a paradigm of free citizenship [long before India's independence] that they never forgot. .... Students realized this paradigm in their own individual ways, in their own gestures of insubordination and their own distinctive forms of creative joy. And because in Tagore's view a deformed conception of masculinity lay at the heart of oppression, both internal and external, the key agents in the creative transformation of society were ... women.[27]

Tagore put a great emphasis on dance and songs for infusing education with passion and delight.

Nussbaum writes:

> The arts are also crucial sources of both freedom and community. When people put on a play together, they have to learn to go beyond tradition and authority if they are going to express

---

[25] Despite their differences on issues such as tradition and modernity, faith and reason, Gandhi was deeply reverential toward Tagore and held his school in high esteem. He visited Tagore at the school several times, often referring to these visits as a "pilgrimage."

[26] Tharoor (1997), p. 9, quoted in Sen (1997), p. 61.

[27] Nussbaum (2013), p. 109.

themselves well. And the sort of community created by the arts is non-hierarchical, a valuable model of the responsiveness and interactivity that a good democracy will also foster in its political processes.[28]

Along with passion and delight, performing in dance dramas gave girl students a new sense of freedom and defiance. Both girls and boys performed together, and often Tagore himself would play a role with them, which they would find inspiring. What is most noteworthy is that Tagore would often assign women to play men's roles—something rather rare until recently anywhere in the world! Also, even in those early days, girl students were instructed in martial arts and they took part in games and sports along with the boys.

The school had yet another unique distinction. Over the years the students were inducted into the practical domain of managing and governing their non-academic affairs. In an election-based democratic process, female students competed shoulder-to-shoulder with their male counterparts and got elected to various leadership roles in the administrative units of the school. Tagore's guidance and inspiration made possible such practical display of democratic self-governance and women's empowerment.[29]

I would like to illustrate this point of women's empowerment in Tagore's education with the example of one student in particular. She is the shy girl in the photo below with her eyes cast down, standing to the left of Tagore nearly 90 years ago on the school campus (see picture 1).

---

[28] Nussbaum (2009), p. 58. Ken Robinson, who preached creativity in teaching and who died recently, echoed Tagore's vision when he said that dance is just as important as math. Robinson was a dynamic and influential proponent of stimulating the creativity of students that he thought is too often squelched by schools in the service of conformity. See Robinson (2001).

[29] I thank Abhijit Chatterjee, a former student at the school, for drawing my attention to this point.

Later in her life this shy girl became the longest-running prime minister of the largest democracy in the world! As India's prime minister, Indira Gandhi was the chief architect of the liberation of East Pakistan from the genocidal oppressive yoke of West Pakistan in 1971. Defying warnings from the United States, which was supporting the dictatorial regime of West Pakistan, India's military intervention and humanitarian help in East Pakistan led to the birth of independent democratic Bangladesh, which has had women as prime ministers and opposition leaders almost all through its history. India's military incursion into East Pakistan has been hailed as one of the two shining examples of commendable foreign interventions in recent times.[30]

What is more, thanks to Indira Gandhi's judicious leadership, more than ten million refugees from East Pakistan were allowed to enter India during the war, and within two months after the war ended, nearly seven million of them went back to liberated Bangladesh. The repatriation was funded by India and coordinated with various international relief agencies and the newly formed Bangladeshi government. The remaining refugees were granted asylum in India— a rare story of exemplary refugee resettlement and repatriation in today's troubled world!

But the amazing tale of courage and democratic leadership of the shy girl in Tagore's school goes much further. One of the core teachings of the school was to go beyond the barriers of group and cultural identities for the common pursuit of human

---

[30] The other commendable example was Vietnam's intervention in Cambodia in 1978 to remove Pol Pot.

dignity. Indira Gandhi took the lesson to heart and made the point vivid to the Indian people and the world by sacrificing her life for it. She was gunned down by two of her own bodyguards—both Sikhs—in the garden of her prime minister's residence in 1984. Defying all advice to not have any Sikhs in her private security because they might pose a threat to her life, she allowed the two men to come back to her security team after they took time off to visit their Sikh community in Punjab.[31]

At that time, the radicals in the Sikh community in Punjab took a vow to assassinate Indira Gandhi because of what they perceived as her grave violation of the sanctity of the holiest of their holy shrines—the Golden Temple of Amritsar in Punjab—when she ordered troops to enter the temple to flush out the leaders of the Sikh militants who were causing mayhem in Punjab and who were hiding in the temple as their last resort to evade the law. She took such a measure after exhausting all peaceful options left at her disposal.

Indira Gandhi did not abide by the advice of her security officials that the two Sikh men could have been radicalized during their time off in Punjab. Sacrificing her own life for the noble cause of putting individuals over their group identities, Indira Gandhi took Tagore's teachings to a new height.

7   Patriotism and Global Citizenship

For Tagore, the path to responsible global citizenship starts early in life. Tagore did not want his students to live in a bubble. He wanted them to expand their vision and inject a global consciousness in their studies and personal endeavors. As much as he was against letting the narrow divides of everyday politics enter the school, he made every effort to see that his uplifting message of hope and refuge in humanity formed the very core of his educational mission and permeated all aspects of the daily lives of the students.[32] Through their literary and artistic programs every week at all levels, as well as through dance, music, and nature studies—along with their studies of humanities and basic sciences—students were imbued with a sense of joy in their daily activities.[33] All this thrived in the simple life that students had in the natural surroundings of the school. The idea was to live simply and think big.

Eschewing the blind euphoria of super-patriotism, which is parochial, tribal, and anti-global, Tagore famously declared: "The God of humanity has arrived at the gates of the ruined temple of the tribe."[34] Repudiation of tribalism requires that we

---

[31] The Sikh religious communities in India and abroad are known for their long history of exemplary community services, including supporting victims of natural disasters and, during the coronavirus pandemic, organizing food drives and grocery delivery for older people.

[32] Ana Jelnikar notes: "[Tagore] stressed the need to understand local problems in a global perspective and seek solutions in worldwide cooperation." Jelnikar (2011), pp. 1051–1052.

[33] Amita Sen, a notable alumna of Tagore's school, puts all this well in her biography titled Joy in All Work (1999).

[34] Tagore (1931b), p. 162.

move beyond conventional patriotism that tends to degenerate into nationalism. Fervent nationalism does not carry democratic legitimacy in a global world where countries must display a shared effort toward a common good. In his lectures on nationalism in the United States, China, and Japan, as well as in his writings and speeches in India, Tagore's message has been to "stand upon the higher ideals of humanity and never to ... [fall prey to the] organized selfishness of Nationalism as ...[a] religion."[35]

The other direction away from nationalism is political cynicism, but this is not patriotic either. Though they have their uses, cynicism and apathy are ultimately as misplaced as super-patriotism. If we care for the collective well-being of our country and the world, we must get involved in the effort to make changes, not simply yield to the status quo that the cynic finds so alienating. This raises new and challenging questions regarding the morality of political allegiance.

At the very least, we must strive to strike the right balance between our duties toward compatriots and our obligation to the world. Patriotic ties, valuable as they are, should be compatible with impartial demands of global justice, just as partiality toward our friends, though commendable in itself, should nonetheless be allowed within the regulative principles of impartial morality. How to work out this nuanced relationship is the challenge of this global era.[36]

As a patriot, Tagore knew all too well that national borders are not just defensive markers of our national sovereignty—they are, to a certain extent, constitutive of our prized national and cultural identity. At the same time, he harbored deep distrust for the idea of a nation-state that lies at the heart of what he called "political civilization ... based upon exclusiveness" and that "enshrines gigantic idols of greed in its temples, taking great pride in the costly ceremonials of its worship, calling it patriotism."[37] For Tagore, "The Nation has thriven long upon mutilated humanity."[38] He declared: "...the idea of the Nation is one of the most powerful anaesthetics that man has invented. Under the influence of its fumes the whole people can carry out its systematic programme of the most virulent self-seeking without being in the least aware of its moral perversion—in fact feeling dangerously resentful if it is pointed out."[39]

---

[35] Tagore (1918), p. 39.

[36] For more on this, see Chatterjee (2003, 2004).

[37] Tagore (1916), pp. 20–21.

[38] Tagore (1918), p. 44.

[39] Tagore (1918), p. 43. Stefan Zweig writes in The World of Yesterday: Memories of a European (Viking Press, 1943): "I have seen the great mass ideologies grow and spread before my eyes — Fascism in Italy, National Socialism in Germany, Bolshevism in Russia, and above all else that pestilence of pestilences, nationalism, which has poisoned the flower of our European culture." On November 11, 2018, French President Emmanuel Macron marked the 100th anniversary of the end of World War I by delivering a forceful rebuke against rising nationalism, calling it a "betrayal of patriotism" and warning against "old demons coming back to wreak chaos and death." (New York Times, November 11, 2018).

Clearly, Tagore's patriotism was not rooted in nationalism, which he called "manufactured abnormality,"[40] but in a global vision of the common humanity that is conducive to fostering egalitarian inclusion and mutual appreciation. For Tagore, "moral law is the law of humanity."[41]

Tagore's longing for a global world was not a call for the abolition of nation-states, nor was Tagore advocating for a world government. He was speaking against the idea of "the Nation" that embodies the excesses of nationalism. As he saw it, fervent nationalism is an antidote to our common humanity—it breaks up our "interlocking commonality"[42] into fragments of exclusion.

In his 1910 poem "Let My Country Awake" (included in the collection of his poems titled

Gitanjali for which Tagore was awarded the Nobel Prize in Literature in 1913),[43] Tagore writes:

Where the mind is without fear and the head is held high;

Where knowledge is free;

Where the world has not been broken up into fragments by narrow domestic walls;

Where words come out from the depth of truth;

Where tireless striving stretches its arms towards perfection;

Where the clear stream of reason has not lost its way into the dreary desert sand of dead habit;

Where the mind is led forward by thee into ever-widening thought and action –

Into that heaven of freedom, my Father, let my country awake.

Some commentators have noted that the final phrase, "let my country awake," could easily be replaced with "let the world awake." For Tagore, then, his dream of this "heaven of freedom" includes both his beloved country India and the world—a "world that has not been broken up into fragments" of exclusion.

As a quintessential poet, Tagore gave us a poetic glimpse of his globalism but not the details. In recent times, it is Amartya Sen, the former student at Tagore's school, who has produced a robust theory of globalism and global justice that reflects many strands of Tagore's vision.[44] Central to Sen's concept of justice is the idea of a shared humanity. In contrast to the Rawlsian "international justice" that relies on partitioning the global population into distinct "peoples," Sen champions the idea of

---

[40] Tagore (1918), p. 29.

[41] Tagore (1918), p. 22.

[42] Martha Nussbaum uses this term for the "circle that defines our humanity." Nussbaum (1996), p. 9.

[43] Gitanjali—a collection of 103 original poems translated to English by Tagore himself and reprinted ten times within a few months after its publication in London in 1912—was a small part of Tagore's 200-plus books of poetry, dramas, operas, short stories, novels, essays, diaries, and letters, along with more than 2000 songs and 3000 paintings and drawings.

[44] Sen (2009). For an account of how Sen's arguments connect with other leading authors in political philosophy, see Chatterjee (2011). See also Sen's response: Sen (2011).

"global justice," which for him means attending primarily to the needs of individuals and not peoples (viewed as political or cultural units). The asymmetry of power and capabilities so starkly evident in the world is a reminder of the need for a more demanding obligation beyond the limitations of a reciprocity-based self-interested cooperation that holds primarily within national borders. Thus, Sen's re-configured notion of relationality—construed not necessarily in terms of the Rawlsian reciprocity between equals but with a broader look at the global realities of entrenched inequalities—is a roadmap from contingent nationalism to principled globalism.

Like Tagore, Sen's great contribution to the culture and human rights debate, as well as to the topic of justice, is that he has opened the way to bridging the divide between the statists and the globalists by situating the arguments of liberalism in the real world of diversity, need, vulnerabilities, and interdependence.

8 Message of Hope

Tagore's vision of democratic citizenship requires us to seriously reflect upon our personal and institutional responsibilities in creating a more just world. For Tagore, such a world not only has no room for nationalism, it eschews liberal internationalism. Scholars have noted that liberal internationalism, with its latent "statist, geopolitical agenda," has been "inexorably drawn toward the norm of war and the instrumental images of the human ... [that] war would engender."[45] As early as 1916–1917, in his lectures on nationalism, Tagore foresaw this flawed civilizational model rooted in Europe's liberal internationalism that would someday engulf the continent and the world in the ruined ashes of violence and war. This is what he saw happening in 1941, when in his last message to the world in his *Crisis in Civilization,* he wrote in anguish: "As I look around, I see the crumbling ruins of a proud civilisation strewn like a vast heap of futility."[46]

For Tagore, the asymmetry of power and resources—made especially acute by the colonial policies of "the Nation of the West"—was an urgent moral issue, and he wanted his students to be aware of it. Things have not changed much for the better since then. Poor countries are being harmed through an inequitable global system that is being continuously shaped and coercively imposed by the political, business and military machines of the rich and the powerful. Our thirst for consumption and the quest for domination over global resources are the causes of much of the conflict in the world. There is a looming global environmental catastrophe as never before, much of it is due to our excessive consumerism. During our life span, millions of human beings, mostly children, will die from poverty-related causes. All this is preventable, yet we do not seem to have the political will to do anything about it.

Tagore wrote about similar issues in his essay, "The Robbery of the Soil," in 1922:

---

[45]Burke (2005), p. 86.

[46]Tagore (1999), p. 726.

> Man has been digging holes into the very foundations not only of his livelihood but of his
> life. … Most of us who deal with the poverty problem think of nothing else but of a greater
> intensive effort of production, forgetting that this only means a greater exhaustion of
> materials as well as of humanity, and this means giving a still better opportunity for profit
> of the few at the cost of the many. … Multiplying materials intensifies the inequality
> between those who have and those who have not.[47]

Because of mass ignorance and apathy that cater to trivia and shun substance, we, the
good people, are accessories to this glaring global injustice. Traits such as curiosity,
imagination, empathy, and critical thinking are mostly missing in today's mass
education, where business and technology have been given priority over the humanities.[48] But these traits that Tagore championed, along with the non-consumerist,
eco-friendly, and minimalist lifestyle that he promoted in his school, are the prized
values in a holistic education for the growth and flourishing of the total person and
for the wellbeing of the world.[49]

What would Tagore's advice be to today's students who are getting disillusioned
by the looming catastrophes they see all around them? Is there any good road open
to them? As anguished as Tagore was by the human follies and cruelties that he saw
during his time, he would still urge the students to endure and carry on. For Tagore,
the very essence of being a human is to not give up but to be resilient and continue
moving forward. In one of his lectures, titled "Man the Artist," he said:

> [Man] is an artist, whose medium of expression is his own psychology. Like all other artists,
> he has perpetually to struggle hard with his materials, to overcome obstructions, inner and
> outer, in order to make definite his manifestation.[50]

The inspiring message in Tagore's famous song that starts with the line: "If they
answer not to thy call walk alone,"[51] had propelled him all through his life. His
message of hope resonated even in the bleak days of 1941 when he said in *Crisis in
Civilization*: "And yet I shall not commit the grievous sin of losing faith in Man."[52]
In his only English poem, *The Child*, Tagore wrote: "Victory to Man, the new-born,

---

[47] Tagore (1975), pp. 39–41, quoted in O'Connell (2003), p. 78. Gandhi said something similar:
"The world has enough for everyone's needs, but not everyone's greed."

[48] Sadly, this is one of the reasons why Tagore's university is routinely passed over today in favor of
other universities in India. In addition, since Tagore's passing, the university has gradually become
a conformist hub where Tagore's ideals are being touted routinely but not vigorously debated or
effectively put into practice in meeting the challenges of today's changing world.

[49] The 2015 Sustainable Development Goals of the United Nations (SDG 16) are indicative of a
global appetite for an alternate approach to human wellbeing that reflects Tagore's ideals of a more
equitable and sustainable future for all. This approach embodies Tagore's vision of what we know
today as positive peace, which is more than just a simple end of warfare. Positive peace is peace
with justice—it is active and transformative. (For more on the prospect of positive peace in today's
troubled world, see Chatterjee 2016).

[50] Tagore (1932).

[51] Translated by Tagore. Published in Bengali in Tagore (1905).

[52] Tagore (1999), p. 726.

the ever-living."[53] In *The Religion of Man*, chapter 3, appropriately titled "The Surplus in Man," Tagore noted: "At a certain bend in the path of evolution Man refused to remain a four-footed creature, and the position which he made his body to assume carried with it a permanent gesture of insubordination."[54]

Indeed, Tagore's uplifting vision of "the marvellous vigour of the indomitable human spirit"[55] transcends the barriers of Nations and Empires.

9   Home in the World

Tagore's school was a testament of a universal poetic vision put into practice. Tagore himself was a living embodiment of this vision. S. Radhakrishnan, the distinguished philosopher and former president of India, considered Tagore as "one of the rarest spirits [that has] ever steered humanity."[56] Albert Schweitzer, who called Tagore "The Goethe of India," wrote:

> Joy in life and joy in creation belong, according to Tagore, to the nature of man. . . .
>
> [Tagore] gives expression to his personal experience that this is the truth in a manner more profound and more powerful and more charming than anyone had ever done before him. This completely noble and harmonious thinker belongs not only to his own people but to humanity.[57]

Tagore's globalism was not a call for vacuous cosmopolitanism. In his lectures on nationalism, he said: "Neither the colourless vagueness of cosmopolitanism, nor the fierce self-idolatry of nation-worship is the goal of human history."[58] Tagore's globalism was a nuanced vision of a shared humanity where the global does not negate or neglect the local. The quest for the far and the grand is a futile venture if it fails to take note of the beauty in things nearby, as Tagore reminds us in this short poem:

> I traveled miles, for many a year,
>
> I spent a lot in lands afar,
>
> I've gone to see the mountains,
>
> The oceans I've been to view.
>
> But I haven't seen with these eyes
>
> Just two steps from my home lies

---

[53] Tagore (1931a), pp. 19–21 (stanzas ix–x).

[54] Tagore (1931b), p. 51.

[55] Tagore (1931b), p. 61.

[56] Radhakrishnan (1918), p. 174.

[57] Schweitzer (1936), pp. 239 and 249.

[58] Tagore (1918), p. 5.

On a corn of paddy grain,

A glistening drop of dew.[59]

Noted ethicist Sissela Bok observes that when children are deprived of a culturally rooted education, "they risk developing a debilitating sense of being exiled everywhere . . . ."[60] On Tagore's educational idea of balancing the local and the global so that the students are "better equipped to work out their stance with respect to interlocking identities, loyalties, and obligations," Bok writes:

> Rabindranath Tagore's philosophy of education was one. . .of encouraging children to reach out 'from part to whole'. . . . The nourishment children draw from culture, inheritance, and tradition should be offered to them freely and thus free them to look beyond their immediate world, not constrain them through rote learning and indoctrination.[61]

Instead of the exclusivity of any singular identity, Tagore's vision makes room for a joyous interplay of multifaceted and overlapping identities. Going beyond the narrow conundrum of conflicting loyalties where the forces of nationalism and ethnocentrism can have an uneasy alliance with the broader vision of our common humanity, as we see in Tagore's novel *The Home and the World*,[62] Tagore's educational mission was to let the students find their home *in* the world.

Tagore himself felt at home in the world both in his ideas and in his travels. Starting in 1912, in the course of the next 20 years when international voyage was not an easy undertaking, he visited 34 countries on five continents, meeting with luminaries in the literary and art worlds as well as scientists, philosophers, and social and cultural icons. He delivered lectures and recitations to spell-bound audiences in small and large groups around the world from Japan to Argentina and engaged in lively conversations with the great minds of his time, such as Albert Einstein, H.G. Wells, Sigmund Freud, and George Bernard Shaw.[63] In the Introduction to the English edition of Tagore's *Gitanjali*, the Irish poet William Butler Yeats wrote:

> I have carried the manuscript of these translations about with me for days, reading it in railway trains, or on the top of omnibuses and in restaurants, and I have often had to close it lest some stranger would see how much it moved me. These lyrics— which are in the original. . .full of subtlety of rhythm, of untranslatable delicacies of colour, of metrical invention—display in their thought a world I have dreamed of all my life long.[64]

---

[59]Translated by Rajib Roy. Published in Bengali in Tagore (1961), p. 253.

[60]Bok (1996), p. 43.

[61]Bok (1996), pp. 43–44. Similarly, Nusbaum writes: "[At Santiniketan] . . . the effort was to root the student's education in the local . . ., and then to expand their horizon to the whole world. . . ." (Nussbaum 2009, p. 56).

[62]Tagore (1921).

[63]"Einstein and Tagore Plumb the Truth," The New York Times Magazine, August 10, 1930. See also Tagore (1931b), Appendix II, pp. 222–225, for a transcript of the Tagore-Einstein conversation. Einstein, along with Mahatma Gandhi, Romain Rolland, and Kostes Palama, was a co-sponsor of The Golden Book of Tagore, which was a homage to Tagore on his 70th birthday in 1931.

[64]Tagore (1913), p. xiii.

Tagore's fans and some early champions in the West included philosopher Ludwig Wittgenstein and literary luminaries W.B. Yeats, Ezra Pound, Romain Rolland, Kostes Palamas, Andre Gide, Victoria Ocampo, Pablo Neruda, and Juan Ramon Jimenez, some of whom later won the Nobel Prize in Literature.[65] Tagore met with many heads of states, including President Herbert Hoover who received him at the White House in 1930, the Shah of Iran who invited him to visit in 1932, and King Faisal of Iraq who hosted a state banquet for him in Baghdad. In addressing a formal dinner in New York in 1930, Tagore's audience included Franklin D. Roosevelt, Henry Morgenthau, and Sinclair Lewis. During his 1928 visit to Czechoslovakia that was hosted by the Czech government, a prominent plaza in Prague was named after him and two of his plays were staged in the Czech National Theatre.

Tagore was awarded the Nobel Prize in Literature in 1913 over the nominations of William Butler Yeats, Thomas Hardy, and George Bernard Shaw. Two years later, he was knighted by King George V, but he renounced the title in 1919 in protest against the British atrocities in India. In conferring Tagore an honorary doctorate in 1940 in a special convocation at his university in Santiniketan, Oxford University—where Tagore had earlier delivered the Hibbert Lectures—cited him as a "myriad-minded" man. Late in his life Tagore took up painting and in 1930 his inaugural art exhibit was held at Galerie Pigalle in Paris with wide acclaim, followed by other exhibitions in London, New York, Moscow, and Tokyo.

Yet this Universal Man who inspired the world was most humble and intimate with his students at his school. They had easy access to him as their close mentor. Tagore routinely included them in his creative endeavors such as participating with him in plays and seasonal festivals, as well as welcoming them to listen to him read his own literary work to campus elders.[66] This interplay of high ideals and creative self-expression was Tagore's recipe for a humanistic education whereby the imperatives of human yearnings are not compromised in the name of local practices or blindly followed while ignoring cultural roots and traditions.

Tagore reframed the entire debate on culture and universal norms in accessible experiential terms, away from its usually contested cultural and foundational juxtaposition. This was his prescient gift to the world as globalization was taking hold in the years after his death, in the second half of the twentieth century. Today, being at home in a global world is the foremost challenge of our time. In Tagore's school, students were imbued with this global vision early in their lives. When work is play and studies are made joyous, as it was in the school, students feel at ease in finding their home in the broader vision of the world community.[67]

---

[65] Some of them, especially Yeats and Pound, were more subdued later on when they realized that their adulation of Tagore as a mystic sage was their own fanciful and one-sided portrayal of a complex and multi-faceted creative genius. For this side of Tagore, they had a limited interest.

[66] For more on this, see O'Connell (2003), pp. 74–78.

[67] Portions of the essay draw on Chatterjee (2022).

References

Bok S (1996) From part to whole. In: For love of country? In a New Democracy Forum on the limits of patriotism. Beacon Press, Boston, pp 38–44

Burke A (2005) Against the new internationalism. Ethics Int Aff 19:73–90

Chatterjee D (2003) Moral distance: introduction. The Monist 86:327–332

Chatterjee D (ed) (2004) The ethics of assistance: morality and the distant needy. CUP, Cambridge

Chatterjee D (2011) Reciprocity, closed impartiality, and national borders: framing (and extending) the debate on global justice. Soc Philos Today 27:199–217

Chatterjee D (2012) Veiled politics: the liberal dilemma of multiculturalism. The Monist 95:127–150

Chatterjee D (2013) Building common ground: going beyond the liberal conundrum. Ethics Int Aff 27:127–150

Chatterjee D (2016) Beyond preventive force: just peace as preventive non-intervention. In: Fisk K, Ramos JM (eds) Preventive force: drones, targeted killing, and the transformation of contemporary warfare. New York University Press, pp 313–340

Chatterjee D (2022) Identity and shared-humanity: reflections on Amartya Sen's memoir. Ethics Int Aff 36:91–108

Das Gupta U (2021) A history of Sriniketan: Rabindranath Tagore's pioneering work in rural reconstruction. Niyogi Books, New Delhi

Fukuyama F (2018) Identity: the demand for dignity and the politics of resentment. Farrar, Straus and Giroux, New York

Jelnikar A (2011) Tagore, Rabindranath. In: Chatterjee D (ed) Encyclopedia of global justice, vol 2. Springer, Dordrecht, pp 1051–1055

Nussbaum M (1996) For love of country? In a New Democracy Forum on the limits of patriotism. Beacon Press, Boston

Nussbaum M (2009) Tagore, Dewey, and the imminent demise of liberal education. In: Siegel H (ed) Oxford handbook of philosophy of education. OUP, Oxford, pp 52–64

Nussbaum M (2013) Political emotions: why love matters for justice. Harvard University Press, Cambridge

Nussbaum M (2018) The monarchy of fear: a philosopher looks at our political crisis. Simon & Schuster, New York

O'Connell KM (2002) Rabindranath Tagore: the poet as educator. Visva-Bharati, Kolkata, India

O'Connell KM (2003) *Siksar Herfer*: Education out of whack. In: Hogan PC, Pandit L (eds) Rabindranath Tagore: universality and tradition. Rosemont Publishing, Cranbury, NJ, pp 65–82

Oldenquist A (2008) The varieties of nationalism. In: Chatterjee D (ed) Democracy in a global world: human rights and political participation in the 21st century. Rowman & Littlefield, Lanham, pp 147–160

Radhakrishnan S (1918) The philosophy of Rabindranath Tagore. Macmillan, London

Ray S (1989) Foreword. In: Robinson A. The art of Rabindranath Tagore. Andre Deutsch, London

Robinson K (2001) Out of our minds: learning to be creative. John Wiley & Sons, New York

Schweitzer A (1936) Indian thought and its development. Holt, New York

Sen A (1997) Tagore and his India. The New York Review of Books, June 26: pp 55–63

Sen A (1999) Joy in all work. Bookfront Publications, Kolkata

Sen A (2005) The argumentative Indian: writings on Indian history, culture, and identity, vol 17. Allen Lane, New York

Sen A (2006) Identity and violence: the illusion of destiny. Norton, New York

Sen A (2009) The idea of justice. Harvard University Press, Cambridge

Sen A (2011) The idea of justice: a reply. Social Philosophy Today 27:233–239

Sen A (2021) Home in the world: a memoir. Penguin Random House, London

Tagore R (1905) Baul. Majumdar Library, Calcutta

Tagore R (1913) Gitanjali: song offerings. Macmillan, London and New York

Tagore R (1916) The message of India to Japan: a lecture by Sir Rabindranath Tagore. Imperial University of Tokyo, Tokyo

Tagore R (1917) Personality. Macmillan, New York

Tagore R (1918) Nationalism. Macmillan, London

Tagore R (1921) Home and the world: translated. Macmillan, London

Tagore R (1922) Creative unity. Macmillan, London

Tagore R (1927) An Eastern university. In: Das Gupta (2010) Rabindranath Tagore: my life in my words. Selected and Edited with an Introduction. Penguin Books, India

Tagore R (1931a) The child. George Allen and Unwin, London

Tagore R (1931b) The religion of man (Being the Hibbert Lectures for 1930). George Allen & Unwin, London

Tagore R (1932) Man the artist: Kirti Mandir Lecture Series 1, Dept. of Education, Baroda State. Baroda State Press, Baroda

Tagore R (1961) Sphulinga. Visva-Bharati, Calcutta

Tagore R (1975) The robbery of the soil. In: Elmhirst L (ed) Poet and plowman. Visva-Bharati, Calcutta, pp 30–41

Tagore R (1999) Crisis in civilization. In: Das SK (ed) The English writings of Rabindranath Tagore, vol III. Sahitya Akademi, New Delhi

Tharoor S (1997) India: from midnight to the millennium and beyond. Arcade Publishing, New York

The "Rights" Road to Inclusion: Disability Rights, Care, and Normalcy

Rachel Levit Ades

Abstract This paper examines the ways in which K-12 schools pass on attitudes towards disability, and argues that schools ought to promote values associated with rights foregrounding rights. Many address disability within education with the goal of creating a culture where disability is treated primarily as a matter of care or made wholly invisible. This paper argues that this approach is misguided. Neither "caring for" the disabled and "normalizing" disability, and argue that neither is sufficient for creating a democratic society where disabled people are treated as equals.

1 Introduction: Kids with Disabilities

Disability rights are absent from many K-12 schools. They are not absent legally, for students are protected by the Americans with Disabilities Act (ADA), Section 504, and especially the Individuals with Disabilities Education Act (IDEA). But educators, families, and even students seem to wish to leave the concept of "disability rights" at the door, and aim to create a culture where disability is treated primarily as a matter of care or rendered invisible. My goal in this paper is not to discuss the way disabled students should be conceptualized in terms of academic supports or even the logistics of inclusive classrooms or mainstreaming. Instead, I wish to examine the particular values and attitudes about disability K-12 schools pass on. I argue explicit and implicit principles about how disabled people ought to be treated must properly foreground rights for disabled students. Specifically, I discuss the values of "caring for" the disabled and "normalizing" disability, and argue that neither is sufficient for creating a democratic society where disabled people are treated as equals. I argue practices and attitudes which seek to "care for" disabled people or

R. Levit Ades (✉)
Arizona State University, School of Historical, Philosophical, and Religious Studies, Tempe, AZ, USA
e-mail: Rachel.LevitAdes@asu.edu

"normalize" disability undermine efforts to create a democratic society in where disabled people are equals.

When one reflects on what "kids with disabilities" might mean, they might initially find themselves at a loss. After all, in the US, we tend to only talk about "special needs kids" or those in "special education." Yet we do not typically differentiate the children in a certain social class with the adults in that class: for example, even if all children themselves have no money, we refer to "poor kids," and even before children consciously assert a particular gender expression or hit puberty, we feel comfortable talking about gender and education. We ought to consider "disability" a type of protected class and ensure that educational environments educate all students about the moral equality of disabled people. This begins with K-12 education that practices a rights-based view about kids with disabilities.

We are unaccustomed to thinking about "kids with disabilities" because of the taboo around the notion of disability in general and the complex history of defining disability within the US. Disability is often conceived as an inability or deficit[1] and it can be odd to apply this to children, compared to adults. There is a sense in which all children are disabled—there are lots of physical and cognitive tasks most children cannot do, and if we turn to a historic, legal sense of "disabled," children are "disabled" from many capabilities in the US, such as the ability to buy alcohol, vote, or marry. (Silvers 1998, p. 55). Because "disability" can be so easy to apply in the abstract to all children, it can seem odd to apply to particular children. If "disabled" is then to be applied to particular children, it must then be about how those children fare in relation to other children, but this too can seem strange—why think this category must then also transfer into adulthood and why not simply state these children merely have extraordinary needs?

"Special needs" is meant to be a euphemism for disability, yet it is an unhelpful one. This is for two reasons. The first is that "specialness" embeds a certain kind of distancing—the very word denotes an exceptionalism. This further stigmatizes disability, by making those who are disabled Othered. This is the explanation from stigma. The explanation from rights also takes issue with this term: to be "special" implies that one also has "special rights." When accommodations are understood as being "special," they become perceived as undeserved privileges, as opposed to civil rights. This is important not only for the rights children with disabilities receive, but also for the way disability rights will be perceived by all students when they leave school, regardless of which disabled people in fact espouse those rights.

The language of "disability," unlike the language of "specialness" is connected to rights, specifically, the disability rights movement. The target of the disability rights movement is equal access and regard for people who have disabilities (Winter 2003). Although there are different ways to *define* disability, for the purposes of this paper, one needs merely agree that disabled people have dignity and deserve equal status under the law. I seek not to offer a way of explaining who is disabled here, but rather

---

[1] For a recent example of this, see Gregory (2020).

some ideas on what we should do once it is clear that "disability" does exist at least as a social category.

This has ramifications for how we treat one another because those considered "disabled" have historically and currently not been treated as moral or democratic equals. People with disabilities have suffered egregious violations of their human rights, from forced sterilization and medical experimentation without consent, to institutionalization and forced labor. Although one can hope that many of these violations are squarely in the past, the equal treatment of disabled people is still a huge issue, whether arising from dangerous police encounters,[2] or adverse treatment performing everyday tasks.[3] Although the causes of this treatment are complex, at least one solution must be targeting the stigma towards disabled individuals.

This makes K-12 education a unique site for interrogation. After all, a school is a place where future citizens learn what they will need to know to participate as equals in a democratic society. This includes not only content, but skills, and perhaps particularly, certain moral values and attitudes. I take it as basic that disabled people are morally equal to non-disabled people—indeed, the two attitudes I examine here originate, I believe, from trying to teach this very notion. However, approaches that treat disability as a matter of "care" or "normalization" do not endorse the full picture of moral equality necessary for combating stigma and creating a community where disabled people are equal citizens. Rights for disabled people can only emerge from a rights-based view. Although we may also wish and hope for a world in which disabled people are cared for and disability is normalized, especially in our educational system, we cannot skip the vital step of first treating disability as a matter of rights.

1.1   The Rights-Based View

By a "rights-based" view, I do not mean that teachers and fellow students should be taught to see kids with disabilities as mini litigants or go out of their way to emphasize the "rights" of these students in a way that is unnatural and neglects the rights of others. Rather, the idea of "rights" here is quite basic: kids with disabilities, like all people, have a right to access the shared social world.

The etymology of the word "accommodation" is useful for understanding how the "accommodations process" is often approached, not just in terms of providing accommodations but what inclusion actually consists of. Accommodation comes into the English language by way of French, originally from Latin. In Latin,

---

[2]For example, consider the recent case of a fourteen-year-old Autistic boy who stated he was "stimming" and a policeman presuming this was a drug reference and pinning him to the ground Albert (2018).

[3]For example, see the recent slate of cases occurring where drive-throughs refuse to serve customers who cannot communicate orally (Simmons n.d.).

"accommodatio" means "an adjustment," and comes from a verb "to make fit." ("Accommodate I Origin and Meaning of Accommodate by Online Etymology Dictionary" n.d.) Yet to what extent should we aim to make students fit into an educational structure? Should it not be the other way around? If so, the true goal of inclusion is access. As Katie Rose Guest Pryal argues, "Accessibility means that "accommodations" are integrated into a space and are not particularized to an individual—but rather created for our society as a whole." (Pryal 2016) Schools must examine which practices are unintentionally ableist—that is, the ways in which they prioritize and prize doing things in an able-bodied way. This applies not only to educating students with disabilities, but creating school environments and expectations for future social environments where disabled people can flourish.

Access consists not only in things like curb cuts, elevators, untimed tests, and captioned videos, or what we might call "basic access." Basic access consists in what is legally mandated by laws like the ADA, and general access considers the technicalities of how to get students into a space or able to understand content or communicate. There is, though often implicit, a second kind of access that is also important: social access (Williamson 2015). In order for disabled people to truly access and be part of a space or a community, respect and equality are vital. Access is not merely a matter of technicalities; we should be asking not only whether someone can get into a space, but how they will be treated once they are there. This is particularly pertinent when it comes to education. Students with disabilities need social inclusion in order to access some of the very things we think are important for every student in K-12 education, such as meaningful peer relationships (Gutmann 1999) and the opportunity to be part of a diverse, integrated social world (Anderson 2010). This social inclusion, I argue, is part of what it means to have a right to access and also that it can only be guaranteed by viewing students with disabilities as rights-bearers.

Part of the appeal of a rights-based approach is that it is relatively easy to understand and can be justified to others. This is meaningful not only philosophically but pragmatically. Recall that part of my argument for eliminating talk of "special needs" was an effort to stop accommodations backlash, or resentment against people with disabilities for taking an unfair share. This is where our attitude towards general access relates to questions of social access. So, for example, one could ask whether services like speech therapy, occupational therapy, orientation & mobility, etc. in fact give students who need these services *more* from their education, or ask why these services must be publicly funded. A rights-based approach can state that these services are provided as part of developing that will serve a student well in their future. Schools should not be trying to "cure" students of their disabilities, even in services like speech, occupational therapy, or orientation and mobility. Rather, schools should view these as measures to provide students with disabilities the same opportunities to develop as individuals and are citizens that are afforded to other students who fit the more traditional curriculum.

2 Rights and Care

Schools often focus on developing the attitudes students have towards each other, and, in particular, disabled students. Teachers may politely request non-disabled students help a disabled student or see the mandate for "inclusion" as one of encouraging non-disabled students to be kind towards students with disabilities. Moral education may indeed be part of what students learn in the classroom—however, *care for* students with disabilities should not replace the need for *rights for* students with disabilities. In this section, I argue that, in the case of fostering inclusive environments for students with disabilities, rights must be an antecedent to care.

Educators may, and perhaps even should, care for all of their students. I do not mean to imply here that general goodwill and support should be halted when it comes to students with disabilities. Rather, we should not expect "care" to be the appropriate way of addressing disability-related issues in education. And, schools should be mindful of the ways in which a caring approach may turn into an approach which treats students with disabilities as pitiful, extra-needy, or while well-intentioned, may be offensive due to social messages (Cureton 2016).

If people with disabilities are equals, we must take seriously their need for access, in general. Our educational systems should model access both on an administrative and interpersonal level. Access is importantly different from care. By treating disability access as a matter of rights, administrators, teachers, and fellow students center what is needed for a disabled person to be part of the shared social world as a matter of *justice* or *fairness*. This creates a robust culture of access, where all students understand the need to then go out, and, as taxpayers, business owners, employers, and voters, make the world more accessible.

If access is a matter of care, it will be provided inconsistently and arbitrarily. When teachers aim to foster "caring" attitudes as avenues of access, be it access to a curriculum or even a social setting, they train students to understand that disability access is, in some sense, optional. Care is a matter of choice, and while it can (and should) be provided whole-heartedly, it has an interesting relationship with prejudice and bias. Leah Lakshmi Piepzna-Samarasinha shows this by explaining that her Black femme friend remarks that she doesn't want to depend on being liked or loved for the right to use the restroom when she wants to (Piepzna-Samarasinha 2018, p. 47).

Even when care is provided, it embodies the wrong attitude. Anita Silvers raises the concern that if accommodations are a matter of care, this will result in even more paternalism for disabled people. (Silvers 1995, p. 40) Nancy Mairs argues that to assume care often assumes a merely downward flowing experience (from the abled to disabled), when in fact a morally mature relationship may depend on some kind of reciprocity (Mairs 2001). And, considering accommodations merely as a matter of care is harmful not only to people with disabilities, but also to caregivers. In an educational setting, it also serves to think of the way we are educating students for the future. If accommodations appear to merely be a matter of care, we make it up to individual students whether they wish to accommodate people with disabilities in their future. And, as Eva Kittay and many others have indicated, this work often falls squarely on women, people of color, and recent immigrants (Kittay 2001).

One may thus argue that rights ought to take place at an administrative level so that care can take place on an interpersonal level. While this may be true for the logistics of access, an attitude of access, I argue, is still vital interpersonally. Care may, at times, stem from dignity, but it is much harder to go the other way. Students should not learn that beneficence creates access-rather, justice creates access.

And yet, the purpose of accommodations cannot be to eliminate the need for care. Kittay takes issue with the way the social model of disability and the disability rights movement seem to suppose that "once the barriers to full [civic] participation are removed, the disabled will be able to be as productive, self-sustaining, and independent as the abled." (Kittay 2001, p. 566). For Kittay's daughter Sesha, who has profound developmental disabilities, Kittay states that there is no accommodation that can make it so that she is not nearly entirely dependent on others (ibid.) The goal of disability rights cannot be to do away with dependency. It seems, though, that when students and communities are made aware of the rights students like Sesha have, they will be better able to respect her and then form a caring relationship. Deborah Rode aptly states, "[rights] express relationships between the individual and the community." (Rode 1993). If we want a society where dependents are cared for, it must be on the basis of their humanity and dignity. Our educational system can model respect for students by ensuring they get the access and accommodations they need.

One way in which the question of care and rights can both be misrepresented is in disability simulations. In a disability simulation, students simulate various impairments, such as wearing blindfolds, using wheelchairs, or attempting to read articles where the letter order is scrambled (to simulate the effects of dyslexia). There is good reason to reject disability simulations based on consequence alone: Supporting the view that care flows from rights, studies of disability simulations have shown that, after the simulations, participants often come to see disabled people with warmth but do not judge them to have capacity[4] and come to see disadvantage as personal deficit.[5] However, the real issue with disability simulation, particularly when it comes to understanding people with disabilities as rights-bearers and as fellow human-beings goes deeper. In the "sin of synecdoche," one aspect of a person, namely their disability, is mistaken for knowledge of the entire person (Asch and Wasserman 2005). Disability simulations perpetuate this sin (Liebow and Levit Ades 2022). This sin is egregious both when it is enacted upon our young people, and when it occurs in an educational setting. It is harmful particularly to young people because it enforces harmful norms about the correct way to perceive others; it tells a person that, as they go through life, there are particular salient characteristics their peers and fellow citizens may have, and it is these characteristics which demand the most attention. These exercises do not teach students the type of care that comes

---

[4]For example, see Nario-Redmond et al. (Nario-Redmond et al. 2017).

[5]For example, see Scullion (1996), Burgstahler and Doe (2004).

from respecting another as fellow human beings. This is harmful because presumably one of the social goals of education is teaching the skills that allow students to respect one another as rights-bearers and hopefully see the potential to form meaningful interpersonal relationships. Synecdoche, in any form, interferes with this.

One might thus think that we ought to adopt some sort of attitude which is directly counter to this: if it is wrongful to pinpoint disabilities, perhaps we should focus on creating a culture where they are erased. The next section examines issues with this view.

3   Not Invisible

The second harmful attitude I wish to discuss is that of the desire to erase disability. Disability erasure has an interesting interaction with normalcy. On the one hand, disability becomes erased when disabled people are forced to assimilate to a normal ideal. On the other, more recently, some schools have responded by aiming to teach students to question normalcy altogether. Although this latter move may appear amenable to radical disability theorists who question the notion of the "normal," teaching students to eschew normalcy is unrealistic, harmful to students with disabilities who in fact are trained constantly to live in "normal society," decreases the possibility for powerful political disruption, and does not in fact reduce disability stigma.

I worked at a school where for Inclusive Schools Week, students were encouraged to wear mismatched socks to show their support for diversity. For most of the students in my class, putting on socks is not an independent activity. I was an aide for a student whose family worked incredibly hard to make sure she was clean and well-dressed. It would have been an embarrassment to them, conceivably because it would have been an embarrassment to my student, if her socks were atrociously mismatched. Perhaps the goal of a "mismatched sock" exercise is that we all are meant to realize socks don't matter—perhaps even that matching socks is some sort of ableist relic. But those who say that socks don't matter have the privilege of people not caring what socks they are wearing. For students already perceived as being "different," it can be of vital importance to blend in with their peers as much as possible, even if in the long-term we could all eschew notions of difference.

Diversity celebrations and disability simulations might be said, at best, to address cultural imperialism as a face of disability oppression; that is, perhaps they "make it OK" to not be measured by the norms of the dominant group. (Young 1990). However, by celebrating abnormality, we perpetuate normalcy. If it really was acceptable to have different socks, people would simply have mismatched socks every day, and there would be no reason for "celebration." As inconsequential as it sounds, matched socks are requisite for being respected, for better or worse. When we play with respectability, instead of take it seriously, we also interfere with the possibility for disruption. In 1990, dozens of wheelchair users abandoned their wheelchairs and other mobility aids and attempted to crawl their ways of the steps of the capital to demonstrate physical inaccessibility and push for the passage of the ADA. It seems clear bodies moving in different, shocking ways drew attention and is often hailed as a catalyst for the passage of the ADA. Different socks to show some kind of solidarity is very different from radical disruption by the very people being discriminated against.

Yet we do not need to create false abnormalities like mismatched socks in order to consider the way we include "the abnormal." What disabled students should get, when a school is truly accessible, is just what any other student gets. The first way we can guarantee rights for students with disabilities is to consider the ways we provide students without disabilities their own rights, and try to widen the way we typically do things. This widening process, and reconceiving what it means to "access" something, should be the focus of any extra funding for disabled students or inclusion weeks.

Pretending that disability stigma does not exist does not solve anything--instead, it entrenches oppressive structures. The goal should not be that students understand the suffering of another or that all students aim to imitate disability. Rather, we should explain clearly what discrimination consists in, and view addressing bullying within schools as an example of how we wish for students to respect each other as equals. Ableism can be expressed not only in how students with disabilities are treated, but how the category of "disabled" functions more broadly. Ableism is often used as a way to justify sexism and especially racism; as Lennard Davis states, disability is porous (Davis 2001), and ableism has been used to justify the subjugation of women, Indigenous peoples, and other ethnic groups. Teresa Man Ling Lee, a Chinese political philosopher living in Canada, has written about her experiences where her speech disability makes it so that people act with racist behavior towards her, for example, saying it is hard to understand "you people" or being met with blank stares after spelling a word when asked for a request (Man Ling Lee 2006, p. 99). The label or perception of disability just makes it harder to be a member of another oppressed group. The tide goes both ways, however: racism can also compound disability stigma (Dolmage 2017, p. 137).

It is not the job of a school to create disability pride. But it may be worth examining the other "pride-related" activities schools encourage, from celebrating Black authors during Black History Month, highlighting the women's suffrage movement during a history lesson, or aiming to create a community for students who identify as LGBTQ+. A rights-based approach to disability makes sense of the notion that these students too might have social struggles, these students too might need support and community, and these students too are ultimately worthy of the belonging and care that previous approaches have aimed for--they just in fact also have rights that guarantee they get the same access to education as everyone else.

4 Conclusion

Sometimes it can seem as if it would be nice to skip rights. It's painful that the rights of disabled people are still a topic of contention and stigma is still a valid concern in the twenty-first century US. Care can feel fuzzier and erasing disability can bring a certain kind of false comfort. But, as I have argued in this paper, the only way out is through. Skipping rights and jumping straight to care, or ignoring disability rights entirely as a way to destroy the badness of the "disability" label is ineffective, and ignores the reality both of students who are disabled and the world all students will enter when they finish K-12 school. The best we can do is prepare them, and continue to educate ourselves, on how we can truly create a society of equals.

References

"Accommodate | Origin and Meaning of Accommodate by Online Etymology Dictionary" (n.d.) Accessed January 29, 2021. https://www.etymonline.com/word/accommodate

Albert V (2018) Cop thought it was drugs. it was a teen coping with autism. The Daily Beast, June 7, 2018, sec. Us-news. https://www.thedailybeast.com/cop-thought-it-was-drugs-it-was-a-teen-coping-with-autism-lawsuit

Anderson E (2010) The imperative of integration. Princeton University Press, Princeton

Asch, A. and D. Wasserman. 2005. "Where is the sin in synecdoche? Prenatal testing and the parent-child relationship." In Quality of life and human difference, edited by David Wasserman, Jerome Bickenbach, and Robert Wachbroit, 1st ed., 172–216. Cambridge University Press. https://doi.org/10.1017/CBO9780511614590.008

Burgstahler S, Doe T (2004) Disability-related simulations: if, when, and how to use them in professional development. Rev Disab Stud Int J 1 (January)

Cureton A (2016) Offensive beneficence. J Am Philos Assoc 2(1):74–90. https://doi.org/10.1017/apa.2015.35

Davis L (2001) Identity politics, disability, and culture. In: Handbook of disability studies, 2455 Teller Road. California 91320 United States: SAGE Publications, Inc. Thousand Oaks, pp. 535–545 https://doi.org/10.4135/9781412976251.n23

Dolmage J (2017) Academic ableism: disability and higher education. Corporealities. University of Michigan Press, Ann Arbor

Gregory A (2020) Disability as Inability. J Ethics Soc Philos 18(1). https://doi.org/10.26556/jesp.v18i1.572

Gutmann A (1999) Democratic education: with a new preface and epilogue. Princeton University Press, Princeton Chichester

Kittay EF (2001) When caring is just and justice is caring: justice and mental retardation. Publ Cult 13(3):557–580. https://doi.org/10.1215/08992363-13-3-557

Liebow N, Levit Ades R (2022) "I Know What It's Like": epistemic arrogance, disability, and race. J Am Philos Assoc:1–21. https://doi.org/10.1017/apa.2021.27

Mairs N (2001) Waist high in the world a life among the nondisabled. Beacon Press, Boston

Man Ling Lee T (2006) Multicultural citizenship and the case of the disabled. In: Pothier D, Devlin R (eds) Critical disability theory: essays in philosophy, politics, policy, and law. UBC Press, pp 87–105

Nario-Redmond M, Gospodinov D, Cobb A (2017) Crip for a day: the unintended negative consequences of disability simulations. Rehabil Psychol 62(3):324–333. https://doi.org/10.1037/rep0000127

Piepzna-Samarasinha LL (2018) Care work: dreaming disability justice. Arsenal Pulp Press, Vancouver

Pryal KRG (2016) Accessibility v. Accommodation (Part 1). Katie Rose Guest Pryal (blog). April 4, 2016. https://katieroseguestpryal.com/2016/04/04/accessibility-v-accommodation-part-1/

Rode D (1993) Feminist critical theories. In: Smith P (ed) Feminist Jurisprudence. Oxford University Press, New York

Scullion P (1996) 'Quasidisability' experiences using simulation. Br J Ther Rehabil 3(9):498–502. https://doi.org/10.12968/bjtr.1996.3.9.14776

Silvers A (1995) Reconciling equality to difference: justice (F)or caring for people with disabilities. Hypatia 10(11):30–55

Silvers A (1998) Formal justice. Disability, Difference, Discrimination: Perspectives on Justice in Bioethics and Public Policy 94:13

Simmons P. A Solution to Drive-Through Lawsuits at the Drive-Thru | Rocky Mountain ADA. Accessed February 10, 2021. https://www.rockymountainada.org/news/blog/solution-drive-through-lawsuits-drive-thru

Williamson B (2015) Access. In: Adams R, Reiss B, Serlin D (eds) Keywords for disability studies. New York University Press, New York

Winter JA (2003) The development of the disability rights movement as a social problem solver. Disab Stud Q 23(1). https://doi.org/10.18061/dsq.v23i1.399

Young IM (1990) Justice and the politics of difference. Princeton University Press, Princeton

Part II
Education Rights and Reasonable Pluralism

The Constitutional Right to an Education

Wade L. Robison

Abstract The right to an education in the United States is grounded on the form of government created by the Constitution. The proper argument for understanding why there is a right to an education is not to show that it is implied by, say, the right to petition the government, a right that does require enough education to read and write, but to see that it is a necessary condition for the structure of government we have. The proper argument is not piecemeal, that is, going from provision to provision to determine which, if any, requires an education, but transcendental, seeing how the very nature of a government of the people, by the people, and for the people depends upon the people being educated.

The Universal Declaration of Human Rights states that everyone "has the right to an education" (Article 26). That the right is not universally recognized should not surprise. What may surprise is that the right is not Constitutionally protected in the United States. It is not a right specified by any provision of the Constitution, and the Supreme Court has not found it implied by any provision. It is certainly arguable that the right is grounded in particular provisions such as the right to petition the government, a right that certainly requires enough education to read and write. But such arguments have not been successful in the cases where the Court has considered the right to an education, and, I shall argue, they are misconceived in any case.

The right to an education is not grounded in some particular provisions of the Constitution. Its proper grounding is in the form of government created by the Constitution. It is a necessary condition for the structure of government we have. The proper argument is not piecemeal, that is, going from provision to provision to see which, if any, requires an education, but seeing how the very nature of a government of the people, by the people, and for the people depends upon the people being educated.

W. L. Robison (✉)
Rochester Institute of Technology, Rochester, NY, USA

© The Author(s), under exclusive license to Springer Nature Switzerland AG 2022
J. McGregor, M. C. Navin (eds.), *Education, Inclusion, and Justice*, Amintaphil:
The Philosophical Foundations of Law and Justice 11,
https://doi.org/10.1007/978-3-031-04013-9_4

1   "All on Equal Terms"

In *Brown v. Board of Education*, the Court held that "education is perhaps the most important function of state and local governments" (347 U.S. 493):

> Compulsory school attendance laws and the great expenditures for education both demonstrate our recognition of the importance of education to our democratic society. It is required in the performance of our most basic public responsibilities, even service in the armed forces. It is the very foundation of good citizenship. Today it is a principal instrument in awakening the child to cultural values, in preparing him for later professional training, and in helping him to adjust normally to his environment. In these days, it is doubtful that any child may reasonably be expected to succeed in life if he is denied the opportunity of an education. Such an opportunity, where the state has undertaken to provide it, is a right which must be made available to "all on equal terms" (347 U.S. 494).

The right the Court recognizes in *Brown* is conditioned by a state's having undertaken to provide an education, but once that condition is satisfied, the right seems broad, sweeping out everything that reeks of inequality and anything that prevents a student from obtaining an equal education. The right may seem broad, but as later cases have made clear, the right is far more limited than the Court's sweeping generalization might suggest.

The Burger Court's 1973 decision in *San Antonio Independent School District v. Rodriguez* countenanced unequal expenditures for education, with the state of Texas spending $1000 for every child in wealthy districts and $370 per child in poor districts (Adelman 2020, p. 10). We may question whether equal funding is necessary to an equal opportunity of an education. The Court said it was not. In his dissent, Justice Marshall argued that it is, saying

> it is inequality—not some notion of gross inadequacy—of educational opportunity that raises a question of denial of equal protection of the laws.... [A]ppellees have made a substantial showing of wide variations in educational funding and the resulting educational opportunity afforded to the schoolchildren of Texas. This discrimination is, in large measure, attributable to significant disparities in the taxable wealth of local Texas school districts. This is a sufficient showing to raise a substantial question of discriminatory state action in violation of the Equal Protection Clause (411 U. S. 90).

In any event, the *Rodriguez* decision surely raises questions about how we are to understand Brown's requirement that, once a state undertakes funding for education, it "is a right which must be made available to 'all on equal terms'."

The Court held in *Rodriguez* that the disparity in funding raised no Constitutional issue. No right to education is provided in the Constitution or the Bill of Rights, the Court claimed, and it is not presupposed by any of the rights that are provided. So what the Court took to be at issue is whether the way in which the state of Texas allocated school funding was "invidiously discriminatory." They held that a classification in terms of rich school districts and poor districts was not "wholly arbitrary or capricious," as Justice Stewart put it (411 U. S. 60). It was for Texas to decide what education it would fund and for Texas to determine how to fund it. No Constitutional issue arose because the classification was not invidious. Only then would it be subject to strict judicial scrutiny.

It was not, the Court held, even though the differences in funding were so significant that the District Court decision it reversed observed that "the current [state aid] system tends to subsidize the rich at the expense of the poor, rather than the other way around" (411 U.S. 81). Funding on those terms is hardly equal, and so *Rodriguez* leaves open the question, if not funding,

1.1 What Is Supposed to be Equal?

And answering that question requires that we answer another:

1.2 How Are We to Measure Whatever It Is That Is Supposed to be Equal?

Measuring school funding per child would be relatively easy, but according to *Rodriguez*, we must measure whether children are getting a "basic minimal educational offering." That is what is supposed to be equal. Not only is the education basic, it is minimal as well, and the state is not to provide it, but only offer it—to "all on equal terms."

The state is to provide funding so that all the children in the state can be offered such an education. No child is left behind, as it were—except that what is equal is an offering. That leaves open enormous leeway on the part of the state to explain, and excuse, the failure in any school district to provide basic minimal education. The state is only funding the opportunity to learn. But that means citizens have no Constitutional recourse if a school system does a terrible job of hiring teachers, offering such low pay, for instance, that they cannot attract even competent ones. With local control, states can argue they are not at fault if school districts fail to provide a real opportunity and students fail to obtain even a basic minimal education.

Even if a student achieves a basic minimal education, that does not sound like much. If you got basic minimal car insurance, you would not get much at all. What is basic and minimal varies from state to state, and if you lived in Florida, that would amount to $10,000 property damage liability and $10,000 personal injury protection—basic and minimal indeed. So much for the sweeping rhetoric of *Brown*.

2 "Basic Minimal Educational Offering"

The court in *Rodriguez* gives a clue, however, as to what it considers a basic minimum education when it claims that in Texas

no charge fairly could be made that the system fails to provide each child with an opportunity
to acquire the basic minimal skills necessary for the enjoyment of the rights of speech and of
full participation in the political process (411 U. S. 90).

Whatever the details, the criterion in *Rodriguez* for assessing whether state funding
meets the minimum standard for offering a basic minimal education is whether those
who achieve that level of education have the "skills necessary" for "full participation
in the political process" and what it calls enjoying the rights of speech. We live, after
all, in a participatory democracy.

Full participation clearly includes voting and, we ought to presume, the ability to
make reasoned choices between alternative candidates and ballot initiatives. It also
includes jury duty. That requires the capacity to understand and assess arguments
and, obviously, a sense of what is fair. The list of what a citizen could do is long—
participating in the deliberations that ought to animate a democratic society, joining
a political party, proposing an initiative, running for office, petitioning for change,
and more.

If this is what the Court means by "basic minimal education," we seem to have far
more than we would have with, say, basic minimal car insurance. The ability to make
reasoned choices is relatively sophisticated. Think here of ballot initiatives, some of
which are worded in such awkward ways that it takes a great deal of work, and an
examination of its history, to determine even what it says, let alone what implications
it will have for society.

It is easy to find examples. California Ballot Initiative 40, in 2012, is a wonderful
example. It was an attempt to overturn the California Senate's redistricting plan and
was originally worded so that voters were to vote in the affirmative to overturn the
plan. But it was reworded in such a way that voting in the affirmative actually left the
plan intact while overturning the plan required a negative vote. Those who pushed
for the initiative ended up having to vote against it, as it were (Lee 2012). It would
take, and did take, a fair amount of research for any citizen to figure out that voting in
the affirmative, far from rejecting the problematic redistricting plan, would
support it.

So if the Court thinks that a basic minimal education is comprehensive enough to
allow for "full participation in the political process," it is actually setting a very high
bar, one seemingly in tension with the phrase "basic minimum"—although we can
find that name used elsewhere for a sophisticated set of skills. Washington State has
a relatively comprehensive set of requirements under the title, "The Goals of Basic
Education":

- Read with comprehension, write effectively, and communicate successfully in a
  variety of ways and settings and with a variety of audiences;
- Know and apply the core concepts and principles of mathematics; social, physical, and life sciences; civics and history, including different cultures and participation in representative government; geography; arts; and health and fitness;
- Think analytically, logically, and creatively, and to integrate technology literacy
  and fluency as well as different experiences and knowledge to form reasoned
  judgments and solve problems; and

- Understand the importance of work and finance and how performance, effort, and decisions directly affect future career and educational opportunities (League of Education Voters).

If this set of skills is thought typical for those who espouse basic minimal education, with the criterion for determining what to include being the capacity of a student to graduate fully able to participate in the political process, the *Rodriguez* decision seems at odds with the high standard it sets.

Several of the dissenting justices agree. In his dissent, Justice Brennan says he disagrees

> with the Court's rather distressing assertion that a right may be deemed "fundamental" for the purposes of equal protection analysis only if it is "explicitly or implicitly guaranteed by the Constitution."...As my Brother MARSHALL convincingly demonstrates, our prior cases stand for the proposition that "fundamentality" is, in large measure, a function of the right's importance in terms of the effectuation of those rights which are in fact constitutionally guaranteed (411 U. S. 62).
>
> He adds that there can be no doubt that education is inextricably linked to the right to participate in the electoral process and to the rights of free speech and association guaranteed by the First Amendment" (411 U. S. 63).

The *Rodriguez* decision is puzzling for two different reasons. On the one hand, there is tension between what seems implied by the phrase "basic minimal" and what is implied by requiring the state to provide an education sufficient for "full participation in the political process." On the other hand, there is the puzzle of how the Court can deny a Constitutional right to an education while seemingly committing itself to a right to an education sufficient for full participation in the political process created by the Constitution.

3   The Value of an Education

There is little doubt about the value of having an education. That has been recognized since colonial days. As John Adams wrote, "Laws for the liberal education of the youth, especially of the lower class of the people, are so extremely wise and useful, that, to a humane and generous mind, no expense for this purpose would be thought extravagant" (Adams 1776, p. 5). He added about his forbearers,

> They made an early provision by law that every town consisting of so many families should be always furnished with a grammar school. They made it a crime for such a town to be destitute of a grammar schoolmaster for a few months, and subjected it to a heavy penalty. So that the education of all ranks of people was made the care and expense of the public, in a manner that I believe has been unknown to any other people, ancient or modern.
>
> The consequences of these establishments we see and feel every day. A native of America who cannot read and write is as rare ... as a comet or an earthquake (Adams 1765, p. 7).

As George Washington put it, "A primary object should be the education of our youth in the science of government" (Washington 1796). This sentiment was held by many of the founding fathers, Jefferson arguing,

> I know no safe depository of the ultimate powers of the society, but the people themselves; and if we think them not enlightened enough to exercise their control with a wholesome discretion, the remedy is, not to take it from them, but to inform their discretion by education. [T]his is the true corrective of abuses of Constitutional power (Jefferson 1820).

John Jay wrote to Benjamin Rush that he considered "knowledge to be the soul of a republic,. . .Education is the way to do this, and nothing should be left undone to afford all ranks of people that means of obtaining a proper degree of it at a cheap and easy rate" (Jay 1785).

Rush was even more emphatic:

> Let our common people be compelled by law to give their children (what is commonly called) a good English education. Let schoolmasters of every description be supported in part by the public, and let their principles and morals be subjected to examination before we employ them. . . .This plan of general education alone will render the American Revolution a blessing to mankind (Rush 1786, pp. 388–389).

Independently of any concern about how requiring a general education for citizens would improve their lives, the founders clearly thought that an education for "all ranks of people" was essential to the Republic. That both sexes were taught "the basics of reading, writing, and numbers" is evidence of how deeply engrained was the idea that *all* citizens, even those who could not vote, ought to be literate (Ricks 2020, p. 66).

We have these founders providing a Constitutional ground for the right to an education that does not depend upon any provision within, or implied by, the Constitution. In his dissent in the *Rodriguez* decision, Brennan might seem to support the view that education is essential to the Republic when he chastises the Court for supposing a right fundamental "only if explicitly or implicitly guaranteed by the Constitution." He argues that the right is presupposed by "those rights which are in fact constitutionally guaranteed." But his argument is piecemeal. In appealing to guaranteed rights, he is simply appealing to more pieces.

His argument is like the argument for the right of privacy in *Griswold v. Connecticut*. That case concerned marriage, "a relationship lying within the zone of privacy created by several fundamental constitutional guarantees" (381 U.S. 485). Just so, Brennan argues that the right to a basic minimal educational opportunity is created by similarly fundamental constitutional guarantees—such as the right to vote and to petition. We cannot exercise those rights without an education sufficient to allow us to understand what voting is and what we are voting for any more than we can have intimacy in marriage without a "zone of privacy."

Brennan is correct, I think, in arguing that a case can be made that a great many of the provisions in the Constitution require an educated citizenry. We find some of these arguments in *Gary B., et al. v. Whitmer, et al.*, the decision of the U.S. Court of Appeals for the 6th Circuit recognizing "that the Constitution provides a fundamental right to a basic minimum education" (*Gary B., et al. v. Whitmer*, p. 33).

The case was brought on behalf of students in "some of the lowest-performing schools in the Detroit Public Schools system'"(Strauss 2020). The suit argued that students blamed "this substandard performance to poor conditions within their classrooms, including missing or unqualified teachers, physically dangerous facilities, and inadequate books and materials. Plaintiffs say these conditions deprive them of a basic minimum education, meaning one that provides a chance at foundational literacy" (*Gary B., et al. v. Whitmer*, p. 2).

The Court in *Whitmer* argued what Brennan argued, that various provisions in the Constitution presuppose a basic minimum education. The 6th Amendment guarantee of a trial by jury requires that defendant be "informed of the nature and cause of the accusation," a requirement that would be impossible if the defendant were not literate. "Without literacy, how can someone...afford a defendant due process when sitting as a juror in his case, especially if documents are used as evidence against him?...Voting, taxes, the legal system, jury duty—all of these are predicated on the ability to read and comprehend written thoughts" (*Gary B., et al. v. Whitmer*, p. 47).

It seems somewhat odd that the Supreme Court has at various times and in a variety of cases rejected this argument, either explicitly or implicitly, when it seems so obvious that literacy is a necessary condition for the exercise of rights and powers that are explicitly guaranteed. The Court in *Whitmer* is the first, citing substantive due process to justify "a fundamental right to a basic minimum education" (*Gary B., et al. v. Whitmer*, p. 33). It uses the two criteria it has found in Supreme Court cases for incorporating substantive rights into the due process clause of the 14th Amendment. The first criterion is that "the Due Process Clause specially protects those fundamental rights and liberties which are, objectively, 'deeply rooted in this Nation's history and tradition.'" The second is that "the asserted right is 'implicit in the concept of ordered liberty,' such that 'neither liberty nor justice would exist if they were sacrificed'" (*Gary B., et al. v. Whitmer*, p. 35).

Whitmer was decided by a District Court, not the Supreme Court, however, and, I would argue, its argument is fundamentally flawed and should not become the basis of any Supreme Court decision. We certainly can go from clause to clause in the Constitution to tease out their dependence on a basic minimal education and then use substantive due process to argue as *Whitmer* did that states are obligated to provide their citizens a basic minimum education. From the 6th Amendment's right of a trial by jury to the 1st Amendment's right "to petition the Government for a redress of grievances," we note how each requires that citizens be literate to exercise those rights.

But we should not tie ourselves to that precedent or to the judicial history that seeks to find the right to a minimal education implied by some particular provision of the Constitution. We should not tie ourselves to the piecemeal form of argument that Brennan and the *Whitmer* court have used. Rather than go from one provision to another to see if it requires an educated citizenry, we should look at what the founding fathers argued.

As the passages from the founding fathers make clear, providing a basic education has been held essential since before the adoption of the Constitution. In his

Democracy in America, Alexis de Tocqueville remarks that "it is in the provisions for public education which, from the very first, throw into clearest relief the originality of American civilization," with no other "people [having] founded so many schools and such efficient ones" (deTocqueville 1966, pp. 38, 83). As the District Court says, near the time of the 14th Amendment's adoption, Senator Charles Sumner argued that "[t]he New England system of common schools is part of the republican form of government as understood by the framers of the Constitution" (*Gary B., et al. v. Whitmer,* p. 43). The proper form of argument recognizes that the Constitution creates a political and legal system that requires that citizens be educated.

Such an argument is transcendental, showing how one thing is a necessary condition for another (Stern 2019). Such an argument does not depend on any of the provisions of the Constitution, but on there being a constitution for a republican form of government, one, as Jefferson put it, that makes "the people themselves" a "safe depository of the ultimate powers of the society." As Madison puts it in Federalist Paper No. 39, a republic

> is a government which derives all its powers directly or indirectly from the great body of the people; and is administered by persons holding their offices during pleasure, for a limited period, or during good behaviour. It is *essential* to such a government, that it be derived from the great body of the society,....(Federalist Papers 2001, p. 194).

A republic is necessarily conditioned on its citizens being educated, literate enough, that is, to read and write and so competent to understand the issues before the nation and knowledgeable enough to make reasoned choices. It is not particular provisions, that is, which provide the ground for the right to at least a basic minimal education, but the very nature of our constitutional system.

This form of argument would require a very different route to hold states responsible for securing the rights of its citizens. The path would run not through the 14th amendment, but through the very nature of having a republican form of government. How many rights would follow the right to a minimum education is a nice question, raising the general issue of what a republic needs to ensure for its citizens. It is surely arguable, on such a ground, that states are obligated to ensure that every citizen has the right to vote and that that right is secured by ensuring that citizens are registered and able to exercise their right without undue hardship. However that may be, this form of argument would realign relations between the federal and state governments as well as relations between them and citizens.

4   The American Revolution

"Some mute inglorious Milton here may rest"

Elegy Written in a Country Churchyard, Thomas Gray

Madison and Jefferson make the main point about why education is essential for the government: citizens are the source of the nation's powers. We have a government by the people as well as of the people and for the people, and government by the people is possible only with educated citizens who appreciate the values that underlie self-government, are independent enough to vote their consciences and further those values as well as their own and to choose the kind of life they wish to lead and those who would govern them to further the interests they have in leading those lives. Madison and Jefferson presupposed the necessity of a certain kind of citizen given the nature of our government.

They presumed individual independence. Jefferson and others presumed that the majority of citizens would be farmers. Jefferson thought them

> the most vigorous, the most independant (sic), the most virtuous, & they are tied to their country & wedded to it's (sic) liberty & interests by the most lasting bonds (Jefferson 1785).

They thus have enough independence to vote their consciences and not be beholden to anyone who might attempt to force or encourage them to vote one way or another. We are long past our rural roots, but Jefferson's point about ensuring that citizens are vested in the government and independent enough to ward off attempts to intimidate them to vote one way rather than another is well-taken, and it provides a reason why at least a basic minimal education is necessary.

Students are learning the basic tools they need to lead economically productive lives. With an education, even a basic one, they can become as self-sufficient and thus as independent as they can be in our economic system. They are the contemporary equivalent of Jefferson's yeoman farmers, not as independent as they were, but presumably independent enough to vote their consciences and not someone else's.

The founding fathers also presumed that education would encourage the values on which our society rests. It is no exaggeration to say that we each begin teaching our children the day they are born. By cooing to smiles and hushing cries, we are rewarding and encouraging certain sorts of behavior and discouraging other sorts. Our children come to speak our language, with many of our mannerisms and the peculiarities of our accents. We are educating them regardless of what we may think we are doing. We cannot help but teach them.

Among other things, we are socializing them into our families and into society and passing onto them, whether we are conscious of it or not, the values we accept— our prejudices and biases, our preferences and loves. The values we pass onto our children is one reason for schooling them. One aim is to ensure that, in meeting children with different values and learning about our common history and heritage, they will come to have the social values they will need in society at large.

They will have a chance to get out of themselves, as it were, to see themselves as a product of the particular upbringing we have given them. In the best of cases, going off to school should be like going to a foreign country and realizing that the social norms are different from those that come naturally to you. They should be like one of my German exchange students who came to me several weeks after classes began and asked, "Can you tell me what's wrong with me?" I asked why he thought anything was wrong, and he said that when he walked around town, people looked at him and smiled. I explained to him that he was in the Mid-west. "That's what they do." He learned something about the friendliness of Americans that was at odds with what he was used to in Germany.

We can see a glimpse of the values he saw and the values upon which the nation rests in the plea by Svetlana Tikhanovskaya, a candidate for President in Belarus,

> We want to live in a free state where no one is afraid to speak freely, where no one is afraid, where there is the right to free meetings on the street, where you don't think about what to say because tomorrow you may be behind bars (Dixon 2020).

We take it for granted that we can speak freely without fear of arrest and that we can meet freely in the street, and it is those values, among others, upon which the society rests. It is those values we want our children to learn when they go to school. Being self-sufficient does not suffice for being a citizen if it is not tied to freedom of expression and association and the other values that distinguish this nation from others.

One value is expressed in the phrase "of the people." Citizens are expected to lead the nation, to serve the country by becoming members of planning commissions, mayors, and representatives in their city councils, state governments, and Congress. They are expected, that is, to become part of the government to further the values of self-government. "Education," the Court argues in *Whitmer*, "and particularly access to literacy, has long been viewed as a key to political power" (*Gary B., et al. v. Whitmer*, p. 44). The students who were the focus of the lawsuit were from a set of schools in Detroit which were so inadequate that most reached high school without a proficiency in English. In one high school, "only 1.8% of eleventh-graders were proficient" in English (*Gary B., et al. v. Whitmer*, p. 12). As the Court put it,

> The affected group—students and families of students without access to literacy—is especially vulnerable and faces a built-in disadvantage at seeking political recourse. The lack of literacy of which they complain is exactly what prevents them from obtaining a basic minimal education through the normal political process (*Gary B., et al. v. Whitmer*, p. 52).

Just because they lacked an education, those in Detroit were not in a position to use the political system to better their lives. The same is true of any group that seeks change in the system. If individuals are denied an opportunity for real literacy, they are unable to know enough about how the political system works to use the levers of power to help themselves.

They are also unable to determine for themselves what kind of lives they would like to lead. Self-determination is not possible without a knowledge of one's own capacities and deficiencies and without a sense of one's possibilities, all of which come through education. It is the assumption of self-determination that underlies Jefferson's vision of a nation of independent farmers. We do not all need to be farmers. The core idea is that we are independent and can do with our lives what we wish. We have no castes, no nobility, no special class of citizens with special powers and rights. We are all to be equal under the Constitution, but that equality extends not just to how we are to be treated as citizens. It extends as well to our each having a real opportunity to decide for ourselves what kind of life we wish to lead. We are not tied to any particular trade or vocation or position. We are all equally at liberty to go wherever our talents and energy can take us.

That is what makes the opportunity for a basic minimal education so valuable. We cannot pursue the dreams we have for ourselves without an education. We need schooling just to realize what is possible for us and how to bend our talents to the end we choose. Our choice can only be informed and so truly free if we have an education that prepares us to achieve our dream.

The value to each individual is obvious. Gray's *Elegy* is a lament about lost lives, about a "mute inglorious Milton" who had no opportunity to be anything more than a simple farmer. The benefit to society ought to be obvious as well. If natural talents are distributed randomly, as we ought to presume they are on pain of being racist or sexist if we do not, then we have no idea who or where the next Milton will be. We will find natural talents everywhere, in the countryside and the ghettos as well as the suburbs and the large cities, among those of any ethnic origin or race, whatever their sex or other natural contingencies.

The presumption that citizens will determine for themselves how they would come to be independent, or at least as self-sufficient as possible within an interconnected economic and social order, is a mark of the new understanding of what it is to be a citizen that powered the American Revolution and is presupposed by the Constitution. We can hardly expect citizens to be independent voters and elect those who will work for their good and the good of all if they are not free to choose their own good.

The contrast with the French Revolution is striking. That Revolution simply carried on the same social and political order, only exchanging a king for an emperor and leaving the French people to serve whatever ends the emperor might choose. It was hardly revolutionary. The American Revolution created a new kind of citizen, with a new kind of relationship to those who govern them. Government exists to serve the citizens. That is what makes citizens the source of the nation's powers.

As Barack Obama said in his eulogy to John Lewis,

> That most American of ideas, the idea that any of us, ordinary people without rank or wealth or title or fame, can somehow point out the imperfections of this nation and come together and challenge the status quo. And decide that it is in our power to remake this country, that we love, until it more closely aligns with our highest ideals. What a radical idea. What a revolutionary notion (Paz 2020).

5   What a State and We Must Provide

We will look in vain in the court cases we have examined for much detail about what would count as a basic minimal education. Literacy, the capacity to read and write, English competency—these are all used pretty interchangeably and leave out any reference to mathematics or science or any other competencies that are necessary in our lives. They also leave out any details of what is to count as, e.g., English competency. The only suggestion to be found is that students are to be competent enough to participate in the political process. That standard is as high, or as low, as we set the bar for what counts as participation.

So we cannot answer either of the two questions *Rodriguez* raised for us. We are unsure what it is that we are supposed to measure, and although the *Whitmer* decision depends upon measurements of English competency, we do not have any insight from these cases about what criterion we are to use to determine if a state's offering is sufficient. It is surely not enough that 1.8% of eleventh graders are assessed as English competent. What about 15% 45%? 78%? Or is it possible that the state need only offer the opportunity to a basic minimal education, with no assumption that any student will achieve it?

Rodriguez led me to ask these questions, and I suggest it misled me and misleads us. The question to ask is whether the state provides the means by which a school district can provide the conditions for an education sufficient to allow full participation in the political process. *Whitmer* answers that question by laying out three conditions a state must provide:

> ... facilities, teaching, and educational materials (e.g., books). For each of these components, the quality and quantity provided must at least be sufficient for students to plausibly attain literacy within the educational system at issue (*Gary B., et al. v. Whitmer*, p. 57).

It would seem that the most important measure is how much funding the state provides each school district so that each can hire the good teachers, maintain their buildings, and provide proper educational materials. The easiest way to ensure that those conditions are met is for the state to provide at least roughly the same amount of funding per student throughout the state—the marker *Rodriguez* rejected.

We do not need to specify what standards must be met for teachers, buildings, and material. As *Rodriguez* pointed out, states and local districts are far better positioned to make those judgments than a court. But if we are to educate students to become informed citizens, capable of making rational decisions, we must do more than simply supply them with books. Much time has passed since *Rodriguez,* and we are now in a technological age that is far different than what the Court considered then.

The remedy for providing entry for students to the information age is for them to have computers to become computer literate—as important in this age as books and English competence. In an age where fake news is readily available online and where, it appears, far too many citizens are unable to think through their beliefs, question the premises from which they start, and reason intelligently to an appropriate conclusion, we should want informed and intelligent citizens, citizens who value the truth and know how to discern good reasons from bad reasons.

We are all of us involved in teaching our children to be good citizens. It is not the state's function alone. We must ourselves do what we can to encourage, and model, the skills and knowledge and values that are central to being citizens in a republic.

The solution starts when children are young, according to John Locke:

> It will perhaps be wondered, that I mention reasoning with children: and yet I cannot but think that the true way of dealing with them. They understand it as early as they do language;

and, if I misobserve not, they love to be treated as rational creatures, sooner than is imagined. Tis a pride should be cherished in them, and, as much as can be, made the greatest instrument to turn them by (Locke 2000, p. 142).

He is not suggesting that we teach them logic, but that even at a very young age, we give them reasons for doing what we do and ask them for reasons for doing what they do. We are to have a continual dialogue of reasoned exchanges when they are very young and ought to continue that dialogue in their schooling. The remedy for succumbing to fake news and conspiracy theories is, as Jefferson put it, "not to take it from them [because we cannot], but to inform their discretion by education." They ought to come to treat as natural providing reasons and assessing them as they mature to become a participant in the political process. Reasoning skills ought to be at the forefront of a basic education.

References

Adams J (1765) A Dissertation on the Canon and Feudal Law. https://thefederalistpapers.org/wp-content/uploads/2013/01/John-Adams-A-Dissertation-on-Canon-and-Feudal-Law.pdf

Adams J (1776) Thoughts on Government. p. 5, https://www.nps.gov/inde/upload/Thoughts-on-Government-John-Adams-2.pdf

Adelman L (2020). The Roberts Court's Assault on Democracy. Harvard Law & Policy Review, February 18, https://papers.ssrn.com/sol3/papers.cfm?abstract_id=3540318

Brown v. Board of Education, 347 U.S. 483 (1954) https://supreme.justia.com/cases/federal/us/347/483/

deTocqueville A (1966) In: Mayer JP, Lerner M (eds) Democracy in America. Harper & Row, New York

Dixon R (2020) Belarus's Lukashenko jailed election rivals and mocked women as unfit to lead. Now one is leading the opposition. The Washington Post, July 23

Federalist Papers (2001). In: Carey GW, McClellan J (eds) Liberty Fund, Indianapolis

Gary B., et al. v. Whitmer, No. 18-1855 (2020), https://law.justia.com/cases/federal/appellate-courts/ca6/18-1855/18-1855-2020-05-19.html

Griswold v. Connecticut, 381 U.S. 485 (1965), https://supreme.justia.com/cases/federal/us/381/479/

Jay J (1785) Letter to Dr. Benjamin Rush, March 24, https://oll.libertyfund.org/titles/jay-the-correspondence-and-public-papers-of-john-jay-vol-3-1782-1793

Jefferson T (1785) Letter to John Jay, August 23, https://oll.liberty.fund.org/titles/jefferson-the-works-vol-4-notes-on-virginia-ii-correspondence-1782-1786

Jefferson T (1820) Letter to William C. Jarvis, September 28, https://founders.archives.gov/documents/Jefferson/98-01-02-1540

League of Education Voters, https://educationvoters.org/2016/07/13/what-is-basic-education/

Lee S (2012) Five of the Most Confusing Ballots in the Country. ProPublica, Nov. 5, https://www.propublica.org/article/five-of-the-most-confusing-ballots-in-the-country

Locke J (2000) In: John W, Yolton JS (eds) Some Thoughts Concerning Education. Oxford University Press, Oxford, p §81

Paz C (2020) Read Barack Obama's Eulogy for John Lewis. The Atlantic, July 30. https://www.theatlantic.com/politics/archive/2020/07/read-barack-obamas-eulogy-for-john-lewis-full-text/614761/

Ricks TE (2020) First principles: what America's founders learned from the Greeks and Romans and how that shaped our country. HarperCollins, New York

Rush B (1786) Letter to Richard Price, May 25, https://www-jstor-org.ezproxy.rit.edu/stable/pdf/j.
ctvhhhddg.32.pdf?refreqid=excelsior%3Abdbe4d46a5e12a74d2ddc36ae8f7e913

San Antonio Independent School District v. Rodriguez, 411 U.S. 1 (1973), https://supreme.justia.
com/cases/federal/us/411/1/.

Stern R (2019) Transcendental Arguments. Stanford Encyclopedia of Philosophy, https://plato.
stanford.edu/entries/transcendental-arguments/.

Strauss V (2020) Federal court rules students have constitutional right to a 'basic' education —
including literary — in historic Detroit case. The Washington Post, April 24

Universal Declaration of Human Rights. Article 26, https://www.un.org/ruleoflaw/files/
ABCannexesen.pdf

Washington, George. Eighth Annual Message, December 7, 1796, https://avalon.law.yale.edu/1
8th_century/washs08.asp

Pluralism, Diversity, and Choice: Problems with School Vouchers

Emily R. Gill

Abstract At a time when regulation of religious schools and other private entities is decreasing, the greater use of school vouchers and scholarship plans like that recently upheld in *Espinoza v. Montana Department of Revenue* is problematic. First, I agree that public schools cannot be purely neutral and nonsectarian. Second, however, indirect aid such as vouchers does not instantiate neutrality; it is simply a different kind of nonneutrality. Finally, if we decide that public funding of private schools is simply a different form of public education, private schools, both religious and nonreligious, should be held to greater accountability, not less, to public values.

1 Introduction

On June 30, 2020, the United State Supreme Court decided the case of *Espinoza v. Montana Department of Revenue* (No. 18-1195). The Montana legislature in 2015 initiated a program of tax credits up to $150 to individuals donating to organizations awarding scholarships for private school tuition. The only participating scholarship organization focused on families with financial hardships or children with disabilities (Roberts, slip opinion, 2). Twelve of the thirteen participating schools were religious ones, and 94% of the scholarships were awarded to religious schools. The Montana Department of Revenue declared, however, that because the Montana Constitution bars the use of government money for any sectarian purpose, students in religious schools were not eligible for scholarships. Following an appeal by three parents, the Montana Supreme Court ruled against them by shutting down the entire program for both religious and nonreligious schools. The government is not required to aid private schools, and if it aids none, religious schools are not excluded (Liptak 2019; Liptak 2020).

E. R. Gill (✉)
Bradley University, Department of Political Science, Peoria, IL, USA
e-mail: gill@fsmail.bradley.edu

© The Author(s), under exclusive license to Springer Nature Switzerland AG 2022
J. McGregor, M. C. Navin (eds.), *Education, Inclusion, and Justice*, Amintaphil:
The Philosophical Foundations of Law and Justice 11,
https://doi.org/10.1007/978-3-031-04013-9_5

In a 5-4 decision, however, Chief Justice John Roberts ruled that withholding aid on the basis of the schools' religious status constituted unequal treatment and therefore violated the free exercise clause of the First Amendment. Unlike *Locke v. Davey* (540 U.S. 712 [2004]), in which the state of Washington was permitted to deny a scholarship to a student who would use the funds to prepare for the ministry, Montana posited a broader denial based upon schools' overall identification as religious. *Espinoza*, argued Roberts, better resembled *Trinity Lutheran Church v. Comer* (137 S. Ct. 2012 [2017]), in which the court overturned Missouri's exclusion of a Lutheran church's learning center because of its religious character from a competitive program using recycled tires to resurface school playgrounds. Unlike the scholarship in *Locke*, this otherwise available public benefit did not finance the direct provision of religious instruction. Although some of the Montana scholarship funds could serve religious ends, the Montana Supreme Court's application of the state no-aid provision was based solely upon status, not use—although some religious uses would not automatically be problematic. In a concurrence, Justice Neil Gorsuch added that status implies use. That is, the status of being a religious person or institution also carries the right within limits to act on those beliefs.

In dissent, Justice Ruth Bader Ginsburg, joined by Justice Elena Kagan, observed that unequal treatment cannot exist when the Montana Supreme Court struck down the program for both religious and nonreligious schools. Parents can still send their children to religious schools at their own expense. The free exercise clause is about "what the government cannot do to the individual, not . . . what the individual can exact from the government" (Ginsburg, slip opinion, p. 3). In another dissent, Justice Stephen Breyer argued that just as *Locke* permitted the state not to fund study for the ministry, Montana should be allowed not to fund an endeavor that is overall religious. Although subsidies through vouchers or tax credits constitute indirect aid, they would go toward the salaries of school personnel who are often considered "ministers" under recent interpretations of the First Amendment (*Hosanna-Tabor Evangelical Lutheran Church and School v. EEOC*, 132 S. Ct. 694 [2012]). Finally, in dissent Justice Sonia Sotomayor noted, "Until *Trinity Lutheran*, the right to exercise one's religion did not include a right to have the State pay for that religious practice" (Sotomayor, slip opinion, p. 8). "Short of ordering Montana to create a religious subsidy that Montana law does not permit" and that the Constitution does not require, "there is nothing for this Court to do" (pp. 3–4; see also p. 11).

Despite assertions that vouchers and tax credits are financed through private contributions, the money either emanates from the government or lowers the amount of tax money that the government would otherwise collect. This mechanism detracts from funds that might otherwise go to public schools. Such a voucher program is among the most recent blurrings of the line separating church and state. The choices it affords purport to increase pluralism and diversity, but under what definitions? The choices made by parents for their children's educations may facilitate the existence of a diversity of options. But because some educational programs may be closed to the values of the larger society, they will not automatically promote a diversity of values to which children may be exposed. Parents may choose private schools, religious or not, on their own dollars. Although the majority of private schools are religiously affiliated, my argument applies both to religious and nonreligious schools. On my view, a liberal democracy should not be allocating funds in ways that appear to endorse the programs being funded. "State funding, even if it is impartial among public and private schools, and even if it is doled out to parents, is ultimately inseparable from endorsement of the value, if not the truth, of religious tenets and practices, secular ideologies, and cultures" (Rosenblum 2003, p. 101; see pp. 101–102).

Ironically, a week after *Espinoza* the Supreme Court decided in *Our Lady of Guadalupe v. Morrissey-Berru* (No. 19-267) that teachers in religious schools may be dismissed in ways that contravene employment antidiscrimination laws. Focused upon the extent to which teachers in religious schools may be considered ministers of religion, it broadened the protection of religious schools under the ministerial exception as established by the court's interpretation in *Hosanna-Tabor*. If funds are increasingly directed toward private schools, religious or nonreligious, the stakes will be higher in many areas. Some private religious schools have refused admission to LGBTQ students or to those with LGBTQ families. A time of less regulation of private entities is not the time to ease up by providing public funds to them. As this funding increases, private schools should be *less* autonomous in setting their own policies and having them upheld, irrespective of one's agreement or disagreement with those policies.

Cogent arguments exist for school choice on grounds of both parental freedom and greater equality of opportunity for families whose children are stuck in inferior or failing schools. Many arguments against school vouchers are based upon concern for maintaining a clear separation of church and state. Although I share these concerns, my argument is a broader one. First, I offer some background to the present controversy. Second, I argue that giving parents educational vouchers does not fulfill the aspiration of greater governmental neutrality concerning education. It is simply a different kind of nonneutrality. Finally, I suggest that public funds for private schools, indirect as well as direct, should lead to greater regulation of these schools rather than less of it.

2   Background

As put by Michael McConnell, the "notion that public schools are neutral and nonsectarian—'merely civic and patriotic'—while private (especially religious) schools are 'parochial, divisive, or separatist'—is the foundational myth of our system of public education" (McConnell 2002, p. 105; see pp. 105–106). Any school will have a viewpoint and will implicitly inculcate values. I agree that no school can be neutral. At the most basic level, schools must decide what to teach and how; they cannot teach everything and cannot do so using every available pedagogical method. Unlike McConnell, however, I do not follow his logic to the conclusion that all education should be privatized.

As a descriptive term, neutrality has no meaning apart from some agreed-upon definition for the purpose at hand. Where neutrality used to connote separationism— no aid to religion lest the government favor some religions over others or favor religion in general—in recent years it has been interpreted as equal access, exemplified by *Widmar v. Vincent* (454 U.S. 263 [1981]), in which the Supreme court ruled that a state university's religious student organizations could not be denied access to campus buildings for their meetings when secular student organizations were admitted. No-aid provisions mean that religious entities are denied benefits available to nonreligious entities. The subject of religion affords a good example of the vagueness of a term such as neutrality. According to formal neutrality, government may cooperate with religion if the application of neutral and generally applicable laws has the effect of benefitting both religion and nonreligion. Religion is singled out neither for special benefits nor for special burdens. Either benefits or burdens may accrue, but only as the unintended, incidental effect of specific policies.

In 2002, for example, the Supreme Court allowed the Cleveland school district to offer vouchers to students in failing schools that could be redeemed in other districts' public schools or in private schools, both religious and nonreligious (*Zelman v. Simmons-Harris*, 530 U.S. 639). The establishment clause was deemed not violated not only because the vouchers were directed by parents and did not go directly to religious schools if those were selected, but also because the policy's intent was not specifically to aid religious practice *because* that practice was religious (Gill 2019, pp. 25–28). "For government aid to religious institutions or individuals to be valid, the religious recipients must be part of a *formally neutral class of recipients* that includes both religious and nonreligious individuals or institutions." Moreover, "aid that goes directly from the government to the religious recipient (*direct aid*) differs from aid that goes first to some private individual or entity who then chooses to funnel it to a religious recipient (*indirect aid*)" (Wexler 2019, pp. 113–114, emphasis original; see pp. 112–120).

Over time, the Supreme Court has been increasingly willing to allow even direct aid to religious schools for nonreligious purposes, basing its judgments upon the character of the aid itself, rather than upon whether the institution is "pervasively sectarian" (Lupu and Tuttle 2014, pp. 105–106). In short, when religion partakes of public benefits, it does so because its mission fulfills a secular purpose or social function that accords with public policy. Its religious nature is irrelevant. *Trinity Lutheran Church v. Comer* exemplifies this willingness even though the money for playground resurfacing was direct aid. In *Espinoza*, the donation-driven tax credits constituted direct aid. Both cases, however, can be described as instances of equal treatment. The outcome is still problematic, however, in that the government picks and chooses among the applicants for benefits, meaning that some religious manifestations will inevitably be favored over others when religious organizations are beneficiaries.

Public schools, as McConnell asserts, have never been neutral and nonsectarian. The ostensibly "common" schools that developed in the nineteenth-century United States were premised on the conviction that the schools should teach moral values and espouse nonsectarianism, or "the claim that there were moral principles shared in common by all Christian sects, independent of their particular theological beliefs" (Feldman 2006, p. 61; see pp. 57–92). Viewed by Roman Catholics as "sectarian Protestantism in disguise" (63), the theory of nonsectarianism denied any reliance on particular religious values, yet propounded a supposedly nonsectarian faith as a necessary grounding for civic morality. This sort of nonsectarianism has not been limited to the field of education. Concerning the historical regulation of sexuality, for example, "the secular state understands itself to be doing so not in the name of religion per se, but in the cause of a universal morality. And yet, time and again, particular religious interpretations provide the state's last best defense for its policies concerning sex" (Jakobsen and Pellegrini 2004, p. 22; see also pp. 13, 21–22, 31, 42, 104, 109–114).

"Nonsectarianism, in other words, was an ideology of inclusiveness that was fully prepared to exclude" (Feldman 2006, p. 85; see also p. 83). The dominant but unstated assumptions that animate American secularism have historically been Protestant. No-aid provisions in state constitutions largely emanated from anti-Catholic prejudice (McConnell 2002, pp. 106–114; Feldman 2006, pp. 71–92; *Pierce v. Society of Sisters* (268 U.S. 510 [1925]). McConnell in fact hypothesizes that if American common schools had allowed the inclusion of Catholic Bibles, religious instruction, and clergy where appropriate, separate Catholic schools might never have been created (McConnell 2002, p. 140 n. 78). Although the origins of no-aid provisions are less than admirable, this does not mean that we should open the floodgates to public funds for private schools, religious or nonreligious.

Indirect aid through vouchers or scholarships may be less straightforward than it appears. Although most private schools befitting from these programs are religious, in some cases church-state separation may not be an issue as donations are collected and distributed by nonprofit scholarship groups. A Georgia program started in 2008, for example, was to help needy students leave failing public schools, an admirable aim of many voucher advocates. Donations to these groups gave Georgians tax credits up to $2500 a couple. In reality, however, only a small portion was reserved for needs-based scholarships. Families could donate, receive the tax credit, and apply for scholarships for their own children. Some parents attempted to enroll their children in public schools in order to qualify for scholarships that would allow them to "leave" for the private schools they were already attending. Families with Georgia relatives could also donate and receive credits, including "swaps" where families could donate for each other's children. Other states such as Florida have strictly regulated scholarships to ensure their receipts by poor families, and only corporations are eligible for tax credits (Saul 2012, p. A1; see also Carey 2017). Close regulation is apparently necessary, and regulation is what private schools do not want.

3   The Nonneutrality of Education Disestablishment

The strongest case for vouchers or scholarships as a complete replacement for traditional public schools analogizes from independent religious choice to independent educational choice. In a liberal, pluralistic society, people hold a diversity of reasonable but irreconcilable views about education, and society is committed to "peaceful coexistence" among these adherents. McConnell therefore asserts that just as government does not prefer any particular religious or nonreligious worldview to any other, it also should not espouse any particular educational philosophy (McConnell 2002, p. 88). Although he notes that pluralism in education supports parental rights, his argument is a broader one. "It is time to discard the notion that democratic control over education is *in principle* the form best suited to a liberal, pluralistic society. It is the public school establishment—not educational choice—that is inconsistent with disestablishmentarian liberal values" (p. 89, emphasis original; see also McConnell 2000, pp. 100–107).

For McConnell, when all parties must adhere to one curriculum, conflict and intolerance result, just as they would if all were forced to adhere to one religious establishment. Why should majoritarian preferences determine educational aims? Although both winners and losers participate in determining outcomes, families who wish to include religious perspectives, for example, find "their own beliefs . . . constitutionally excluded from the outset" (McConnell 2002, p. 100). Although the ideal of democratic education is supposed to inculcate certain values and virtues that should be held in common in a liberal pluralistic society, conflict abounds as to what these are and how they should be interpreted. Imposing a thin understanding of democratic values through accreditation standards is reasonable, but prescribing a thick understanding of democratic virtues is not (pp. 101–104).

Simply designing a better curriculum, McConnell asserts, will not help. An effective presentation of democratic values in a pluralistic society can be accomplished, but like the Protestant-inflected one, only at the price of suppressing dissenters. Contrary to secularist stereotypes, for the most part religion and religious education have not been antidemocratic and intolerant, but have been forces for egalitarianism, justice, and democratic participation (McConnell 2002, pp. 122–129). Private school classrooms often encompass greater diversity than that found in public schools. And the success of some charter and magnet schools within public systems undermines arguments against choice outside of them (pp. 129–133). In sum, argues McConnell, just as in religion, the way forward for education in a pluralistic society is not a more diligent search for a "neutral" public curriculum, but a recognition that our diversity requires public support for private education. As put by Joseph Viteritti, "It is not the suppression of public schools by private schools that is at stake in the choice debate. It is rather a redefinition of what is meant by a public education" (Viteritti 2003, p. 21). I disagree. As the product of 6 years in an Episcopal preparatory school, I emphatically believe that private schools, both religious and nonreligious, can inculcate democratic values and also teach young people to think for themselves. My disagreement is with the use of public funds in private schools.

First, McConnell does not oppose the inculcation of democratic values. He simply believes that these values may be better conveyed by schools rooted in particular religious and moral principles than by traditional public schools (McConnell 2002, p. 125). This position is supposed to reflect neutrality more accurately than a system that espouses principles ostensibly shared in common among those of all worldviews. As noted by Amy Gutmann, however, although voucher advocates such as McConnell distrust those who claim expertise as to what educational principles are best for democracy, their advocacy of choice with minimal standards is itself a claim about what principles are best for democracy and about how these should be conveyed. Rather than promoting neutrality, educational pluralists are simply making a different claim. On her view, "If the time comes when citizens of a constitutional democracy should not as citizens say what principles we think are best for the education that we are publicly funding, then we will probably be ready for the end of public funding for schooling. This would be a sad day for constitutional democracy" (Gutmann 2003, p. 135).

Gutmann advocates what McConnell would view as a thick understanding of democratic values. The goal of civic education, she argues, both authorizes and obligates professional educators "to cultivate in future citizens the capacity for critical reflection on their culture" (Gutmann 1989, p. 85). More specifically, a liberal democratic society must inculcate the capacity "to choose rationally (some would say 'autonomously') among different ways of life" (p. 77), and it "must aid children in developing the capacity to understand and to evaluate competing conceptions of the good life and the good society" (Gutmann 1987, p. 44; see pp. 30, 44–45, 78–80). Her specific goal is that of preparation for citizenship in a society that advantages those who can participate in collective deliberation on public policy (pp. 34, 42). If children cannot evaluate competing ways of life—including modes different from those of their parents—the pluralism of families who may each represent a different unreflective consciousness "serves as little more than an ornament for onlookers" (p. 33; see pp. 30, 44, 14; see also Callan 1997, pp. 162–195; Gill 2001, pp. 220–229). For Gutmann, the civic virtue of mutual respect does not deny the value of diversity but instead promotes it by exposing children to the potential value inherent in different ways of life.

A thinner understanding of democratic values—and therefore more in keeping with McConnell's position--is represented by William Galston. For him, a public commitment to the development of the capacity for autonomy threatens individuals and groups that do not place a high priority upon critical reflection. "Liberal freedom entails the right to live unexamined as well as examined lives" (Galston 1989, p. 100; see pp. 153, 130). To valorize choice rather than protect diversity "is in fact to narrow the range of possibilities available within liberal societies. It is a drive toward a kind of uniformity, disguised in the language of liberal diversity" (Galston 1991, p. 329 n. 12; see also pp. 129, 256). The focus of civic education should be on "education within, and on behalf of, a particular political order" (Galston 1989, p. 90; see also Galston 1991, pp. 242–243). This calls for instruction in "a core of habits and beliefs supportive of the liberal polity" (Galston 1989, p. 96), rather than through training in the exercise of critical reflection. Although Galston's liberal state is not a neutral one, it is a minimally committed one. "The liberal state rests solely on those beliefs about the good shared by all its citizens, whereas every other state must coercively espouse some controversial assumptions about the good life" (Galston 1991, p. 93; see also pp. 82–97, 116, 180; Galston 2002, pp. 3–27, 93–109; Galston 2005, pp. 45–71, 187–196). Tolerance of others, for example, is a core virtue in liberal democracy, but this need not require critical reflection upon one's own commitments.

In actuality, both Gutmann's and Galston's accounts of civic education are thick. Neither is neutral; rather, each is nonneutral in a different way. And McConnell's advocacy of a thoroughgoing disestablishment of public education in favor of public funding for private education represents still a different version of nonneutrality. Moreover, if the United States were to move toward education disestablishment, this would happen at the behest of the sort of majoritarian preference that McConnell eschews. On some level, decisions about whether public education should be offered and, if so, what sort, are made in a liberal democratic republic through public authority informed by voters' choices. Conflict will still exist about the virtues of each alternative and about how each might be implemented.

Pierce v. Society of Sisters (268 U.S. 510 [1925]) ruled against a Ku Klux Klan-inspired anti-Catholic Oregon law requiring that all children attend public schools. Most well-known is its protection of parents' rights to direct their children's educations. A child "is not the mere creature of the State." Less noticed, however, is that although the state does not possess the authority to "standardize its children" (p. 535), it has the authority to prescribe reasonable regulations for all schools and teachers and to require certain subjects central to good citizenship. This requirement is congruent with Galston's belief that civic education should operate on behalf of a particular political order. If all schools, both public and private, both religious and nonreligious, are subject to state regulation and must also adhere to minimal standards for accreditation as McConnell notes, why should they not all be publicly funded? Why do they not all, in Viteritti's terms, fit the definition of public education? Even complete education disestablishment would still qualify.

The key question is what the particular political order of the liberal democratic polity actually is. On one account, the liberal state is committed only to "beliefs about the good shared by all its citizens" (Galston 1991, p. 93). One of these, apparently, is the right of parents to direct their children's education. "The ability of parents to raise their children in a manner consistent with their deepest commitments is an essential element of expressive liberty" (Galston 2002, p. 102). Regarding education, however, there seems to be little agreement as to what goods are shared by all, whether about the content of public education or about whether public education in the traditional sense should even exist. Although McConnell's position is more broadly based than one grounded on parental rights, his argument inevitably returns to them because education disestablishment would principally empower parents.

Along these lines, for example, Harry Brighouse and Adam Swift argue that although adults have a right to parent, parents' rights are fiduciary ones and are entirely derived from and justified by appeal to children's interests. Parents may confer some economic advantages upon their children and shape some of their values, but they should do so much less extensively than many currently believe. The advantages and values that parents may transmit are instrumental to the relationship, not intrinsically valuable. Regarding values, therefore, parents must endeavor "to do what they can to ensure not only that their children are properly equipped to function as citizens in a liberal democracy but also that they develop the capacity for autonomy" (Brighouse and Swift 2014, p. 150; see also pp. 151, 153). Some overlap in parents' and children's interests and values is a necessary basis for intimacy, and in the early years these are necessarily those of the parents. If children eventually reject some of their parents' values, moreover, they will do so based on some understanding of them (Brighouse and Swift, pp. 150–161). As adults, however, they need the ability to make independent and critical judgments and to act upon them (pp. 164–168; Gill 2001, pp. 13–30).

This description is a thinner definition of autonomy than that offered by Gutmann. Critics such as Galston, however, argue that an emphasis on the capacity for critical reflection on different ways of life is a comprehensive and therefore controversial notion of the good. It cannot and need not claim the allegiance of all liberal democratic citizens. Adherents of religious doctrines that require close control over individuals' formative sociopolitical environments, for example, view the traditional liberal hostility to these worldviews as a restriction on the free exercise of religion. Most individuals and groups in a liberal society will find expression for "their distinctive conceptions of the good. But for those who are left out, it is hard to see how liberalism can be experienced as anything other than an assault" (Galston 1991, p. 149; see pp. 143–149, 277, 259). Although Roman Catholicism in no way resembles a small sequestered group such as the Old Order Amish, the Catholics who established parochial schools undoubtedly experienced "nonsectarian" public schools this way.

On my view, any school with legitimate claims on public funding should incorporate in some form education in the *capacity* for autonomy, or what Brighouse terms an autonomy-facilitating education as opposed to an autonomy-promoting one. Children should be taught that diversity is a fact and to engage other views about the good life seriously, not that diversity is desirable or that they should be sympathetic toward other views. Autonomy-facilitating education "does not try to ensure that students employ autonomy in their lives, any more than Latin classes are aimed at ensuring that students employ Latin in their lives. Rather, it aims to enable them to live autonomously should they wish to" (Brighouse 2002, p. 268; see pp. 255–272; Gill 2001, pp. 25–30). A number of individuals make autonomous choices to live nonautonomous lives, as in those who choose cloistered lives of poverty, chastity, and obedience. What is key is that they had the ability to understand other options.

Some critics will regard even this autonomy-facilitating education as a controversial notion of the good. I do not argue that autonomy-facilitating education is neutral. What I do contend is that education—public or private—within any polity must be grounded in a set of commitments. As Galston states, the liberal state is not neutral, but minimally committed. Even a liberal polity cannot allow choice among all preferences that might conceivably exist. It does offer choice within the range of preferences entailed by its core commitments, or those that a given interpretation of liberalism puts forward. As put by Patrick Neal, "The positive defense of liberalism cannot be that it is neutral among preferences; it must be a defense of the *kind* of preferences liberalism produces" (Neal 1997, p. 28; see pp. 34–47). What remains are the implications for vouchers of a commitment to autonomy-facilitating education.

4   Be Careful What You Wish For

It appears that all parties agree that some degree of regulation and minimal standards of accreditation should apply to all schools, public or not. The problem is in determining what these should be. Although McConnell analogizes from independent religious choice to independent educational choice, we do not regulate or "accredit" houses of worship as we do schools. Moreover, public funds are not the foundation of support for houses of worship that they are for schools. One alternative would be to use some form of autonomy-facilitating education—or for that matter some other type—as a standard for determining which schools, religious or not, are eligible for public funding through vouchers. The standard would apply to a formally neutral class of recipients that comprised both religious and nonreligious institutions. It is not difficult to foresee, however, a great deal of contention over various degrees of autonomy-facilitating education offered by various educational programs. Because a great deal of regulation might be required, the temptation would be to water down whatever standards were developed to accommodate all comers.

Even voucher opponents do not oppose private schools. They do not support what Nancy Rosenblum terms the logic of congruence, or the idea that the health of liberal democracy requires voluntary associations to reflect democratic principles in their own internal life (Rosenblum 1998, pp. 36–41). Opponents do believe, however, that those who provide funds to private associations are entitled to hold the recipients accountable. A crucial distinction exists "between the entitlement to have one's rights respected, and the right to have one's viewpoint funded" (Brettschneider 2012, p. 120; see pp. 118–120; Tebbe 2017, pp. 255–256 n. 19), a conviction reflected in Sotomayor's dissent in *Espinoza*. This point is now reflected in the Sotomayor dissent in *Espinoza*. All voluntary associations, including private schools, need not themselves embrace internal pluralism. But they should expect to be held to particular standards if they are to receive public funds, whether direct or indirect, whatever these might be.

In this area, we could decide that no distinction should be made between religious and nonreligious schools. Religious choice would be neither endorsed nor penalized. Religion would be singled out neither for special benefits nor for special burdens. If these accrue, they would do so only as the unintended, incidental effects of specific policies. If religious schools received benefits such as religious exemptions unavailable to secularly orientated schools due to their religious character, nonreligious schools would not labor under regulatory burdens not shared by religious ones. By accepting even indirect public funding, religious schools would be understood to have agreed to these terms.

Based on this admittedly controversial proposition, I suggest that the right to freedom of association, here extending to both religious and nonreligious private schools, does not automatically preclude a degree of regulation. The extent of regulation depends upon the function of the group. The more a group exercises public functions as well as private ones, the weaker its claim to complete autonomy (Flanders 2016, pp. 105–115). Political parties, for example, are private organizations, but under a publicly run electoral system they also hold primaries that select nominees for general elections, and they therefore exercise a public function (p. 113). Similarly, corporations under the 2010 Affordable Care Act were mandated to provide health care insurance for their employees, and therefore they "were now the vehicles of a state program" and "were now in reality state actors" (p. 113). Chad Flanders concludes that a functional account of associational freedom perhaps best explains what political parties, religious organizations, and even businesses share in common. "The relevant question about whether we can regulate parties or religious organizations is not 'does this regulation interfere with the rights of the group?' but rather, 'will this regulation interfere with the ability of the group to serve its function, or can it better serve that function when it is relatively unregulated?'" (p. 116).

The existence of any public function or purpose does not automatically extinguish claims to associational freedom or the right of expressive association. Rather, "On the functional account, associational rights aren't trumps, but must instead be justified in terms of the goods they promote or fail to promote" (Flanders 2016, p. 118). In this context, the goods promoted by political parties are external to the group, or instrumental to the good of the political process. The goods promoted by religious organizations are intrinsically valuable—that is, instrumental to the good of religion for its participants. Yet religious organizations may have varied purposes, some private and some public. A church provides worship services, for example, but many also operate food pantries. When groups exercise public functions as well as private ones, "this accordingly weakens their claim to religious autonomy on the functional account. Their ability to advance *their* unique good competes with other goods at play" (p. 121; see pp. 115–121). Educational institutions assuredly serve public functions. This issue is especially salient when public funds are at stake.

The point can be illustrated by *Christian Legal Society v. Martinez* (561 U.S. 661 [2010]), in which the Supreme Court upheld Hastings College of Law of the University of California in depriving the Christian Legal Society (CLS) of its registered student organization (RSO) status when it refused to follow the school's accept-all-comers policy. Adherence to this policy was required to access school funds and certain channels of communication, and it mandated that any student be allowed to participate as a member or leader in RSOs regardless of the student's status or personal beliefs. The national organization of which CLS was a chapter required members and officers to sign and adhere to a statement of faith, including the tenet that sexual activity should occur only within marriage between a man and a woman. CLS challenged its own exclusion on grounds that Hastings' policy violated its right to free speech, expressive association, and the free exercise of religion (p. 661).

The Supreme Court ruled, however, that CLS's rights were not violated. By foregoing the benefits of official recognition, it could exclude anyone that it chose without compromising its principles. The all-comers policy was viewpoint neutral, as it ensured "that no Hastings student is forced to fund a group [through mandatory student activity fees] that would reject her as a member," as well as incorporating state antidiscrimination laws (*Christian Legal Society v. Martinez*, pp. 664, 689–690). Educational institutions should be able to select pedagogical principles consistent with their missions (pp. 686–687, 694–697). The dissent responded that Hastings' reliance on its all-comers policy was a smokescreen for a policy that discriminated against religious groups with a particular viewpoint (pp. 708–715). The majority's position was one of formal neutrality in that all groups were treated the same, but Hastings' policy exerted a disparate impact by burdening some organizations more than others.

The crux of *Martinez* rests upon the fact the CLS received public funding. When public funds are at stake, if the courts were to exempt dissenters from the application of antidiscrimination laws because of their "disparate impact" on those who wish to discriminate, "it would bring the application of antidiscrimination law, as we know it, to a grinding halt" (Ball 2017, p. 219; see pp. 218–221). Moreover, CLS was not an independent organization within the larger society, such as the Boy Scouts, but an organization within a larger entity with rights of its own, Hastings Law School of the University of California. Religious organizations often have the right to include or exclude members or leaders for their own reasons because this autonomy may be necessary to the very definition of the group's identity. The court in this case, however, regarded CLS not as an independent voluntary group, but "as an-association-within-a-university" (Flanders 2016, p, 109; see also Lupu and Tuttle 2014, pp. 188, 202–203). Because it was in part expressive of Hastings' values as well as its own, it was not simply a private actor but also a quasi-public one.

Martinez provides a lesson for those who advocate either direct or indirect funding for private schools, either religious or nonreligious. An organization's ability to exercise a recognized liberty right is not contradicted by a government refusal to support its activity, although the refusal may increase the cost of its exercise (Tebbe 2017, pp. 184–191). The government has discretion in refusing to support discriminatory groups even when some may be religious in nature. If Hastings had made the same argument with regard to a secular organization—for example, one supporting prochoice viewpoints concerning abortion that excluded antichoice advocates—I believe that the Supreme Court would have decided the same way. If in *Zelman v. Simmons-Harris*, a benefit—vouchers eligible for religious schools—was conferred on private religious schools but not because the schools were religious, in *Martinez* a benefit was denied, but again, not because of religion. Rather, the point that all student organizations should be open to all students took precedence over the fact that CLS was a religious organization. Religion is not thereby suppressed. "Instead, religion is merely asked to make concessions in return for taking advantage of public resources. If it refuses to do so, religion is still free to step back to the private realm" (Joppke 2015, p. 186; see pp. 182–186).

More generally, if public funds are increasingly directed toward private schools, both religious and nonreligious, the stakes will be higher not only in this area but also in others. Private schools, both religious and nonreligious, may and should become less autonomous than currently in setting their own policies and having them upheld, irrespective of whether one agrees or disagrees with them. Is this result worth the price? The reaction of some evangelicals in 2001 to President George W. Bush's Faith-Based Initiative, enabling faith-based organizations to apply for public funds for nonreligious purposes such as soup kitchens and after-school programs, is telling. These groups were allowed to retain their religious character and to use religious criteria in selecting employees. Yet with public money comes public surveillance and accountability. Some evangelical leaders objected to awarding money to non-Western religions; other leaders rejected the idea that funds could be directed to religious agencies that discriminated in hiring. Some of these objectors were the same ones that had long complained that the government discriminated against religious social service programs in favor of secular ones (Goodstein 2001). Despite the fact that eventually some of this aid was provided through vouchers, some programs received aid and some did not, meaning that some religions were favored over others.

Equal treatment or equal access advocates too often desire the same benefits as secular groups, but they also want exemptions from generally applicable laws for which secular groups are ineligible. They should not be able to have it both ways. I would make the same point regarding secular groups desiring exemptions on the basis of particular philosophical commitments. Education in a liberal democratic polity can never be neutral, even if it is completely disestablished or privatized. If privatized, it will in large part still be publicly funded. This calls for public accountability to voters and their representatives. Whether private or public, publicly funded education should be based on public purposes worth pursuing.

References

Ball CA (2017) The first amendment and LGBT equality: a contentious history. Harvard University Press, Cambridge, MA

Brettschneider C (2012) When the state speaks, what should it say? how democracies can protect expression and promote equality. Princeton University Press, Princeton, NJ

Brighouse H (2002) School vouchers, separation of church and state, and personal autonomy. In: Stephen M, Yael T (eds) Moral and political education (NOMOS 43). New York University Press, New York, pp 244–274

Brighouse H, Swift A (2014) Family values: the ethics of parent-child relationships. Oxford University Press, New York, New York

Callan E (1997) Creating citizens: political education and liberal democracy. Oxford University Press, New York

Carey K (2017) Arizona's shady tale of tax credit vouchers. New York Times, March 3: p. A13

Christian Legal Society v. Martinez. 2010. 561 U.S. 661

Espinoza v. Montana Department of Revenue. 2020. No. 18-1195

Feldman N (2006) Divided by God: America's church-state problem and what we should do about it. Farrar, Straus & Giroux, New York

Flanders C (2016) Religious organizations and the analogy to political parties. In: Micah S, Chad F, Zoé R (eds) The rise of corporate religious liberty. Oxford University Press, New York, pp 103–122

Galston WA (1989) Civic education in the liberal state. In: Rosenblum NL (ed) Liberalism and the moral life. Harvard University Press, Cambridge, MA, pp 89–101

Galston WA (1991) Liberal purposes: good, virtues, and diversity in the liberal state. Cambridge University Press, New York

Galston WA (2002) Liberal pluralism: the implications of value pluralism for political theory and practice. Cambridge University Press, New York

Galston WA (2005) The practice of liberal pluralism. Cambridge University Press, New York

Gill ER (2001) Becoming Free: autonomy and diversity in the liberal polity. University Press of Kansas, Lawrence, Kansas

Gill ER (2019) Free exercise of religion in the liberal polity: conflicting interpretations. Palgrave Macmillan, Cham, Switzerland

Goodstein L (2001) For religious right, Bush's charity plan is raising concerns. New York Times, March 3: pp A1, A10

Gutmann A (1987) Democratic education. Princeton University Press, Princeton, NJ

Gutmann A (1989) Undemocratic education. In: Rosenblum NL (ed) Liberalism and the moral life. Harvard University Press, Cambridge, MA, pp 71–88

Gutmann A (2003) Assessing arguments for school choice: pluralism, parental rights, or educational results? In: Alan W (ed) School choice: the moral debate. Princeton University Press, Princeton, NJ, pp 127–164

Hosanna-Tabor Evangelical Lutheran Church and School v. EEOC. 2012. 132 S. Ct. 694

Jakobsen JR, Pellegrini A (2004) Love the sin: sexual regulation and the limits of religious tolerance. Beacon Press, Boston

Joppke C (2015) The secular state under siege: religion and politics in Europe and America. Polity Press, Cambridge

Liptak A (2019) Justices will weigh in on Montana conflict over aid to religious schools. In: New York Times, December 24:A11

Liptak A (2020) Court weighs aid to religious schools. In: New York Times, January 23: A23

Locke v. Davey. 2004. 540 U.S. 712

Lupu IC, Tuttle RW (2014) Secular government, religious people. William B. Eerdmans, Grand Rapids, MI

McConnell MW (2000) Believers as equal citizens. In: Rosenblum NL (ed) Obligations of citizenship and demands of faith. Princeton University Press, Princeton, pp 90–110

McConnell MW (2002) Education disestablishment: Why democratic values are ill-served by democratic control of schooling. In: Stephen M, Yael T (eds) Moral and political education (NOMOS 43). New York University Press, New York, pp 87–146

Neal P (1997) Liberalism and its discontents. New York University Press, New York

Our Lady of Guadalupe v. Morrissey-Berru. 2020. No. 19-267

Pierce v. Society of Sisters. 1925. 268 U.S. 510

Rosenblum NL (1998) Membership and morals: the personal uses of pluralism in America. Princeton University Press, Princeton, NJ

Rosenblum NL (2003) Separating the Siamese twins, "pluralism" and "school choice." In: Wolfe Alan (ed) School choice: the moral debate. Princeton University Press, Princeton, NJ, pp. 79-103

Saul S (2012) Public money finds back door to private schools. In: New York Times, May 22: pp. A1, A14

Tebbe N (2017) Religious freedom in an egalitarian age. Harvard University Press, Cambridge, MA

Trinity Lutheran Church v. Comer. 2017. 127 S. Ct. 2012

Viteritti JF (2003) Defining equity: Politics, markets, and public policy. In: Alan W (ed) School choice: the moral debate. Princeton University Press, Princeton, pp 13–30

Wexler J (2019) Our non-christian nation: how atheists, satanists, pagans, and others are demanding their rightful place in public life. Redwood Press of Stanford University Press, Stanford, CA

Widmar v. Vincent. 1981. 454 U.S. 263

Zelman v. Simmons-Harris. 2002. 530 U.S. 639

Part III
Opportunity and Inclusion in Education

Interculturality, Justice and Inclusion: Key Educational Values for a Pluralistic Society

Columbus N. Ogbujah

Abstract To destroy a nation, as is visibly emblazoned at the entrance to a South African college, does not need the use of atomic bombs or long range missiles. It only requires lowering or destroying the educational standards. In other words, the growth or collapse of a nation depends on her educational system; on the skills and values the academe inculcates in the members of society. This essay identifies the myriad crises in modern Nigeria and most multiethnic societies as arising from an ineffectual educational system that tacitly promotes greed, unhealthy rivalry, and the tendency to view reality through a bifurcating lens that pitches humanity into "I-thou", "we-them" conflict trajectory. It highlights the harm done to society by various forms of injustice, exclusionary practices, and attempts at cultural homogenization; and concludes by noting that the adoption of the values of intercultural dialogue, justice and inclusion as key educational modules will help quell the tide of decay and promote growth in our pluralistic societies.

1 Introduction

Nigeria, like most nations of the world, is a multiethnic society, with segments espousing divergent values. These values sometimes jostle for supremacy, making it tough for members to arrive at compromises. At other times, perhaps because of weak institutional frameworks, bureaucrats easily subvert the rule of law and illicitly promote particularized or sectional interests. These have caused, between component elements, recurrent unhealthy rivalry, acrimony, and conflicts that not only mar cohesive living, but stunt the overall growth of the nation.

Now and again, scholars and policy makers attempt to rejig the system with policy thrusts intended to jumpstart the assimilation of new good values. At first, the

C. N. Ogbujah (✉)
Rivers State University, Department of Philosophy, Faculty of Humanities, Port Harcourt, Nigeria
e-mail: ogbujah.columbus@ust.edu.ng

effort was to reform and rename old institutions and programs: the Oil Mineral Producing Areas Development Commission (OMPADEC) established in 1992 to rehabilitate and develop the Oil Mineral Producing Areas of the country was renamed the Niger-Delta Development Commission (NDDC) in 2000, with perhaps, worse output. The recent Parliamentary probe of the agency's financial scandal is a big eye-opener. In a similar way, the poverty alleviation initiatives have undergone several transmutations before ending with its current name—*National Poverty Eradication Programme* (NAPEP). Yet, there is little to show for the billions of dollars expended in the programme. On the contrary, Nigeria, within this period, became the poverty capital of the world,[1] with nearly 50% of her estimated 180 million people living in extreme poverty.

In other areas, the effort is simply to copy and replicate policies of foreign nations adjudged to be efficient, without regard to due diligence and local relevance. This explains the constant shift in the education system. To equip youths with skills that will enhance self-reliance, the government made the transition from the 6-5-4 to the 6-3-3-4 system in 1982. In 1976, the Universal Primary Education, *UPE*, replaced the educational policy inherited from the British. Subsequently in 1999, the *UPE* was replaced with the Universal Basic Education, *UBE*, purportedly to provide FREE and COMPULSORY basic education for every child during the first nine years of schooling. This switch gave rise to the apparent 9-3-4 system that is currently running. In spite of these, the level of decay in the education sector, and society in general, is alarming: schools are grossly underfunded, with millions of drop-out children roaming the streets. Regrettably, this sterile policy flip-flop pervades most government institutions and agencies.

At the wake of these, every discerning mind has begun to ask questions: why, regardless of huge investments, is the nation on the path of decay? Why, after several lofty institutional reforms, is Nigeria on the verge of another civil war? Although there isn't a one-size-fits-it-all answer to these questions, a glimpse at the values espoused by the people and tolerated by society might give us a clue. Every society, as prescriber of values, determines what is good or bad, acceptable or unacceptable by its members. In other words, every society has its core values which it tries to transmit to its members through the educational system, either formally or informally. In the end, what is transmitted comes back to influence the norms and values of the society. The variety of transmissible educational values ensues from the assortment of existing societal values. In this sense, the educational values a society imbibes, for the most part, determine the attitudes and behaviors of her citizens, and in consequence, are responsible for her growth or decay. This essay looks at intercultural dialogue, justice and inclusion as key educational values that are fundamental to unity and growth. In doing so, it highlights certain values that are inimical to unity and progress in Nigeria, as well as in any multiethnic nation in the world.

---

[1] This conclusion was arrived at by World Bank after using various socio-economic indices to calculate the standard of living in world countries. See Kharas et al. (2018) article, para 9.

2 The Making of a Civic Nation

The concept 'nation' by nuanced step, is open to a variety of meanings. Originally, it entailed the agglomeration of a group of people with common ancestry, and a shared culture. The common ancestry explains the propinquity of its members since life in preindustrial world revolved around the immediate community. Members of a nation generally lived within the shades of an identified territory. The shared culture implied that members are united in such key elements as language, values, arts, folklores, etc. Thus, prior to the eighteenth century, the term nation signified a group of interdependent people from a common descent with ethno-linguistic and cultural commonalities. Nations did not necessarily have stratified territories or governments, but were comprised of people generated within specific situation, community, language, or culture. This is the reason we can find members of a nation in diverse regions of the world. Currently we have Biafrans (members of Igbo nation) residing in some states of the Niger-Delta region of Nigeria, in America, Europe, and other parts of the world. Similarly, we have the Kurds in both Syria and Turkey, and elsewhere. The original portrait of the concept 'nation' was strewn with ethnic and cultural frames.

But in everyday usage, *nation* has often been wrongly taken as a synonym for 'state' or 'country', especially in delineating specific terrains with governing structures. To be clear, state or country is a term that applies precisely to a self-governing political entity. In the course of time, two theories—*constitutive* and *declarative*, have been adduced to explain away the elements of statehood. The constitutive is a nineteenth century model that recognized a State as a juridical person in international politics if it is so recognized as sovereign by other sovereign States. In other words, what constitutes an enclave into a State is the fact of its being recognized by other already existing States as such. Conversely, the declarative shifted the emphasis from recognition to the fulfillment of some criteria. This was ratified in the 1933 Montevideo Convention, where it was approved that a State must have a permanent population, defined territory, governing structure, and the capacity to engage in interstate relations. Such a self-governing entity possesses statehood in international law, whether or not it is recognized by other States.[2]

So, whereas nations have dominant ethnic or cultural cores, States are strung together by their political or administrative character; whereas a nation might not have sovereignty over any particular territory (as members of the Jewish nation are scattered all over the world), a State is a self-governing entity with defined territory (like the State of Israel). The confluence of nation with State has given rise to one of the most popular coinages of modern political history—nation-state. A Nation-State is a territory inhabited by members of a single ethnic or cultural group, and whose sphere of influence is coextensive with the borders of the group;[3] it is the outcome of a racial drive that establishes a distinct political unit. Here, the two—*nation* and

---

[2] See articles 1 and 3 of the 1933 Montevideo Convention.

[3] See Smith (1995), p. 86.

state—coalesce to form a political structure based purely on ethnic lines. In reality, only few modern States like Somalia, Germany or Japan can actually fit into this 'pure' frame. All others either adopt the values of a dominant culture over those of the minorities, or are outright multinational States, with no epistemic privilege given to any of the constitutive ethnic groups.

To further deconstruct the concept, scholars distinguish two types of nations: *ethnic* and *civic*. Ethnic nation pertains to an administrative mass of people sharing common ancestry, language, culture, religion, a sense of cohesion and history that separate them from other stratified groups. In other words, it is a nation-state. This was the dominant assumption prior to emancipations that trailed the end of slave trade. By limiting its membership and influence to people of an identified cultural group, ethnic nation became the springboard for the emergence of nationalism. Ethnic nationalists seek for political autonomy and self-determination over specific lands and are oriented toward developing a national identity based on common features. But this orientation leaves it vulnerable to abuse, and the support of ethnocentric and protectionist posturing—twin charges for which it has been derided.

The alternate—*civic nation* is a contraption centered on the willingness of different ethnic groups to forge a unity with defined leadership structures. This happens either by war, as in when a powerful State defeats another and forces it to be part of its body politic (e.g. Russia's annexation of Crimea); or by the collective will of contiguous micro nations; or still by the express fiat of colonial lords, as did happen in the creation of most African States. In the West, the emergence of civic nations was propelled by the abolition of slavery. To grant citizenship to the erstwhile slaves was to grant them national identity; and to grant them national identity entailed that the parochial basis upon which nations were delineated had to be discarded for new criteria, new terminologies. A nation came to be defined not just in terms of language and ethnic descent, but much more on the basis of physical boundaries and recognized leadership. Thus, people of diverse ethnic groups, living within a milieu, with central leadership structures, came to be referred to as a *civic* nation.[4]

The *civic nation* is a cultural-political community that has become conscious of its coherence, unity, and particular interest.[5] The driving motif is the unity of constituent multiethnic groups, not by forceful assimilation but by promoting individual acceptance of guiding societal norms and values. The idea of *civic nation* has given rise to *civic nationalism* which contrasts its *ethnic* equivalent by insisting on inclusive principles that promote otherwise liberal values of justice, equality, tolerance and freedom. Whilst ethnic nationalism is stuck in its link with the closed lineage of specific peoples, civic nationalism is grounded on liberal-democratic ethics that are open to inclusion and dialogue.[6] When civic nationalists insist on

---

[4] See Ogbujah (2014a), pp. 53–60.
[5] See Smith (1983), pp. 128-132.
[6] See Markell (2000), pp. 38–63.

the preservation of national identity, it is not for the furtherance of exclusive tribal ethics, but for the safeguard of commonly accepted national ethos, since identity bolsters the capacity of individuals to lead autonomous and meaningful lives.[7] Moreover, liberal-democratic society cannot function optimally except in a stable *civic* nation.

Since they are multicultural in character, civic nations do not prioritize any culture over others. Even though individual groups have their peculiarities, members generally espouse shared sets of values and political culture, and are marked by attachment to civic institutions, justice and the rule of law. Nationhood is by citizenship, and citizens, as Jürgen Habermas insists, should not be forced to assimilate into a dominant culture.[8] Habermas decries genetic arguments that reinforce cultural hostility to immigrants as poison,[9] and like Brubaker, identifies the acceptance of provisions of a State's guiding rules as the legitimate basis for membership into a civic nation. Civic nationalism provides the legal and social frameworks to bolster political participation and intercultural dialogue which nurture understanding, inclusion and growth.

3 Blips with Ineffectual Educational System

There are few concepts in the world that are as popular as education, and perhaps, fewer that can influence the growth trajectory of the world, as it does. This is well captured by Jean Jacques Rousseau as he notes:

> Plants are shaped by cultivation and men by education.... We are born weak, we need strength; we are born totally unprovided, we need aid; we are born stupid, we need judgment. Everything we do not have at our birth and which we need when we are grown is given us by education.[10]

From as simple as Stone Age tools used by *Homo Floresiensis*, to as complex as genetic engineering and information technology of this age, education has been the bedrock of change and progress. It sparked the profound wisdom generated and transmitted in the valleys of the Nile, Tigris and Euphrates, as well as the postulations of Pre-Socratic materialists of classical antiquity. It influenced the Byzantine preservation of classical texts at the collapse of the Roman Empire and birthed the first University (Bologna) in Christian Europe. Its renaissance gave insights to the explosive scientific-technological discoveries of the twentieth and twenty-first centuries. Education is key to creating and sustaining unions, promoting justice and

---

[7] At several fora, I had highlighted the importance of identity in human life and growth. See also Kymlicka (1995).

[8] See Habermas (1989); see also the beautiful piece by Stilz (2009), pp. 257–292.

[9] Jürgen Habermas' denunciation of arguments that reinforce racism was cited in Taspinar (2010), para 8.

[10] See Rousseau (1762).

harmony, and turning aspirations into reality. When Aristotle observed that "all who have meditated on the art of governing mankind have been convinced that the fate of empires depends on the education of youth",[11] he was not merely restating the inestimable worth of learning. His concerns were perhaps, more directed to the sort of values transmitted, especially to future leaders of societies, because values can make or mar the growth of society.

Nigeria, like every nation, has its own educational values, some of which are implicit, while others are explicit. The implicit revolves around acceptable norms and practices transmitted in families and by other informal agents of socialization. The explicit are generally couched in the goals set for the formal educational sector. For the most part, the educational goals are set to help accomplish the overall National Development Plan, which entails building a free and democratic society, a just an egalitarian society, a great and dynamic economy, a united strong and self-reliant nation, and a land of bright and full opportunities for all citizens.[12] These are lofty ideals with the potential to transform any society. But in reality, the nation currently posts abysmal records in all of these indices. Rather, some of the values espoused and transmitted informally are antithetical to, and in fact inhibit the actualization of these educational goals.

The first of these hostile values is ethnicism—prejudice based on ethnic origin. Here, the average pre-school child is groomed to espouse ethnic bias, with little sense of national patriotism. At schools, the bias is amplified and reinforced in subtle and multiple ways by educators, administrators, and policy makers, by their acts of preferential treatment to students of preferred ethnic or religious extraction; or by accepting inducements to reward indolent or mediocre students. This, by no means, is peculiar to Nigeria, as history shows the US African-American children were never given the same opportunities as white children; or as the recent court files charging several people in college admission scandal involving bribery, money laundering and document fabrication to unfairly get students admitted to elite colleges in the US, indicate.[13] The difference perhaps, is in currently sustaining some of these anomalies as part of state policy thrust. The absurdity in the skewed use of 'quota' for college admissions and staff recruitments in Nigeria is but a ploy to enthrone ethnic hegemony. Besides the claim of 'righting' historical 'wrongs' (which is strongly contestable), its use readily sacrifices excellence at the altar of tribal sentiments, elevating mediocrity over and against national growth. In this seeming cycle of doom, the system generates segregated citizens entrenched in ethnic prejudices and corrupt practices.

Added to the disaster of ethnicism is the burden of dysfunctional processes. John Dewey identified educational aims with its processes, noting that a separation of the

---

[11] This piece of information is gleaned from Aristotle's quotes on the art of governance.

[12] These educational goals are enshrined in the National Policy on Education. See Federal Republic of Nigeria (1981), p. 7.

[13] The court filling reveals a long-drawn college admissions' cheating scandal that recently rocked some American Universities. See Shamsian and Mclaughlin (July 27, 2020).

two cannot be sustained without causing harm to the goals. In reality, what this means is that the objective of learning cannot be isolated from the structure of the curriculum, methodology, discipline, quality of instructors and their reinforcements, instructional materials or the schools themselves through which the ideals are impacted.[14] In their current sorry state, Nigeria's educational processes need to be revamped. With very low budgetary support, it is impossible to provide sufficient instructional materials, enforce discipline, care for the needs of teachers, or provide an atmosphere conducive for teaching and learning. Education aims to promote learning, but the theory of learning-conditions stipulates different types of instruction for the identified five diverse categories.[15] Each of the categories has different internal and external conditions of support. With the dearth of requisite conditions and materials of support in the nation's educational processes, the prospect of attaining the desired educational goals remains a mirage.

Perhaps, a more potent threat posed by a dysfunctional educational system comes from its ability to infuse the populace with divisive identity sentiments that apparently foreclose intercultural dialogue. Society prescribes educational values that are transmitted to younger generations. After being assimilated by the citizens, these values, in turn, become standards for making future judgements regarding the society. In this mutually reinforcing relationship, the values transmitted informally are very crucial because they serve as the bases for accepting or rejecting the values transmitted in the formal settings. Whereas in pluralistic nations like the United States, the blips arising from diffused divisive attitudes are often seen in systemic racism and sundry White-collar frauds, in Nigeria, as in most of Africa, they manifest in unabashed nepotism, greed, unhealthy rivalry, and the tendency to view reality through a bifurcating lens that pitches the citizens into the "I-thou", "we-them" conflict trajectory. The Nigerian civil war, the Rwandan genocide, and recently the Rohingya massacre are but small examples of the upshot of ethnic bigotry. Without educational reorientation, these entrenched glitches will not cease to clog the wheel of society's quest for survival and inclusive growth.

4 Interculturality, Justice and Inclusion: Didactic Ideals for a floundering Nation

There are a plurality of values that could be taught in families and schools which, in my opinion, can avert the slippery slope of Nigeria, or any multiracial society, into the abyss of self-destruction. Although they may overlap at some point—being individual ideals capable of generating harmony in their own respects, these values are distinct from each other and should not be substituted for one another. As the needs of different societies manifest in diverse ways, perhaps, due to national or

---

[14] See Dewey (1938), in Mortimer A.J. (ed.), (1992), vol. 55, pp. 100–120.

[15] See Gagne (1985), p. 243.

regional peculiarities, so would be the required educational values to satisfy the needs. Nonetheless, ideals with universal appeal will always be relevant to all societies either to enable them break new frontiers, or to help consolidate the feats they had already attained. To this end, I propose three values—interculturality, justice and inclusion as essential ideals to fill the educational needs of Nigeria, or other pluralistic societies facing similar challenges.

Interculturality or intercultural dialogue is to be understood in opposition to multiculturalism. Ordinarily, one would think that pluralistic societies are those with multiethnic leanings, and as such should benefit more when multiculturalism is adopted as a guiding ethic. This sort of thinking exposes the hollow in our delineation of the subtleties within the concepts, leading to unqualified equiparation of one with the other. Multiculturalism, as an ideology that accommodates mutual respect and harmonious living of people of diverse cultures, is premised on the non-acceptance of rankings among the committee of cultures. Its philosophy decries the ideal of a "melting pot" into which minority groups are required to assimilate, but rather promotes a model of seemingly unhindered freedom that ennobles members of minority groups in their distinctive collective identities and practices.[16] In support of this, theorists' arguments range from tolerating minority groups, to leaving them free from state interference, to recognition and positive accommodation in what has been labelled "group-differentiated rights."[17]Ironically, to admit of "group-differentiated rights" ultimately leads to endorsing "identity politics," or "the politics of differ-ence" which, is at the heart of xenophobic feelings.

Evidently, by promoting nationalist feelings, multiculturalism puts a knife across the very heart of intercultural dialogue. More so, its unqualified respect of divergent cultural values is a recipe for cultural relativism. Multiculturalism is often conflated with cultural diversity – passive admission of the empirical reality of differing cultures within a social space. But its "group-differentiated rights" component, which is exclusionary in structure, is pivotal to post-modernist orientation enmeshed in particularist underpinnings that directly oppose all forms of universal strictures. By accentuating the preeminence of lives lived in different, culturally constructed worlds—which is the essence of multiculturalism, postmodernism rejects every universal claim to knowledge, value and reality as a whole, and thus obfuscates the possibility of meaningful dialogue across cultures.

The term interculturality, on the contrary, designates a connection or relationship between culturally diverse people. Its core, according to UNESCO, lies in advancing a fair interaction of diverse cultures and the prospect of couching common cultural expressions through dialogue and mutual regard.[18] Scholars like Martha Nussbaum, Hans-Georg Gadamer, Marek Hrubec, etc., corroborate this view, though with emphasis on the import of mutual dialogue. Nussbaum, for instance, describes

---

[16]See Song (Spring 2017 Edition), para 1.

[17]See Kymlicka (1995).

[18]See article 4.8 of the Convention on the Protection and Promotion of the Diversity of Cultural Expressions.

interculturality as the idea involving "the recognition of common human needs across cultures and of dissonance and critical dialogue within cultures."[19] Her views are in direct contrast to current multicultural policies which fail to create inclusion, but rather legitimize and accentuate the specificity of isolated cultures within the same society. In more ways than one, multiculturalism has the potential to create conflict. My personal experience of this at a parish community in the summer of 2018 was an eye opener. Members of the two-station Parish in Bryson City—a suburb of North Carolina where I served, virtually had no interaction with each other: Masses were celebrated in English in one, and Spanish, in the other; they ran parallel programmes, hardly knew each other, and in some instances, shunned having to mingle with one another. Yet, they belonged to the same Catholic Parish community. It was absorbing and sometimes frustrating coordinating a multicultural Parish community without a community life.

Gadamer, in his turn, envisions the overlapping of different horizons through intercultural dialogue.[20] The aim of this overlap is not to create a 'melting pot' or cultural homogenization which is oppressive to alternative views of reality, but to provide an avenue for the appreciation of diverse values in a cosmopolitan world. In general, interculturality supports cross-cultural dialogue, challenges isolative tendencies of ethnic groups within civic nations, and engages further than simple acquiescence with the multicultural fact of multiple cultures inhabiting a society.[21] Its openness to value systems' interaction is a departure from multiculturalism; and its willingness to dialogue elevates the possibility of arriving at commonly shared 'transcultural' consensus that is significant for promoting understanding and cooperation in multiethnic societies.

Students need to know that it is not sufficient to be closed-up in themselves, and in their pursuit for "group-differentiated rights" which further isolate them from each other. They need to be inspired to be open-minded and curious about others' cultures through intercultural dialogue. By encouraging students in multiracial communities to freely interact with one another through group assignments, interfaculty quizzes, and social/extra curricula activities, value education engenders a deeper appreciation of the differences and commonalities of the respective cultures. This is a successful peacebuilding strategy in Ukraine and the United Kingdom,[22] and it is obvious that if properly implemented in a fractured heterogeneous society like Nigeria, youngsters will begin to better understand the underlying motifs behind each other's thoughts and actions, share in each other's experiences, and respect each other's values. They will then infuse this new narrative of tolerance into their families and communities.

---

[19] Here, Nussbaum is cited by Kolapo (2008), p. 134.

[20] See Gadamer (1997), p. 305.

[21] Interculturality goes beyond the mere recognition of multiple cultures dwelling within a society. See Penas-Ibáñez and López-Sánez (2006), p. 15.

[22] Here, Rattansi argues for the preference of Interculturalism over multiculturalism, and goes on to buttress his thoughts by providing important evidence of how projects of interculturality in the UK have, beyond expectations, promoted multi-ethnic civility. See Rattansi (2011). See also the Council of Europe's position paper on Interculturality (2020), paras 5–6.

To educate with intercultural values is certainly a potent strategy for reducing tension and promoting peace in pluralistic communities.

The second ideal essential for value education—*justice*, is central to ethics, law and social engineering. For this, John Rawls calls it "the first virtue of social institutions".[23] Its scope is wide, and its reach extensive, touching on every policy and action emanating from individuals, groups or the state. All policies and actions are adjudged just or otherwise depending on their relation to public morality or extant laws. This stretch complicates the efforts at mounting a comprehensive definition of the concept, leading to the rise of four strands, namely: distributive (fairness in the distribution of rights or resources), procedural (fairness/transparency of the processes of decision making), retributive (fairness in the punishment of wrongs) and restorative (fairness in restoring relationships to rightness). Each of these plays a significant role in the establishment of peace and prosperity in pluralistic societies.

Distributive justice pertains to fair sharing of the rights and responsibilities, resources and burdens of society; the impartial allocation of assets and liabilities. While most people do agree that resources and burdens should be fairly distributed, there is not a consensus as to what constitutes the criteria for fairness. In their essay, "Types of Justice", Maiese and Burgess draw everyone's attention to the import of equality, equity and need as determinants of fairness: *equality* means that everyone should get the same share, regardless of inputs; *equity* means reward should be in measure of one's contribution; while *need* implies that people should be rewarded according to their necessities in life.[24] So, whether seen as equality, equity or need, those who carry the burden of grooming youngsters must understand and teach them that distributive justice or fair allocation of resources and burdens is vital for creating a stable and prosperous society. When people feel they are not given fair treatment in the distribution of assets and liabilities of society, as is perceived in the skewed resource allocations in Nigeria, or the racial bias that led to the killing of African-Americans like George Floyd, they will, more likely than not, engage in actions capable of disrupting civic order.

Whereas procedural justice emphasizes the need to formulate an impartial and consistent process that enlists representations of all stakeholders, retributive justice deals with the fair punishment of offenders. The idea is to even-up the injuries inflicted on victims in order to satisfy aggrieved parties, deter prospective offenders, reinforce societal moral boundaries, and incapacitate offenders from causing more harm to society.[25] Restorative justice, on the other hand, seeks to (re)establish relationships to rightness by means that repair hurts on victims, restore offenders to good standing, and heal damages to interpersonal and communal relationships caused by crimes. In point of fact, fairness, and its acuity in the distribution of resources and liabilities, in decision-making processes, and in punishment of

---

[23] See Rawls (1999), p. 3.

[24] Maiese and Burgess (2020), para 2.

[25] See Ogbujah (2014b), pp. 42–29.

offenders is key to having a safe, peaceful and just society. Justice, however it is viewed, will always involve a set of ideas, values and social practices that ensure all persons and groups enjoy social security, can contribute in decision-making processes, exercise mutual respect and care for one another, and engage in actions that preserve the natural environment for future generations.[26] This can be achieved for the overall benefit of societies, if care-givers, teachers and administrators make fairness not just the nexus of pedagogy, but their undergirding canon of praxis. Injustice of any kind is recipe for solicited violent conflicts.

The third important value—*inclusion* refers to the non-discriminatory policy of accepting and supporting people in the exercise of their franchise under the law. In most societies, there are multilayered systems of social categorizations. Beyond the distinct features that make a cultural group unique from others within a milieu, there are elements that separate individual human beings from each other, and by reason of which there is diversity. These elements include race, gender, age, religion, sex, political affiliation, etc. Not to discriminate in access to employment, resource allocations and other opportunities on the basis of these elements of diversity, is called inclusion. Inclusion is the fair and respectful treatment of all in the distribution of assets and liabilities; the granting of equal access to resources and opportunities to everyone.

The questions of who should be included, and where, are very critical to pedagogy in a fractured multiethnic nation. Most people are familiar with the "caste" system in India but seem to overlook its ignominious equivalence in the United States which, till now, has remained the instrument of subjugation of black race. In understudying America's method of race subordination in order to shore-up its Aryan race, even the Nazi Germany was appalled at their hypodescent or 'one-drop-rule' of exclusion. For the racist American or Nazi German, inclusion was for the 'White race in a White land.' Similarly, the component ethnic groups in Nigeria have constituted themselves as identity blocks, with somewhat ridiculous belief in the purity of tribal members, akin to those of the Nazis and White supremacists. This has fueled nepotism in the allocation of resources, employment opportunities and promotions; religious bigotry; and a culture that supports systemic corruption in political life. As a result, there are palpable tension and anger among the populace, unhealthy ethnic rivalry, breakdown of law and order, and radicalization of youths and groups. In the essay, "Ethics of exclusion and its impact on Nigeria's trudge to Democracy", we already noted how the exclusive policies of the current president Buhari's administration have cascaded the revival of separatist movements, such that within one calendar year of its inception (May 29, 2015–August 2016), the number of militant groups agitating against the Federal Republic of Nigeria rose from two to twenty.[27] With the recent brutal dispersal of the #ENDSARS protesters by security agents, and the apparent genocide at Oyigbo in retaliation of alleged killing of security officers by the Indigenous People of Biafra (IPOB) members, there is

---

[26] See the work of Hulbert and Mulvale in M. A. Hurlbert (ed.). (2011), pp. 9–22.

[27] See Ogbujah (2020), pp. 75–88.

every reason to expect the emergence of more resistant groups. Thus, exclusion and indiscretion widen the ethnic, regional, religious, and generational gulfs amongst clusters within a multiethnic nation. They promote corruption, and increasingly constrict the paths to national integration and growth.

Value education, using the ideal of inclusion, sets out to ensure no one is excluded from their common patrimony; from the 'livewire' of the society to which they belong. This begins by formulating legislations to empower agencies like the Equal Employment Opportunity Commission (EEOC) in the US, or the Federal Character Commission (FCC) in Nigeria, to enforce Non-Discriminatory rules in workplaces. In turn, parents, teachers, and administrators have the onerous task of applying these rules by exuding inclusion in words and deeds, so as to properly mentor their wards, students, and staff. The vision is to protect individuals who face discrimination due to social categorizations. Creating an inclusive culture, much like administering justice, is helpful to intercultural dialogue and supportive to citizens' productive engagements. Promoting same in schools may perhaps be the way out of the seemingly cyclic conundrum Nigeria faces.

5   Conclusion

Every culture, every society prescribes values which determine what is good or bad, right or wrong, acceptable or unacceptable within the society. The prescribed societal values are then expressed and transmitted through the educational system either formally—through the schools, or informally—by other agents of socialization. Although there are some universal values applicable to all in different cultures, the existence of peculiarities leads to divergent educational values across nations. To preserve their identity, every society transmits her cherished core values to her progenies. The rise and fall, growth and decay of any society, for the most part, depend on the sort of educational values shared and transmitted to her members. In this sense, society is the determinant of its fortunes.

Protests following the death of George Floyd, and the recent #ENDSARS protests have rekindled discussions regarding racism in the United States, and endemic institutional impunity in Nigeria. Nigerians are livid with injustice and corruption that somewhat leverage on ethnic bigotry. Racial and ethnic biases have stealthily permeated the lives of successive generations in both countries, such that to make positive changes, the value system needs to be restructured. Education has the potential to erase these "home errors" by stressing the futility of traditional stereotypes and prejudices, and the attendant harm they portend; and by projecting the benefits of harmony and collaborative living.

Beyond advocating for the use of interculturality, justice and inclusion as values for transformative education, special attention needs to be paid to teachers: what they know, and what they do in and out of classrooms. Teachers are the most essential drivers of what and how much students learn. A learning boom has, at its core, a teaching boom, and vice versa. The public is entitled to good, value education to overcome the crises of racism and ethnicism. The English philosopher—Francis Bacon was apt in noting that "knowledge is power." So, if the public is armed with the right kind of knowledge, citizens will come to terms with their real struggles and find ways to overcome racial and ethnic prejudices that have for long, held them hostage.

References

Aristotle (2020) A quote by Aristotle. https://www.goodreads.com/quotes/30596-all-who-have-meditated-on-the-art-of-governing-mankind

Council of Europe (2020) Interculturality: a value for citizens. https://www.coe.int/en/web/interculturalcities/interculturality. Accessed 30 July 2020

Dewey J (1938) Experience and education. In: Mortimer AJ (ed) 1992. Great Books of the Western World, vol 55, 3rd edn. Ency. Britannica Inc., Chicago

Federal Republic of Nigeria (1981) National policy on education. Federal Ministry of Education, Lagos

Gadamer H-G (1997) Truth and method. Continuum, New York

Gagne R (1985) The conditions of learning, 4th edn. Holt, Rinehart & Winston, New York

Habermas J (1989) Political culture in Germany since 1968. In: Nicholsen SW (ed. and trans.) The New Conservatism: Cultural Criticism and Historians' Debate. MIT Press, Cambridge, pp 257–292

Hurlbert M, Mulvale PJ (2011) Defining justice. In: Hurlbert MA (ed) Pursuing justice: an introduction to justice studies. Fernwood Publishing Co. Ltd., Manitoba, pp 9–22

Kharas H, Hamel K, Hofer M (2018) Rethinking global poverty reduction in 2019. https://www.brookings.edu/blog/future-development/2018/12/13/rethinking-global-poverty-reduction-in-2019/.

Kymlicka W (1995) Multicultural citizenship: a liberal theory of minority rights. Oxford University Press, Oxford

Maiese M, Burgess H (2020) Types of Justice. https://www.beyondintractability.org/essay/types_of_justice. Accessed 30 July 2020

Markell P (2000) Making affect safe for democracy?: On "Constitutional Patriotism". Polit Theory 28(1):38–63

Montevideo Convention (1933) Articles 1 and 3. https://en.m.wikipedia.org/wiki/Montevideo_Convention

Nussbaum M (1998) Cultivating Humanity, cited in Kolapo FJ (2008). Immigrant academics and cultural challenges in a global environment. Cambria Press, New York

Ogbujah C N (2014a) Fostering national integration: a guide from Nyerere's philosophy of Ujamaa. Res Human Soc Sci 4(26): 53–60

Ogbujah CN (2014b) Ethics, law and justice in Achebe's Things Fall Apart. IOSR J Human Soc Sci 19, Issue 12(1): 42–29.

Ogbujah CN (2020) Ethics of exclusion and its impacts on Nigeria's trudge to democracy. J Afr Stud Sustain Dev 3(6):75–88

Penas-Ibáñez B, López-Sáenz C (2006) Interculturalism: between identity and diversity. Peter Lang AG, Bern

Rattansi A (2011) Multiculturalism: a very short introduction. Oxford University Press, Oxford

Rawls J (1999) A theory of justice, Revised edition. Harvard University Press, Cambridge

Rousseau JJ (1762) Émile, On the Philosophy of Education. https://www.spaceandmotion.com/Philosophy-Education.htm. Accessed 14 July 2020

Shamsian J, Mclaughlin K (July 27, 2020) Here's the full list of the people charged in the college admissions cheating scandal, and who has pleaded guilty so far. https://www.insider.com/college-admissions-cheating-scandal-full-list-people-charged-2019-3

Smith AD (1983) Ethnie and nation in the modern world. Millennium 14(2):128–132

Smith AD (1995) Nations and nationalism in a global era. Polity Press, Cambridge

Song S (2017) Multiculturalism. In: Zalta EN (ed) The Stanford Encyclopedia of Philosophy. https://plato.stanford.edu/archives/spr2017/entries/multiculturalism/

Stilz A (2009) Civic nationalism and language policy. Philos Public Aff *37*(3):257–292

Taspinar Ö (2010) Multiculturalism and Integration in Europe. BROOKINGS. https://www.brookings.edu/opinions/multiculturalism-and-integration-in-europe/

UNESCO (2020) Diversity of Cultural Expressions. Interculturality. https://en.unesco.org/creativity/interculturality

The Concept of Opportunity and the Ideal of Equality of Educational Opportunity

Alistair M. Macleod

Abstract My aim in this paper is to explore some of the conditions under which the concept of opportunity is intelligibly applicable (including some of the respects in which it both resembles and differs from the closely related concept of freedom) in order to (a) provide an account of the diversity there is in the kinds of educational opportunities any society has good reason to make available to its members and (b) draw a distinction between two dramatically different ways in which the ideal of equality of educational opportunity must be understood.

For educational opportunities of certain kinds, the ideal of equality of educational opportunity requires opportunities to be provided on the same basis to everyone in society. For educational opportunities of certain other kinds, the ideal requires restriction of effective access to the opportunities: only the members of (often quite small) sub-classes of the members of a society can be represented as having the opportunities, but the rules restricting access must satisfy certain demanding normative conditions.

For the full realization of the first version of the ideal, there are familiar economic and socio-cultural hurdles to be overcome. For the second, there are, in addition, the exacting normative requirements embedded in the competitive processes that have to be established.

I am grateful to all who took part in the discussion of earlier versions of this paper, including Nathan Brett, Deen Chatterjee, Owen Clifton, Sue Donaldson, Ben Ewing, Arthur Hill, Colin Farrelly, Kyle Johannsen, Will Kymlicka, Andrew Lister, Colin Macleod, Margaret Moore, David Rondel, and Christine Sypnowich.

A. M. Macleod (✉)
Department of Philosophy, Queen's University, Kingston, ON, Canada
e-mail: macleoda@queensu.ca

1   The Concept of Opportunity

The concept of opportunity can be meaningfully applied only if answers can be provided to two questions: (1) opportunity to what? and (2) opportunity for whom?

1.1   Opportunity to What?

The "X" in "opportunity to X" must, in any context in which the notion of opportunity is meaningfully applied, have some determinate value. It's a mistake, consequently, to suppose that no such determinate, context-specific value need be provided because "X" in "opportunity to X" can always be glossed as "X for any value of X." There is no such thing as opportunity to X for all values of X: talk about opportunity as such (or opportunity sans phrase) is meaningless. If politicians or political parties claim to be committed, as they sometimes do, to the creation of an "opportunity society" or a society in which "opportunity" (*sans phrase*) will be created or fostered, the claim would have to be dismissed as meaningless if it couldn't be glossed as "opportunity to X" with some specification (at least contextually) of the determinate values of "X" for which a commitment to the creation or fostering of opportunity was being flagged.

If the (logical) requirement for specification of the value of "X" in "opportunity to X" is to be met, recognition must be given to the indefinitely large number of quite different ways in which, context by context, the value of "X" can be specified. The opportunity to increase the number of places in a school system is quite different, for example, from the opportunity to liberalize the criteria for admission to the emergency department of a downtown hospital.[1]

Numerous, and diverse, though the values of "X" can be in "opportunity to X," the logically permissible values can be divided into at least two instructively different sub-classes. On the one hand, there are values of "X" in "A has an opportunity to X" in which it stands for something A is in a position to do (an action, an activity, or a decision, perhaps). A may, for example, have an opportunity to apply for a credit card or to play tennis or to accept a job offer. On the other hand, there are values of "X" in "A has an opportunity to X" in which A has an opportunity to be treated in some determinate way—the opportunity, for example, to be provided with health-care services whenever needed or to be supported financially when disabled or unemployed. The difference between the opportunities in these two sub-classes is marked, grammatically, by the fact that in the first set of cases what follows "to" (in "opportunity to") is a verb in the active voice (an act or

---

[1] These are rather specific examples of what the "X" in "opportunity to X" might mean in municipal election debates in which rival candidates both claim to be committed to expanding the opportunities of town residents. Less specific examples might mark the distinction between enhancement of educational opportunities on the one side and, on the other, expansion of healthcare opportunities.

action of some sort), whereas in the other cases what follows "to" is a verb in the passive voice (a mode of treatment of some sort).

While most ordinary references to "opportunity" are reasonably upbeat—because the opportunities in question are assumed to be welcome or desirable in some way— it's a mistake to think of opportunity as itself an inherently normative notion. While many of the opportunities we routinely refer to are indeed valued opportunities, it's only contingently that this is the case. We sometimes have occasion to talk about opportunities we don't want to see realized, opportunities which, if they happen to exist, we would prefer to get rid of. For example, given an increase in the incidence of burglaries in certain urban districts, burglaries that are taking place during daylight hours and not under cover of darkness, the explanation may be that, in the areas targeted by burglars, most of the houses are vacant during working hours and consequently the "opportunities" for undetected break-and-enter crimes are much greater than they would be if more residents were at home during the day.[2] There can also be opportunities about the value of which there is room for debate. An example is the opportunity, within a hierarchy of some kind, "to rise" or "to get ahead"—a frequently-cited opportunity in discussions of "social mobility." Despite the confidence with which it is cited as a valuable opportunity, its value can easily be contested when it is noted how problematic the presupposed "hierarchy of positions" can be, not only because some of the positions may themselves be objectionable or because the rungs in the social ladder may be too far apart, but also because access to even the lowest of these rungs may be unavailable to some members of society.

If opportunities can be desirable or undesirable, how is this to be accounted for? It's implausible to suppose—in a last-ditch attempt to defend the idea that the notion of opportunity is an inherently normative notion—that the term "opportunity" itself just happens to have both a favorable and an unfavorable connotation. It's more reasonable to recognize that opportunity is itself an evaluatively-neutral—a merely descriptive—notion and that consequently the normative "coloration" (so to speak) of the opportunities that, in particular contexts, are taken to be desirable or undesirable, as the case may be, is attributable to special features of the contexts in which the notion is applied. For example, where the "X" in "opportunity to X" is either a (in principle) desirable action of some sort (as it is when it's a stand-in for "take care of children while their parents are at work") or where "X" stands for some desirable mode of treatment (as when it means "receive treatment for a painful injury"), the opportunity will understandably be a welcome opportunity. However, where the "X" in "opportunity to X" is an action or mode of treatment there's good reason to deplore (as when it's either the opportunity to perform burglaries undetected or the opportunity to become the leader of a racist organization like the Ku Klux Klan), the opportunity will not surprisingly be regarded as a decidedly undesirable opportunity.

---

[2]Examples of this sort can easily be multiplied. Thus, it's something of a commonplace that **opportunities** for becoming addicted to dangerous drugs are more numerous in communities with a high incidence of poverty and unemployment.

1.2 Opportunity for Whom?

Attention to the specific contexts in which individuals can be said to have, or to lack, certain identifiable "opportunities" also serves to show that the class of those who have, or who lack, given opportunities often has to be specified with some care.[3] Consider, for example, policies designed to foster opportunities for post-secondary education. The proper interpretation and assessment of the opportunity-promoting policies that a political party may be proposing make it crucial to determine whose opportunities for post-secondary education are in the event going to be fostered if the policies are implemented. While educational policies for the provision of the opportunity to acquire specialized job-related skills can defensibly restrict such opportunities to only the members of certain sub-classes of a society, it matters to their defensibility which particular sub-classes are to be given access to the opportunities. It's one thing if the intended beneficiaries of the expansion will be those who are likely to fill the relevant jobs most acceptably; it's quite another if the opportunities are to go to friends, or relatives, or colleagues of the sponsoring politicians.[4]

Once the "whose opportunity?" question is asked, however, it becomes clear that it's a mistake to assume that the only possible—the only coherent—answer will specify the individuals (be they many or be they few) who either already have or might in the future come to have an opportunity of some specified kind. It is of course very often individuals whom we must identify as the actual or potential possessors of some specific opportunity. But it's perfectly acceptable—wholly consistent with the conventions governing ordinary, non-stipulative, "opportunity" talk—for groups, or organizations, or governments to be singled out as the (actual or

---

[3] It clearly doesn't follow from the fact that an individual A in community C has (ascertainably) the opportunity to X, that this is only because **any** individual in community C (let alone **any** individual—anywhere) has that opportunity. How the opportunity to X is in fact distributed among the members of C is a question to which many different answers are possible—and it's at least in part an empirical question which of these answers is correct in any given situation. It should go without saying, consequently, that the existence, here or there, in some society, of the opportunity to X does **not** imply that **everyone** in that society has an opportunity to X. This point is so obvious—and so seemingly trivial—that it might well be wondered what, if anything, makes it worth making at all, even in passing. However, it is worth recalling the frequency with which politicians—and ordinary citizens who are echoing what politicians say—speak of the policies they favor as creating "opportunity" or as part of a commitment to creating an "opportunity" society, when "opportunity" is intended as shorthand for "opportunity **for all**." It may become clear when this sort of political claim is scrutinized or challenged that the policies being championed are by no means policies that will foster "opportunity" (even the specific sort of opportunity that may be taken, contextually, to be at issue) for **everyone**. It may become clear, indeed, that the beneficiaries of the policies in question are certain (perhaps rather narrowly circumscribed) sub-classes of the members of society.

[4] For example, it's not uncommon even in otherwise quite benign jurisdictions, for additional openings in programs for the education of aspiring members of highly regarded professions to be filled not on the basis (strictly) of the comparative merit of would-be applicants but rather on the basis, at least in part, of such extraneous considerations as wealth, social standing, and family background.

potential) possessors of some specific opportunity. Consider such examples as the following: (a) "The investment opportunities enjoyed by financial firms are much ampler in societies with weak rules for the regulation of business activity"; (b) "While the individual members of tenant protection associations have little clout against unscrupulous landlords, collectively they have an opportunity to offer effective resistance to rent-gouging"; and (c) "While the government had an opportunity to enact tough environmental protection legislation in the months immediately following its election, that opportunity no longer exists."

One reason for taking special note of cases where answering the "Whose opportunities?" question needn't take the form of identifying the individuals who have the opportunities is that, even when individuals can (and should) be said to be beneficiaries of opportunities of certain sorts, the opportunities in question may have to be regarded, simultaneously, as opportunities ascribable to certain groups to which the individuals in question belong. Thus, when the individual members of a democratically-organized society are said to have an opportunity to vote periodically in society-wide elections, this opportunity is systematically linked to an opportunity that is enjoyed by the society as a whole when its members are seen, collectively, as being in a position to help determine the general direction (to be) taken by the government. The opportunity the individual members have to "vote" is an institutionally-facilitated opportunity they have to participate in a collective decision-making process—the process whereby the election of members of the society's legislature gives the members some (perhaps in practice rather small) measure of control over the laws the government enacts, the policies it adopts, and the institutions it creates or maintains. While the members of a society, when they vote, are taking advantage, individually, of an opportunity the constitution gives them, it is only because this enables them to participate in a collective decision-making process that they can be said to be taking advantage, simultaneously, of an opportunity to help determine the political orientation of the government. The opportunity to vote is thus both an opportunity they have as individuals and an opportunity they have only as members of an electorate.

2 Concepts of Opportunity and Freedom: Similarities, Differences, and Connections

2.1 Similarities

Despite the fact that it's not uncommon in many contexts for the notions of opportunity and freedom to be regarded—mistakenly—as virtually equivalent notions, their identification is in part traceable to several striking features they share.

Just as it makes no sense to talk about opportunity **as such** (opportunity *sans phrase*)—as though the opportunity "to X" could be glossed as opportunity to X for **any** value of X—so too it's a condition of the intelligibility of freedom talk for it to be clear, contextually, what sort of freedom is being referred to. Just as the question "opportunity to what?" is a question to which a broad range of answers can in principle be provided, so too it is essential for it to be recognized that the question "freedom to what?" admits of a large number of very different answers.

Again, meaningful talk both about "opportunity" and about "freedom" requires that determinate answers be available to the questions "opportunity for whom?" and "freedom for whom?" and in neither case can it be assumed that "for all" (or "for everyone") provides the obvious—all-purpose—answer. On the contrary, even when it's clear from the context what the boundaries are of the group or class within which certain opportunities or certain freedoms are (to be) enjoyed, it's not uncommon for the specified opportunities or freedoms to be within the reach of only the members of specifiable sub-classes of the groups or classes in question.

Yet again, while it's tempting for the notion of freedom, like the notion of opportunity, to be regarded as a normatively-toned notion, it has to be recognized that—on the contrary, and in line with what was said in Sect. 1.1 about the notion of opportunity—it is a normatively-neutral or merely descriptive notion. It's true that in many familiar contexts, freedom, like opportunity, is highly valued and its absence regretted. The explanation, however—as in the case of the notion of opportunity—is that when the contexts in which freedom is favorably regarded and its absence regretted are fleshed out (through specification of the relevant answers to both the "freedom to what?" and "freedom for whom?" questions) it becomes clear that the normative work is being done, not by the term "freedom" itself, but rather by certain features of the contexts that have been supplied. Thus, if in given circumstances A is identified as a member of a democratically-organized society and X as the act of expressing an opinion about the government's most recent legislative decisions, A's being free to X will be celebrated because democracy is an approved form of government and the right of citizens to provide public assessments of the government's actions is a highly valued right. A's freedom to X will be favorably evaluated, in short, because of the values assignable to "A" and "X" in "A's freedom to X", not because the term "freedom" must itself be viewed in this context as an inherently normative term. On the other hand, however, in a context in which A's freedom to X is deplored rather than celebrated – as is the case when A is identified as a criminal gang and X as the act of extorting protection money from small grocery stores – the explanation for our refusal to approve of A's freedom to X is our knowledge that "A" is a criminal gang and "X" an act of extortion, not any inherently normative role played by the term "freedom" in this context.[5]

---

[5] Indeed, if—*per impossibile*—an attempt is made, in the "gangster" case, to identify the word "freedom" in "A's freedom to X" as doing even part of the normative work done by this phrase, it would have to be given a pejorative connotation. Not only would this be a remarkably counter-intuitive interpretation of its meaning but it would also be strikingly at odds with any attempt to represent "freedom" as an inherently approval-expressing term.

2.2 Differences

There are, however, several differences between the notions of opportunity and freedom, differences that stand in the way of their being regarded as more or less interchangeable notions.

One of these is that, whereas any comprehensive specification of the sort of freedom to which reference is being made in any context calls for an answer to be given to the question "freedom from what?"—a question that looms large in the articulation of the various versions of the doctrine of "negative freedom"—there is no such counterpart question in the case of the concept of opportunity. It makes no sense to ask the question "opportunity from what?"

A second important difference has to do with the range of possible answers that can be returned to the question how "X"—in "opportunity to X" and "freedom to X"—can be specified. Whereas "freedom to X" makes sense only when "X" stands for an action, or activity, or decision of some sort (that is, only when "X" is a verb in the active voice), the "X" in "opportunity to X" can stand for either an action (or activity, or decision) of some sort or a mode of treatment of some sort. That is, "X" (in opportunity "to X") can be a verb either in the active or in the passive voice. For example, someone can be said (close to indifferently, it might be thought) either to have the opportunity to express disagreement with some government policy or to be free to express this sort of disagreement. However, whereas people can have the opportunity to be admitted to a hospital for needed surgical treatment or to have the opportunity to be voted into office in a municipal election, it makes no sense to talk about their being free to be admitted to a hospital for surgery or about their being free to be voted into municipal office.[6] Neglect of this distinction is responsible for failure to notice that, despite the similarity there is between the questions "opportunity to what?" and "freedom to what?", the range of available answers is much greater to the former than to the latter.[7]

---

[6] Sue Donaldson pointed out in discussion that talk about someone being "free" (and not only having an opportunity") to be admitted to a hospital for surgery—or about being "free" (and not only having an "opportunity") to **be elected** to municipal office—doesn't breach, strictly, any ordinary language rule. Such uses, however, are somewhat unusual (calling, perhaps, for a special context of some kind). So although the linguistic distinction between someone's being "free" **to X**, where "X" is a verb in the active voice, and someone's having an "opportunity" **to X**, where "X" is a verb In the passive voice, may need to be drawn more circumspectly, these uses are so much commoner that it's tempting to regard them as "standard" (or even "paradigmatic") even if the temptation should perhaps be resisted.

[7] It's also arguable that failure to appreciate the significance of this point contributes to the prevalence in some quarters of the idea that **all** "rights" are **freedom** rights—rights to freedom to X, for some value of X.

2.3   Connections

These similarities and differences between the notions of freedom and opportunity show that it's a mistake to suppose that freedom and opportunity are substantively identical notions and that consequently the terms "freedom" and "opportunity" should be treated as strictly synonymous (and inter-substitutable) terms. Nevertheless, in most (if not all) contexts they are closely connected (perhaps even necessary linked) notions—a fact that helps to explain why they are often treated as identical notions. The tightness of this connection between freedom and opportunity is perhaps best illustrated by noting that whenever, in a broad range of familiar situations, A is said to be free to X, it will not only be the case that A can be said to have an opportunity to X, but also that A's having an opportunity to X is among the necessary conditions of A's being said to be free to X. For example, if A, in given circumstances, is "free" to express an unfavorable opinion about the government's most recently announced policies, it'll also be the case—to make the point in "opportunity" language—that A has, in this situation, an "opportunity" to voice public criticism of the government's recent policies. Moreover, if there were any reason to think that A did not have this sort of opportunity in the circumstances, the claim about A's being "free" to criticize the government publicly on this occasion would be false.

3   An Ambiguity in the Concept of Opportunity?

3.1   Do Opportunities Admit of Degrees?

It's clear from some—but only some—familiar uses of the notion of opportunity that it admits of degrees. For example, when a certain kind of technology is introduced into poorly equipped primary schools, the pupils will typically have better opportunities for (say) the rapid acquisition of basic mathematical skills. Again, when nurses are added to an otherwise understaffed hospital, patients recovering from surgery will normally have better opportunities to acquire the strength they need to be safely discharged. Applicants for skill-demanding positions will generally have better opportunities for appointment if they have given serious attention to development of the relevant skills. And so on.

However, it's equally clear from certain other familiar uses of the notion of opportunity that it doesn't always admit of degrees. Uses of the notion of opportunity can be readily cited that do not accommodate questions about "how good" a given opportunity happens to be. Thus, if A is given a ticket for a concert she would very much like to go to (and if tickets are no longer available at the box office), she will have an opportunity to go to the concert that she wouldn't otherwise have had at all: all she needs to do is turn up at the appointed hour at the concert venue with the ticket in hand. An opportunity of this sort (in these circumstances) is an opportunity someone either does or does not have. It makes no sense to think of it as an opportunity that admits of degrees. The opportunity can of course be characterized in a wide variety of ways—as a "good" opportunity, or as an "unexpected" opportunity", or as a "welcome" opportunity—and each of these qualifying terms admits of degrees. The opportunity can be a "very" good or a "very" welcome opportunity, or a "somewhat" unexpected opportunity, and so on, but the opportunity itself doesn't admit of degrees.

One interesting feature of the distinction between uses of the term "opportunity" in which the opportunity does not admit of degrees and uses that accommodate questions about "how good" opportunities are is that it points to what seems to be a crucial ambiguity in the notion of opportunity.

3.2   Two Senses of "Opportunity"

On the one hand, there are uses of the term "opportunity" in what might be said to be the "strong" sense of the term. These uses link "having an opportunity to X" with "having the ability to X" (whether straight away or in due course)—where having the ability to X is, at least roughly, equivalent to being in a position to "choose" to X, either without further ado or only after certain other (mediating or "bridging") choices have been made.

Examples of cases where an opportunity (in this strong sense) can be seized "without further ado" would include not only the "gift-concert-ticket" case which was cited earlier, but also the sort of case in which someone who has received a firm job offer has an opportunity to take up the job by simply deciding to do so, or in which (to take the sort of opportunity to X where the "X" is not an action or activity of some sort but a service that's available on request to all who ask for it) someone who needs some (universally available) service has an opportunity to take advantage of it.

Examples of cases where preliminary steps have to be taken by the possessor of an opportunity to X before the opportunity can be seized would include cases where a long-distance runner has an opportunity to compete in a demanding marathon that is still several months away or where an opportunity comes up to spend an upcoming summer holiday at a remote mountain cottage.[8]

---

[8]While in these cases the opportunity that is available can be seized only after certain preparatory steps have been taken, the opportunity can still count as an opportunity in the strong sense because the agent is herself assumed to have the power to take—that is, to be in a position to choose to take—all the intermediary steps. The long-distance runner, for example, may have to undertake and maintain a suitably demanding training regime, and the person with the opportunity to holiday at a remote mountain cottage may have to adopt and execute a travel plan to get there What's important in these cases is that it should be within the power of the agent who has the opportunity to take all the required intervening steps by herself.   ˙

On the other hand, there are uses of the term "opportunity" in what might be called the "chance" (or, better, the "one chance in N") sense of the term. In this sense, the putative possessor of the opportunity to X—an individual A, say—cannot take advantage of the opportunity simply by choosing or deciding to X. This is because she lacks the power or ability in the circumstances to make any such choice all by herself (either straightaway or in due course) and is consequently dependent on unfolding events that are beyond her control (including events controlled by decisions others must make) if she is to have, at some future date, an opportunity to X in the strong sense. Applicants for a job, for example, have an "opportunity" to secure appointment, not in the sense that it's "up to them" to take up the position, whether straightaway (by simply deciding to do so) or in due course (after steps have been taken to try to secure it), but in the sense that, as applicants, they at least have a "chance" of landing the job.[9] Similarly, if we hark back to the "recovering patient" and "early mathematics education" cases, to say that a patient has a better opportunity of recovery after surgery if a hospital has a large complement of nurses, or that a child has a better opportunity of developing mathematical skills if she has access to I-Pads or computers, is to say that the patient's chances of early discharge from hospital or the child's chances of consolidating the ability to carry out arithmetical calculations quickly and accurately, will be better than they would be if nurses weren't added to the hospital's staff or if the primary school weren't provided with the relevant electronic devices.

4   The Goals of Education and Kinds of Educational Opportunity

Recognition is commonly given to at least three broadly distinguishable goals of education and there is corresponding diversity in the kinds of educational opportunities a society needs to foster.

Sometimes—in the case of (what might be called) education for **employment**—the goal is the acquisition of the sorts of knowledge and the development of the sorts of skills that are essential to the playing of some role within, and the making of some contribution to, a society's economy (on a fairly broad understanding of what counts as its "economy").

Sometimes—in the case of (what might be called) education for **self-fulfill-ment**—the goal is one the members of a society have as individuals with a wide range of distinctive potentialities, the goal of developing their unique capacities and interests with a view to engaging in activities that give texture and meaning to their

---

[9] As was noted earlier, this sort of opportunity admits of degrees because the chance of landing the job may, for some applicants, be a rather remote chance and for others a very good chance.

lives, especially in areas outside any formal role they play in their society's economy.[10]

Sometimes—in the case of (what might be called) education for **citizenship**—the goal is one the members of a democratically-organized society have a stake in pursuing, in order to be in a position to take part, effectively and on an equal basis even if only in various indirect ways, in a society's collective decision-making processes, especially those that give shape to the policies, laws, and institutions that provide the framework for individual and social life. While education in these contexts is particularly closely related to enabling a society's members to enjoy the political benefits and discharge the political obligations they have as citizens, recognition should also be given to important non-political dimensions of citizenship. For example, citizens have a wide range of non-political rights and duties that enable them to play important roles in the associations, organizations, and clubs of the many kinds that make up (what is often referred to compendiously as) "civil society."

While this three-part account provides reasonably accurate coverage, if only in a rather general and somewhat skeletal way, of the major goals of education, it's important to give proper recognition both (i) to the many respects in which these goals intersect and overlap, and (ii) to ways in which these goals, if too narrowly construed (as they not infrequently are), may fail to cover important education-related activities.

For possible examples of (i), consider the many overlaps there are in the educational strategies that are geared to pursuit of the educational goals identified in this three-part account. Thus, strategies that promote more effective citizen engagement may be valued also for their contribution to the living of a life of flourishing. Strategies that enhance personal well-being can also contribute to success in the pursuit of job-related goals. Successful pursuit of occupation-related educational objectives can overlap with effectiveness in the exercise of the rights (and in the discharge of the obligations) of citizenship. And so on.

Despite their obviousness, there is some danger of such overlaps being overlooked, not only when only one of these educational goals is being emphasized in some context, but also when, in that context, the goal itself is too narrowly conceived.

As for (ii)—apropos the risk that the specified goals of education, if too narrowly conceived, may fail to cover important education-related activities—consider the role education can play in the lives of those who pursue knowledge **for its own sake**. While knowledge in its different forms—in the many branches of the physical, biological, and social sciences, and in non-scientific disciplines of different kinds (historical, literary, philosophical, etc.)—has a crucial role to play not only in the

---

[10]Since "self-fulfillment" is also often related to the contribution individuals can make to their society's economy in some official capacity, the sort of self-fulfillment absolutely **all** the members of a society have a stake in **just as individuals** is self-fulfillment through participation in (what might be regarded as) **leisure**-time (or "off-duty") activities.

development of a society's economy (again, on a broad understanding of what its "economy" comprises), but also in the successful pursuit of individual self-fulfillment and in the effective exercise of the rights (and discharge of the obligations) of citizenship, and while educational strategies for the advancement of knowledge in all these ways give content to a great deal of what we have in mind when we highlight the importance that attaches to education in any society, there's a risk that associating education too exclusively with the proffered three-part account of the goals of education will leave out the sorts of educational strategies that might be crucial to the pursuit of knowledge **for its own sake**. Scientists whose education focuses too narrowly on the practical role science can play in facilitating economic success, personal fulfillment, and effective political engagement, may be ill-equipped to make the kinds of break-through scientific discoveries for which no practical application can yet be envisaged. In non-scientific disciplines too—in the educational programs provided in the "Arts" departments of colleges and universities—educational opportunities can be problematically restricted when too much importance is attached to their "relevance."

The more broadly—and thus comprehensively—the goals of education have to be understood, the more diverse the educational opportunities are to which recognition must be given if effective strategies for the achievement of these goals are to be adopted. It is then a matter of importance to distinguish between (A) the kinds of educational opportunities that can be made available to everyone and (B) the opportunities that can only be provided to (often quite small) sub-classes of a society.

Examples of educational opportunities on both sides of the line between (A) and (B) can easily be provided. For example, the opportunity to receive a primary school education[11] is clearly an opportunity that can (in principle, and in any society) be made available to all young children.[12] On the other hand, the educational opportunities needed for admission to the medical profession (or for that matter, to

---

[11] An interesting feature of this sort of educational opportunity is that the beneficiaries—whether these are identified as the children who are in a position to benefit from a primary school education or as their parents or guardians—are normally not free to choose whether or not to take advantage of the opportunity. On the contrary, they normally have a **duty** to do so. The educational opportunity to receive a primary school education is thus—in a sense, as well as somewhat paradoxically—a **mandatory** opportunity. (I am indebted for this point to Will Kymlicka.) While recognition should be given to "mandatory" opportunities, it should be noted that while such opportunities can be identified (at least roughly) as opportunities their putative beneficiaries have a "duty" to take advantage of, by no means all "mandatory" **duties** are describable, simultaneously, as mandatory **opportunities**. When a state has the power to impose a military draft, those who are ordered to report for military service can be said to have a "duty" to do so. But while the duty can be characterized as "mandatory," it would be grossly misleading to try to describe draftees as being provided with a "mandatory" **opportunity**.

[12] There can, of course, be a failure in some societies for strictly universal primary school policies to be adopted, either because an under-developed economy makes them unaffordable or because heartlessly elitist policies are adopted by reactionary governments. But these kinds of failure obviously don't show that primary school educational opportunities cannot in principle be provided to **all** children in **any** society.

any skill-demanding occupational group) are clear examples of the sorts of opportunity that can be made available to only some members of any society: they are opportunities that only the members of certain (typically quite small) sub-classes of any society can enjoy, and the opportunities will consequently be provided, typically, on a competitive basis of some kind.

5 The Ideal of Equality of Educational Opportunity

Since some educational opportunities can in principle be provided to all the members of any society and others to only some members on a competitive basis, no single account can be given of the ideal of equality of educational opportunity. A distinction has to be drawn between what it takes to secure equality of educational opportunity when the opportunities in question can in principle be provided to everyone and what is involved when competitions for the opportunities in question have to be staged and monitored. In cases of the first sort, the equalization of educational opportunity calls for the opportunities in question to be made universally available. In cases of the second type, equalization of opportunity is a matter of making opportunities available to only those who emerge as winners of appropriately structured competitive arrangements.

If equalization of educational opportunities in these two kinds of cases is taken to be a desirable and not merely a possible objective—and its assumed desirability is a given if equality of educational opportunity is to be represented, as it commonly is, as a socio-political **ideal**—what does it take to show that both versions of the ideal are defensible?

5.1 The Defence of Equalization of Opportunity for Everyone

For one familiar version of the ideal—the version that takes universality of access to opportunities to be a veritable hallmark of what equalization of opportunity requires—demonstrating its defensibility involves at least three steps. First, since not all the educational opportunities that could in principle be provided are desirable opportunities—the opportunities provided by the sponsors of a variety of (moral, religious, or political) **indoctrination** programs being plausible examples[13]—the

---

[13] It's implausible to suppose that indoctrination can't intelligibly be taken to be a form of "education" when the term "education" is used correctly—since ordinary educated usage doesn't support any such restrictive definition—and nothing is gained by simply stipulating that a sharp distinction should be drawn between education and indoctrination. In any case, there are lots of other examples of educational opportunities that fail the desirability test: the job-related educational opportunities states may provide to facilitate research into, as well as manufacture of, internationally prohibited chemical gases; the training programs provided sales representatives who are paid by

acceptability in principle of the opportunities to be promoted in the name of the ideal has to be confirmed. Second, since not all in-principle-acceptable educational opportunities that a society has the power to underwrite are opportunities that it ought to underwrite, a case must be made for including candidate opportunities among those that are to be protected under the ideal. A society's failure to provide support in school sports programs for development of the skills needed for the playing of some such minority sport as water polo can't plausibly be cited as a violation of the ideal of equality of educational opportunity. Third, since even universally available educational opportunities may disproportionately benefit some members in ways that are unfair, the opportunities must be fairly distributed if the ideal of equality of educational opportunity is to be satisfied. The ideal can be breached, for example, even when an educational opportunity is provided for all the members of a society, if access to the opportunity (the opportunity to receive a primary school education, say) is provided on terms that give easier access to some families than to others.

5.2 The Defence of Competitive Equality of Opportunity

For the second version of the equality of educational opportunity ideal—the version that applies to educational opportunities that cannot in principle be made universally available—a somewhat different set of conditions must be met if a society's educational arrangements are to pass muster. The first of these conditions is the same as one the first version of the ideal has to meet: the educational opportunities to be protected must be benign opportunities. The opportunity to go to medical school or to acquire carpentry skills will be covered, but not the opportunity to master burglary techniques or the opportunity to develop embezzlement skills. Second, since the educational opportunities in question can be provided for only some members of a society, competitive arrangements of some sort must be established to determine the membership of the favored subclasses. Third, these arrangements will normally have two ingredients. On the one hand, there will be arrangements to determine who is to be eligible to apply for the limited educational opportunities that are on offer. On the other hand, there will be arrangements to determine which of the eligible applicants is to be selected, in the event, to take advantage of these opportunities. Fourth, while the rules governing competitive arrangements of both these kinds must be normatively defensible if the arrangements are to satisfy the ideal of equality of opportunity, there can understandably be difference of view (especially when relevant social circumstances are acknowledged to be diverse) as to both the interpretation and application of the criteria of defensibility. Thus, while both "capacity" (understood

---

their employers to boost demand for marketable goods among ignorant or gullible consumers; the educational opportunities political parties provide their employees to enable them to establish data banks about the potential vulnerabilities of voters; and so on.

as highlighting the need for applicants to be capable of successfully completing limited-access educational programs) and "aptitude" (understood as covering the personal qualities that enable applicants to make effective use of these programs) are perhaps the most obvious of the required defensibility considerations,[14] they can be invoked in different ways by advocates of different versions of the equal opportunity ideal. Allowance should be made, for example, for both (a) versions of the ideal for which educational opportunities should be provided for all who can contribute, through the jobs they do, to maximization of the welfare of society, and (b) versions for which the ideal is essentially a justice-based ideal. In the case of versions of the first sort, there can be differences of view as to what should count as contributing to the welfare of society—about whether, for instance, what maximizes a society's GNP can be a proxy for maximization of a society's welfare.[15] In the case of versions of the second sort, there can be differences of view as to whether equality of educational opportunity is a free-standing principle of justice (as it perhaps is in Rawls's **A Theory of Justice**[16]) or whether it's better viewed as a subordinate principle, whether derivable from a more general equal opportunity principle[17] or from a more fundamental principle of justice of some other sort.[18]

---

[14]While it's uncontroversial that such considerations as race, religion, ethnicity, socio-economic status and family connections would be inappropriate determinants of success in the securing of job-training-related educational opportunities, there's some room for difference of view about how and how far "capacity" (or competence) and "aptitude" considerations should be allowed to determine success. For example, the nature of the occupations for which educational opportunities are to be provided—as well as the circumstances in which competitions for these opportunities are being mounted—may help to determine whether the relevant "capacity" (or competence) standard is a "threshold" standard or one that calls for **extent** of capacity or **degree** of competence to be determined. How important "aptitude" considerations should be taken to be may also depend on how crucial to occupational success reliability in the carrying out of long-term job commitments is taken to be: for many jobs, once the required threshold of competence is reached, reliability in the execution of job-related tasks is what matters.

[15]When equality of educational opportunity is defended on economic efficiency grounds by members of the business community and the defense is assumed to be consistent with their commitment to GNP-maximization, a charitable interpretation of their view would be, not that they think GNP-maximization is an intrinsically desirable social goal, but that they think of it as worth aiming at **because (and so far as)** it can be taken to be a reliable means of maximizing the welfare of society as a whole.

[16]Rawls (1971). While the equalization of educational opportunity isn't represented by Rawls as a derivative principle of justice—as deriving from some more fundamental principle, whether of justice or morality—it's problematic whether this implies that he regards it as a "freestanding" principle. Moreover, in the canonical formulations Rawls provides of the "principles of justice as fairness", the requirement that (job-related?) educational opportunities are to be "open to all" is embedded in what he refers to as his "second" principle, and this principle has at least as much to say about just economic distribution as about justice in the distribution of educational opportunities of certain kinds.

[17]As would be the case if it were a specification, for a certain range of cases, of a more general principle that calls for equalization of opportunities for the living of a satisfying and fulfilling life.

[18]As might be the case if "impartiality" of treatment were thought to be the most fundamental requirement of justice.

5.3   Equalization of Opportunity in Education for Employment, Education for Self-Fulfilment, and Education for Citizenship

How, then, do these two models of what it takes for the ideal of equality of educational opportunity to be sponsored help to facilitate effective pursuit of the three broadly distinguishable goals of education that were described earlier—education for employment, education for self-fulfillment, and education for citizenship?

While a fine-grained answer to this question would no doubt have to incorporate various qualifications (to allow for special features of the specific contexts in which each of these goals can be pursued), a rough-and-ready answer might be as follows. On the one hand, when arrangements are being made to educate the members of a society for employment in the skill-demanding positions any society must aim to fill and when, consequently, opportunities for the acquisition of the requisite skills have to be provided on a competitive basis only to certain sub-classes of the population, conformity to the ideal of equality of educational opportunity must take the form of arranging for the competitive rules controlling access to the relevant opportunities to be defensibly structured. On the other hand, when the educational goals to be pursued have to do either with enabling individuals to achieve self-fulfillment over time or with facilitating effective citizen participation in socio-political decision-making processes on all issues that have an impact on their general well-being, the version of the ideal of equality of educational opportunity that must be applied is the one that calls for the required educational opportunities to be made available on the same basis to all the members of a society.

6   Concluding Remarks

While I have merely gestured (in passing) towards some of the normative questions that must be tackled if a systematic defense is to be mounted of the ideal of equality of educational opportunity in its two most intriguingly different versions, and while parts of this defense are bound to be somewhat controversial, full implementation of the ideal also requires many recalcitrant obstacles to be overcome.

In the case of the version that calls for certain kinds of educational opportunities to be made universally available, there are familiar economic and socio-cultural obstacles to be overcome. For example, even generously-funded school and college programs can turn out to be inadequate in face of unpredictable (and sometimes intractable) differences in the economic circumstances of potential beneficiaries.[19]

---

[19]Laudable attempts to eliminate financial barriers to effective access to "universally available" school and college opportunities cannot, for example, be entirely successful. Individuals can suffer from debilitating illnesses, economic misfortunes (like prolonged periods of unemployment) can interfere in irremediable ways with the educational opportunities of affected family members,

Moreover, some of the inherited advantages and disadvantages that are impervious to even the best-intentioned of the morally permissible "levelling" strategies that "equal opportunity" societies may adopt provide formidable obstacles to the provision of strictly equal access to educational opportunities that ought to be universally available.

In the case of the competitive version of the ideal, there are also—in addition to these familiar obstacles—the hurdles presented by the demanding normative requirements embedded in the competitive processes that would have to be established. For example, while it may be relatively uncontroversial for admission to specialized training programs to be restricted to those who have the capacities and aptitudes needed for successful completion of the programs, agreement is bound to be difficult to secure both about the devising of administratively usable criteria for the identification of potentially successful applicants and about the degree to which the ranking of candidates who meet these threshold criteria is either desirable or feasible.

Reference

Rawls J (1971) A theory of justice. Harvard University Press, Cambridge

---

society-wide economic disasters have a differential impact on the life prospects of differently-situated groups, and so on.

Part IV
Race, Inclusion, and Education

Institutional Racism and the Ethics of Inclusion: What Does Justice Require to Transform Institutions of Higher Education?

Rebecca Tsosie

Abstract This article describes what "institutional racism" means within public institutions of higher education, arguing that transformative change is possible only if we link "justice" to the "diversity, equity and inclusion" framework that most Universities have adopted. The DEI framework replaced the earlier call for "affirmative action," which required active efforts to secure inclusion. DEI offers a broad, and often purely symbolic commitment to "inclusion" as "belonging." Appeals to "justice" are currently contested by those who are seeking to ban the instruction of "critical race theory" within institutions of higher education. The article argues for recognition of the rights and experiences of distinctive groups as well as the epistemic forms of injustice that have been experienced by specific groups, including Indigenous, Black, and Latinx peoples within institutions of higher education.

1 Introduction

In the summer of 2020, public Universities were pulled into the national dialogue on racial justice that followed the murder of an African American citizen, George Floyd, by a White police officer who "detained" him by sitting on his neck until he died. In the wake of the murder, many University presidents issued proclamations in support of racial and social justice, and some pledged a renewed "commitment" to "diversity, equity, and inclusion."[1] One year later, over 26 states have enacted laws banning the teaching of "Critical Race Theory" in state educational systems due to its allegedly "divisive" nature and unfair treatment of "Whites."[2] Critical race theory (CRT) emerged among legal scholars in the 1990s to examine the ways in which

---

[1] See, e.g., statements of President Michael Crow at Arizona State University and President Robert Robbins at University of Arizona.

[2] See, e.g., McKellar (2021).

R. Tsosie (✉)
University of Arizona, Tucson, AZ, USA
e-mail: rebeccatsosie@arizona.edu

© The Author(s), under exclusive license to Springer Nature Switzerland AG 2022   111
J. McGregor, M. C. Navin (eds.), *Education, Inclusion, and Justice*, Amintaphil:
The Philosophical Foundations of Law and Justice 11,
https://doi.org/10.1007/978-3-031-04013-9_8

racism is perpetuated by the supposedly neutral practices and norms within our legal and social institutions. In particular, CRT examines how the law uses "race" to construct hierarchies of power within social institutions. The work of CRT scholars is linked to a larger effort to overcome epistemic forms of injustice within academia.[3].

The "anti-CRT" movement rejects the notion that "past forms of racism persist today" and maintains that CRT is "divisive" because it "pits races against each other and teaches White people that they are responsible for past injustices."[4] Some of the state laws pertain only to K-12 education and some would extend the ban to higher education as well. Arizona's legislature banned teaching CRT in public K-12 education systems, as well as government-sponsored trainings that invoke the contested concepts of "implicit bias," "privilege" or "structural racism."[5] The state movement was preceded by former President Trump's 2020 Executive Order on "Combating Race and Sex Stereotyping," which sought to withhold federal funding from institutions that engage in training on "bias," "structural racism" or "privilege." President Biden rescinded the federal Executive Order, promoting many state legislatures to pick up the attack, asserting that recognition of "collective social and political identities" represents a "destructive ideology" that jeopardizes "American" values.[6]

Although the perspectives are polarized, it seems clear that race is relevant to public education. It is not clear how or if "justice" is part of the equation. Racial justice advocates contend that "institutional racism" thrives, often covertly. The term "institutional racism" refers to structural forms of inequity that persist despite the presence of "neutral" laws and regulations because the practices of exclusion are deeply engrained within the institution. Within our postsecondary education system, this inequity is visible in the declining numbers of students from domestic underserved populations who are eligible for admission to 4-year colleges or universities following high school, who can finish their postsecondary education within 4 or even 6 years, and who can navigate the competitive admissions process for a Ph.D. or professional degree program.

As former President Barack Obama noted, post-secondary education is vital to the success of our Nation and it is an essential prerequisite for many of the most lucrative jobs that are available in the U.S. economy. Statistically, we haven't moved the needle on "diversity" within our institutional cultures, and some would assert that gender and racial bias is as much of an issue today as it was 30 years ago. The problems are particularly severe for women of color, who suffer from "double bias"

[3] See Crenshaw (1995).

[4] Christie and Cooper (2021).

[5] Arizona House Bill 2906 (2021) (preventing government entities from requiring employees to undergo training that would suggest that they are "inherently racist sexist or oppressive, whether consciously or unconsciously").

[6] Executive Order on Combating Race and Sex Stereotyping (issued September 22, 2020).

and yet are frequently omitted from consideration within the statistics for their racial or gender group.[7]

Institutional racism within our educational system merits special consideration because educational institutions manage the "pipeline" to the future for our youth. With this power comes responsibility. This was apparent 50 years ago, as proponents of affirmative action lobbied for change in the 1970s. At that time, there were very few, if any, students from racial minority groups at the country's leading public and private universities. Affirmative action "opened the door" to university admission for many students of color in the 1980s and early 1990s. Many of those graduates became the "first" members of a minority group to hold positions of authority, for example, within academia, the courts, and the medical profession. As a policy movement, however, affirmative action lasted a short time, dating from the *Bakke* decision in 1978 to the mid-1990s, when the Supreme Court tightened the analysis of "beneficial" racial classifications.

In 1978, the Supreme Court affirmed that strict scrutiny was the relevant analysis for affirmative action programs at public universities, but struck down the UC Davis admissions policy because it relied on "racial quotas" and was not "narrowly tailored" to serve the asserted purpose.[8] By 2013 and 2016, when the Supreme Court decided the *Fisher* cases, filed against the University of Texas by an unsuccessful White applicant, the Court found that educational diversity is a compelling interest, but the use of "race" as a factor in admissions decisions "must play no greater role than is necessary" to meet the University's interest.[9] Moreover, the Court found that the University must regularly evaluate its data to ensure that this necessity still exists.

Harvard University's admissions policy recently came under attack for allegedly limiting the number of Asian-American students who can be admitted. The federal district court and First Circuit Court of Appeals upheld Harvard's admissions policy as necessary to secure student diversity, but the case is now pending in the United States Supreme Court.[10] Yale and other elite universities have similar policies, so the Harvard case tests the current viability of affirmative action policies. In many states, "affirmative action" is considered an outmoded "diversity strategy" of doubtful Constitutional validity, unless it is used as a narrowly-tailored remedy for specific and proven instances of unlawful discrimination. Some states, such as Arizona, have

---

[7] See American Bar Association Study, "Left Out and Left Behind: The Hurdles, Hassles, and Heartaches of Achieving Long-Term Legal Careers for Women of Color," (June, 2020); Debra Cassens Weiss, "Majority of minority female lawyers consider leaving law; ABA study explains why" (Diversity, "Your Voice", ABA Journal, June 22, 2020).

[8] Regents of the University of California v. Bakke, 438 U.S. 265, 291 (1978).

[9] Fisher v. University of Texas (Fisher II), 136 S.Ct. 2198, 2209 (2016).

[10] Students for Fair Admissions, Inc. v. Pres. and Fellows of Harvard Coll., 261 F. Supp. 3d 99 (D.Mass. 2017), aff'd 980 F.3d 157 (1st Cir. 2020), cert. granted, 142 S. Ct. 895 (2022).

banned affirmative action programs at public universities through state Constitutional amendments.[11]

The discourse of "diversity, equity, and inclusion" (DEI) has replaced the earlier call for "affirmative action." Affirmative action invoked racial justice by requiring active efforts to secure inclusion. DEI, in comparison, offers a broad and often purely symbolic commitment to "inclusion" as "belonging" in an effort to foster multiculturalism and equitable access to public goods provided by the state. DEI aligns with the discourse of a "post-racial" America, where everyone is "equal." Under this frame, a University should welcome students of all races, genders, ethnicities and religions so long as they are qualified for admission, and it should provide equitable access to academic resources. Many "DEI" programs are essentially student services programs that promote multiculturalism and are led by a "diverse" university administrator who serves as the "public face" of diversity for the University. Diversity Officers rarely have a significant role in faculty hiring or the academic affairs of the departments. In sum, DEI often exists as a diversity management strategy and not a substantive basis for inclusion within higher education Institutions.

Many racial justice proponents have adopted an "anti-racist" platform to identify and eradicate institutional racism.[12] The "anti-racist" platform includes a more active interrogation of structural racism, consistent with the intellectual movement associated with CRT. "Anti-racism" requires recognition of how "race" has been socially constructed over time to justify practices of exclusion, subordination, and exploitation. It requires an intentional effort to "de-center" Whiteness and promote marginalized voices, including those of scholars of color. Anti-racism also requires intentional actions that foster racial justice and social justice, including recognition of implicit bias and privilege in hiring, promotion, and admissions decisions, as well as a commitment to identify and transform institutional practices that promote "racism."

Academia has been slow to admit that it harbors "institutional racism," and DEI is typically linked to student recruitment and retention, rather than substantive change at the structural levels of the University. Universities continue to adhere to conventional standards for excellence, hiring faculty members who hold similar credentials to the senior faculty, and privileging the scholarship that meets the disciplinary standard. Although proponents of DEI have attempted to instill a notion of "inclusive excellence" as a goal of the University, most faculty are unable to say what this concept means or align the goal with any substantive part of their work.

This essay offers an account of what "institutional racism" means within American educational institutions and argues that transformative change is possible only if we link "justice" to the DEI framework. The article argues for an "ethics of inclusion" based upon justice and recognition. An ethics of inclusion must foster

---

[11] In 2010, Arizona voters passed a constitutional ban on government-sponsored affirmative action through Proposition 107. The ban extends to public schools and state Universities.

[12] See Kendi (2019).

an understanding of the historical context of public education and its role in contemporary society, as well as an understanding of the challenges to inclusion that are and have been experienced by specific groups, including Indigenous, Black, and Latinx peoples.

An ethics of inclusion must be shaped by the needs and circumstances of different groups, so in practice, it is not a "one size fits all" proposition. In all cases, however, we must understand of the dynamics of institutional racism and the harms caused by historic trauma, as we acknowledge the experience of particular groups within contemporary U.S. society. This essay develops a rights-based framework for recognition, and I draw on law, legal history, and political and moral theory to explore the potential components of an "ethics of Inclusion."

Part I of the essay presents an account of education as a "civil right" and discusses the historical contours of structural racism within U.S. educational institutions. Part II of the essay probes the nature of racial injustice, examining what is meant by "racial trauma" and what form of "moral repair" should ensue. Part III of the essay examines the concept of "reconciliation" and develops a working framework for an "ethics of inclusion."

2 Understanding Structural Racism Within U.S. Educational Institutions: Education as a "Civil Right"

As Professor Joel Olson argued in a 2002 essay, there is an active and on-going tension between "inclusion" and "participation" within domestic institutions that struggle to justify the dominance of "Whiteness" within their structures.[13] Citing the achievements of the Civil Rights Act of 1964 and the Voting Rights Act of 1965 to facilitate the participatory rights and access of citizens from racial minority groups, Olson notes that the statistical data about "Black disadvantage" and "White advantage" has stayed consistent, thus challenging the notion that we have achieved "inclusion." According to Olson, "whiteness persists at every level of American society, continuing to operate as a norm that sediments accrued white advantages into the ordinary operations of modern society, making them seem like the 'natural" result of individual effort."[14] Without a notion of "racial privilege," the "politics of inclusion" cannot "grasp the full scope of whiteness."[15] Consequently, a mere commitment to "access" as participatory inclusion will fail because it cannot shift the structural imbalance in power relations that is the cornerstone of "whiteness."

Olson's critique provides a workable foundation for the discussion about institutional racism within our domestic educational institutions. I will first engage the

---

[13] Olsen (2002).

[14] Id. at 385.

[15] Id.

construct of institutional racism as "injustice," and then I will provide a brief survey of the legal history that informs our current commitment to "inclusion." Our current civil rights laws, such as Title VI and Title IX are designed to preclude overt discrimination against racial minorities and women. They are the product of our Constitutional transformation and effort to define "equal" citizenship. The civil rights guarantees are important in many ways, but they fall short as a mechanism to achieve inclusion. Structural forms of racism are distinctive and do not depend upon intentional discrimination by an individual actor. In that sense, civil rights law alone cannot ensure justice for racial groups.[16]

2.1 Institutional Racism and the Commitment to Justice

The discussion of institutional racism requires an account of "race" and "racism," as well as a theory about why it should be morally unjust to continue institutional systems that perpetuate racism. By "race," I mean the "socially constructed categories of difference" that have come to represent the race consciousness of America. What it means to be "White," "Black," "Native American," "Asian" or "Latino" within U.S. society has been shaped by the discourse of race that is embedded within the terms of the original U.S. Constitution and then specifically addressed by the post-Civil War Amendments. In particular, the construct of the "citizen" as a rights-holder, as opposed to those who are not eligible for citizenship or have not secured it, has always been tied to race, as exemplified by the original restriction on naturalization to citizenship as belonging only to "Free White persons."[17]

The Constitution was intended to "establish Justice" for "ourselves and our Posterity."[18] Although "justice" is a foundational principle of our Nation's history and creation, the Constitution did not construct an "equal" commitment to justice for all persons within U.S. jurisdiction. Rather, the framers developed a hierarchy of rights in association with the various categories of "persons" who might be subject to the law. Structural racism is embedded within the Constitution and formal legal exclusion persisted for the first century of this Nation's existence. Structural racism deploys racial difference to "include" some persons and "exclude" other persons from equal access to the rights and benefits extended to members of the U.S. as a civil society. When structural racism becomes embedded within institutions, such as the courts or educational systems, it perpetuates inequality. Over time, that inequality may become invisible as it becomes normalized within specific institutional practices. For example, the Fair Housing Act bans discrimination in the housing

---

[16] For example, to prevail in an employment discrimination case, a plaintiff must prove that there was intentional discrimination in an employment decision because of his or her race, gender, national origin, or other protected status.

[17] See Tsosie (2016).

[18] U.S. Const. Prmbl.

market, yet residential patterns of segregation persist. The nation's formal commitment to "equality" has not dismantled the structural racism that perpetuates residential segregation.

The U.S. Constitution does not mention slavery, and yet, as it was originally drafted, it distinguishes between persons who enter the country as immigrants and those who are "imported." The document also distinguished between "Free persons," who count as a full person for purposes of determining a state's share of congressional representatives, and "other" persons, who only constitute 3/5 of a person. [19] The Constitution guaranteed free persons the right to travel throughout the states as a fundamental liberty, while persons who were "held to service or labor" must be returned to their owners if they "escape. "[20] These provisions enshrined the denial of legal personhood to African American slaves, and the *Dred Scott* opinion normalized this distinction as founded upon the notion that Black people are inherently inferior and lack the capacity for citizenship.[21] Consequently, slaves were not entitled to an education or any civil rights because they would never become citizens.

This legal reality shifted with the post-Civil War Amendments. The 13th amendment banned slavery within U.S. borders. The 14th Amendment required states to accord all persons "equal protection of the law," and extended citizenship to all persons born within the United States, as well as those naturalized to citizenship. American Indians were considered "wards" and did not become citizens by virtue of the 14th Amendment. Rather, Congress naturalized American Indians to citizenship through a 1924 statute.[22] The 15th Amendment precluded racial restrictions on voting rights, though states quickly turned to "proxies" such as literacy or property ownership requirements. By the latter part of the 19th century, our Constitutional law no longer supported the exclusion of Black Americans from U.S. citizenship, but a new structural form of racism quickly developed.

2.2 The Construction of Racism as a "Social" Issue

Under the logic of the *Plessy v. Ferguson* case, decided in 1896, states could lawfully enforce segregation based on race, even in public accommodations such as railroad cars.[23] The Supreme Court reasoned that the 14th Amendment secures "political" equality among the White and "colored" races, but not "social" equality. Moreover, the state could legitimately prescribe the standards for what constitutes a "White" citizen versus a "Colored" citizen, even if the distinction is as arbitrary as

---

[19] U.S. Constit. Art. 1, sec. 2.

[20] Art. IV, sec. 2, cl. 3.

[21] Dred Scott v. Sandford, 60 U.S. (19 How.) 393 (1857).

[22] The Indian Citizenship Act of 1924.

[23] Plessy v. Ferguson, 163 U.S. 537 (1896).

the "one drop" rule of some states. The notorious "Jim Crow" laws institutionalized racial segregation within the developing state public education systems, as well as other institutions. Black citizens were restricted to separate restaurants, bathrooms, swimming pools, and hotels by law. Their political rights were understood as "equal." Their lived experience was far from this.

The twisted logic of *Plessy v. Ferguson* persisted until the Supreme Court issued its 1954 opinion in *Brown v. Board of Education*, holding that segregation within K-12 public education systems violates the 14th Amendment because it denies children "equal educational opportunity" and stamps them as "inferior" by barring access to public schools based on their race.[24] The Court said that this exclusion would cause irreparable damage to the "hearts and minds" of the children, and would also undermine American democracy, given the important role of public education in training children to assume their role as citizens. *Brown v. Board* explicitly linked inclusion within public educational systems to participatory access within society's democratic institutions.

Although the *Brown* case is extraordinarily important in the development of U.S. Constitutional law, it was unable to generate a lasting notion of *racial justice as "inclusion."*[25] First, the courts struggled with their role in "implementing" the law because it was virtually impossible to enforce a lasting "remedy" for decades of formal segregation. Forcible attempts to "desegregate" neighborhood schools led to residential changes and a shift to private education that have now resulted in a *more* segregated America than 1954. Today, however, this pattern is linked with economic disparities and not formal segregation, which poses the second challenge to racial justice as "inclusion." The prevailing social narrative is that all citizens are free to live where they choose and can make rational choices about where their children will be educated. As the Supreme Court found in *San Antonio School District v. Rodriguez* (1973), some citizens will choose to live in areas where property values are low and schools are underfunded, but these social realities do not create a "legal problem" that the courts can solve.[26]

The *Rodriguez* case held that "education is not a fundamental personal right" under the U.S. Constitution, and a state may permissibly use property taxes as a mechanism to allocate funding for public schools even though the schools in poor districts received a fraction of the amount allocated to wealthy districts. This resulted in a demonstrably "inferior" education for the disadvantaged students, who were overwhelmingly minority, as compared to the advantaged students, who were overwhelmingly White. The inequities were not actionable under the Court's deferential standard, however, because they were the product of a permissible "economic" classification rather than an impermissible "racial" classification. Some states have

---

[24] Brown v. Board of Education, 347 U.S. 483 (1954).

[25] See Bell (1980) (arguing that *Brown* did not represent a transformation of American race relations, but rather represents a moment in time in which segregated public schools were simply "bad for America," give the context of its national and global agendas at that time).

[26] San Antonio Independent School District v. Rodriguez, 411 U.S. 1 (1973).

rejected this approach and require funding equity through their own state Constitutions, but the *Rodriguez* analysis is applicable to the federal Constitutional claim.

To return to Olson's argument, the norm of whiteness within state public educational systems is not contested or seen as problematic, because it is the product of "economics" and not "racism." This system has persisted. We have a formal commitment to legal equality and "access" to public education. Yet, we have marked disparities in the quality of education available in our K-12 schools, and these disparities have only intensified in the wake of the pandemic because affluent parents can support their children with computers to do Zoom classes and hire tutors, and poor parents cannot do this. This lack of access will be very apparent in the near future, as the disabilities associated with poverty and race intersect in the wake of COVID-19.

In sum, the public education system is broken at the K-12 level in many states because there is not "equal access to educational opportunity." This reality necessarily affects access to and the quality of postsecondary education in many states. Universities address this problem in different ways. Some universities still use race as a factor in their admissions decisions, a practice upheld by the Supreme Court in *Grutter,* and they continue to recruit and admit students from domestic underserved groups. Some Universities have relied upon international students for their "diversity" component, although this has become notably more difficult due to travel restrictions associated with the pandemic. Some universities have liberal "open access" requirements, and in some cases this is tied to the University's online education programs. Some private corporations have exploited these deficiencies by creating "open access" online universities that charge high tuition to disadvantaged students, who must take out large loans to fund their education and then cannot complete their academic programs. It is not uncommon to see 6-year graduation rates under 10% in these schools, and yet they defend their mode of operation as "inclusive."

Nationally, there are still very few Black, Latinx and Indigenous students within the U.S. higher education system. The numbers of Black students have actually decreased at many postsecondary institutions within the past decade. Native students at most Universities constitute less than 1% of the student population, and many Universities show the number as "zero". The deficiencies are most pronounced at the upper levels of each part of the system. The more prestigious the University, the less likely it is to have significant student diversity. Graduate education programs are markedly less diverse than undergraduate programs. Racial disparities also exist among University faculty and administrators. White males hold most of the prestigious faculty or administrative positions at most Universities, while greater numbers of women and minority faculty members are in non-tenure track positions or serve as "contract" faculty. Our post-secondary Institutions have not modeled "inclusion" even if they purport to have a commitment to equal "access."

The problem of institutional racism continues, yet it is very difficult to identify what practices will be sufficient to correct the problem and which entities have this responsibility. Universities must grapple with at least three forms of "structural inequity."[27] The first category relates to the university's own institutional history and practices, including the composition of their departments, their required curriculum, and their processes for hiring, promotion, and admissions. This category is fully within the responsibility of the specific institution. The second category relates to inequities within the educational "pipeline," including disparities in K-12 education, residential segregation, and wealth disparities. These are broad issues that affect universities, and yet the universities do not have the power to correct the multiple levels of injustice. Finally, there are broader national and global considerations, including regional disparities due to population demographics, migration patterns, and changing economies. The dynamics of colonialism, for example, continue to cause global disparities, and yet no single country or institution has the power to correct that level of injustice. The fact is that structural injustice exists in multiple locations, and it is often difficult to engage accountability for the harm.

3 When the Past Becomes Present: Racial Trauma and "Moral Repair"

Civil rights laws cannot remediate institutional racism because they only apply to intentional acts of racial discrimination against individual plaintiffs. Structural racism continues because unjust practices have become normalized within the system. They are part of the everyday fabric of our society, and the harms often disproportionately burden marginalized groups. In order to achieve transformative change we must engage the multiple frameworks that inform—and challenge--our temporal sense of "injustice." The dialogue on reparations for historic injustice, for example, freezes "injury" in the past and is unsuccessful in obtaining redress in the "present," given that no current living person is responsible for past harms, such as slavery. Similarly, many citizens today view group requests for reparative justice as linked to a "victim" mentality among underperforming groups, who are seen as attempting to alleviate their own responsibility to "get an education" or "get a job" and instead want to "get a check" for historic wrongs done to their ancestors.

Reparative justice is distinct from "transformative" justice, although overcoming institutional racism likely requires attention to both.[28] Transformative change requires action, but what type of action will be required and who should decide? Professor Eric Yamamoto's work on "social healing through justice" identifies the importance of "legal consciousness" as a combined sense of what the law is and what it should be.[29] Specifically, the American experience of race focuses on Black/White relations and has been shaped by the legacy of slavery and segregation. The modern

---

[27] I am grateful to Dr. Mark Navin for sharing his perspective on the issue of accountability, which inspired this more nuanced approach to "institutional racism."

[28] See Brophy (2006).

[29] See Yamamoto et al. (2007).

"civil rights movement" attempted to "transform" that legacy, but, as a society, we have not created a coherent account of racial injury and reparative justice. The position of Indigenous and Latinx peoples with "race" and "rights" is both linked to the legal consciousness associated with Black/White relations and also shaped by other historical and cultural factors.

Margaret Walker has offered an account of "moral repair" that links justice with institutional responsibility.[30] In a 2016 lecture, she commented that Nations often don't like to examine the negative aspects of their past, and they may even attempt to "erase" the past, for example, by not teaching about slavery or genocide. They may also engage in denial, claiming that "we are all equal" or that "we are post-racial." As Professor Walker noted, citizens within our society are not equal, nor are they equally situated. They have different historical experiences and different contemporary experiences, and the combination of those factors can manifest as "injustice."

How do we address this reality? For persons who are the beneficiaries of Whiteness, this is a difficult question. Do we look at police brutality leading to the murder of African Americans as an aberration, the work of a rogue "bad actor," or perhaps just a law enforcement officer using "poor judgment" about how long you can restrain a human being by sitting on their neck? Or do we see it for what it is: the product of a society that was trained to see human difference as a means to give some lives less moral weight, and less legal protection, than others? If we take the latter road and recognize continuing racial injustice, we must be willing to acknowledge injustice in the past as well as the present, because the experience of injustice for many groups is a continuing phenomenon. In a recent lecture at Arizona State University, Dr. William J. Barber, III, stated that "racism is a cultural problem" and Black people "do not suffer from PTSD, but rather from DOTS, Daily Ongoing Traumatic Syndrome."[31] They are always on alert for signs of danger, always fighting to be seen, recognized, and valued in the ways that White Americans take for granted.

Professor Walker claims that those who have experienced injustice have a "right to the truth about the past," and there is a corresponding duty placed upon public educational institutions, as the repository of "knowledge," and public archives, which serve as a collective repository of "memory." Walker argues that the "duty to remember the past" falls upon states and their respective institutions. American "history," for example, represents a complex and often painful set of experiences that all students should learn and acknowledge. The past is part of the present for communities that have experienced long histories of injustice. As Professor Walker says: "We have a duty to remember what our fellow citizens cannot be expected to forget."[32]

---

[30] Walker (2006).

[31] William J. Barber, III, "Heal the Nation," Delivering Democracy Lecture sponsored by ASU's Center for Race and the Study of Democracy (Apr. 17, 2021).

[32] Margaret Walker, lecture on "Justice and Responsibility," ASU 2016, citing work of Pablo DeGrieff.

The current movement by states to ban CRT constitutes a form of "epistemic silencing."[33] Policymakers seek to ban from public education any form of acknowledgement of race or racism as a *continuing phenomenon* in American society. The laws permit discussion of race in teaching American history, such as the history of slavery and the Civil War. However, contemporary forms of "race" are recast as "culture" within the pluralistic American democracy, unified under a "color-blind" Constitution. In fact, however, speaking about "race" often requires engaging "racism." Racial hate speech, for example, has an entirely different character than other forms of speech directed at other maligned groups, such as communists or socialists. Some Americans may disagree with the political ideologies of those groups, but they do not consider them "subhuman." Critical Race Theorists do not believe that racism ended when formal laws authorizing slavery or "separate but equal" public accommodations were repealed. "Covert" racism continues and it is present in "the less visible procedures of institutions and norms of a system."[34] Critical Race scholars broaden the lens to examine the *lived experience* of people of color. They often interrogate what is behind the statistical disparities between racial groups, and they identify the "neutral" procedures and practices that assure us that we are a "just" society, despite the differential burdens that impair equal access to justice and opportunity. This is the truth of our society as it currently operates. It is not an "ideology."

Institutional racism will persist until Institutions are ready to engage their embedded practices of racism and until they have the courage to address the historic and continuing trauma associated with racism. As Dr. Barber acknowledged in his lecture, racial trauma is intergenerational and it has social, psychological and physical manifestations, although these are frequently disregarded at the institutional level. Scholars point out, for example, that people of color in police detention are frequently over-medicated for "aggression" even to the point of death, while people of color in emergency health care settings are often denied pain medication upon the suspicion that they are seeking prescription medical to fulfill their desire for recreational drug use.[35] Health institutions are completely unrelated to law enforcement institutions, yet both are affected by deeply engrained biases that affect the standard of care that is used to deal with people of color.

Racial trauma "shatters the self."[36] It does so at the individual level and it does so at the group level. Racial trauma matters. It matters to individuals and to groups. We may think of ourselves as autonomous agents in our social interactions, assessed on the basis of our individual "merit," but we are all bound together in the same web of implicit bias and constructed social narrative that has always masked racial violence

---

[33] Dotson (2011).

[34] Chin (2015).

[35] Racial Trauma Panel (Monday July 6, 2020), sponsored by University of Arizona Health Sciences and featuring Dr. Noshene Ranjbar, MD, Dr. Patricia Harrison-Monroe, PHD, and Dr. Tommy K. Begay, PhD, MPH.

[36] Dr. Noshene Ranjbar, M.D., University of Arizona Panel on Racial Trauma, See supra note 35.

in this country. How can we start to address racial trauma as part of an ethics of inclusion? The first step is to realize that racial groups are not equally situated, and the requirements of justice must be particularized to their needs.

4   Reconciliation: What Does an Ethics of Inclusion Require?

There are many views about what "justice" requires, of individuals, institutions and governments, and how we, as a society, ought to measure compliance with the norm of justice.[37] Most accounts emphasize the need for a fair distribution of goods and freedoms, as well as a principled adherence to "social welfare, freedom, autonomy and virtue."[38] There is often a tendency to associate "equality" with "identical moral recognition."[39] On this view, human beings should be given equal regard because of their common humanity, and to do otherwise, could encourage mistreatment, denial, or hypocrisy. Margaret Walker describes this "fully symmetrical" model of 'humanity" as fictional, and she claims that Western cultures have always understood humanity as comprised of "different human kinds" and authorized forms of "hierarchy, domination, or exclusion."[40] There is a "moral gap" between the members of a community and those who are nonmembers, and the standard of "justice" often reflects power relations between those who dominate and those who are oppressed. Walker contests the idea that social virtues such as "respect" or "sympathy" can intervene to accord justice within a society that relies on this symmetrical model of equality.

According to Walker, it is relatively easy to "think in particular ways morally without contradiction or even significant strain *if you live that way*."[41] In comparison, she says, the "epistemologies and logics of inequality and domination that are a central study of feminist, race critical, and postcolonial theory are also essential to ethics. For ethics must look at actual languages of morals to grasp how people can in fact think and live."[42] Walker contends, for example, that "moral knowledge is open-ended, fallible and indefinitely revisable" under the "naturalized view of moral knowledge" that explains the multiple forms of gender bias that are revealed within feminist scholarship. Similarly, our knowledge of "race" is merely a product of what we *think* we know about how members of racial groups live. Moral knowledge is situated, and it is made visible by those members of a group who *actually* live that experience.

---

[37] See Sandel (2009), pp. 19–20.

[38] Id. at 19–21.

[39] See Walker (2002), p. 208.

[40] See id at 211.

[41] Id. at 216.

[42] Id. at 216.

Policymakers who seek to "ban" Critical Race Theory are seeking to ban an entire category of moral knowledge from being transmitted within a public education system. The formal equality of the law ensures that the society is "just," and policymakers do not worry about the vast gaps and inequities that persist within institutions of higher education. The symmetrical notion of equality tracks the "ideal moral theory" that exists only at an imaginary level. A non-ideal, naturalistic moral theory can better capture the experience of "different human kinds" that was built into the Constitution and persists in the covert mechanisms that secure institutional racism. Public universities must undertake active efforts to dismantle systemic racism, as well as building more just and inclusive structures. "Inclusion" embodies an *ethics*, a way of knowing, acknowledging, and engaging groups and communities, around shared goals, with respectful attention to difference. Inclusion also embodies a set of *practices*. Inclusion results when institutions are restructured through collaborative and intercultural processes that engage justice as "healing." In sum, "diversity, equity, and inclusion" efforts, alone, will not result in institutional transformation. Rather, the goal of DEI must be linked to racial justice and social justice, and those who are most affected by systemic racism must have agency in the process of transformation.

Shaping an ethics of inclusion requires attention to several continuing themes and challenges. First, there is an ever-present movement to shift the discussion of institutional racism into a "political" or "social" issue. In that way, racial justice activists can be marginalized and silenced, which is a form of "epistemic violence," as defined by philosopher Kristie Dotson.[43] Today, racial justice proponents associated with the Black Lives Matter Movement are accused of dismantling "civil society" to air their "grievances." Of course, the act of political protest is a carefully guarded liberty within the U.S. Constitutional democracy. On the other hand, "racial hate-mongering," has also become politicized. It is no surprise that the state bans on CRT have been accompanied by laws restricting voting rights, which are intended to protect the "political rights" of White majorities. Racial injustice is a reality of life in America. Until we collectively engage the issues of racial injustice and racial violence, they will remain the dark side of our American "democracy."

Second, we are conflicted on the need to publicly acknowledge the issue of systemic racism or engage in a strategy to "repair" or reconcile racial injustice. On June 4, 2020, Rep. Barbara Lee of California introduced a bill that would establish the first United States Commission on Truth, Racial Healing and Transformation, to "properly acknowledge, memorialize, and be a catalyst for progress toward jettisoning the belief in a hierarchy of human value based on race, embracing our common humanity, and permanently eliminating persistent racial inequalities." Four days later, more than 100 members of Congress had signed on as co-sponsors, leading to a national set of dialogues about racial disparities and the need for reconciliation. Although the bill was not enacted into law, the national dialogue is long overdue and public universities could play an important role in that process.

---

[43] Dotson (2011).

Third, the discussion about racial justice is an intersectional discussion. Native American Congressional Representative Deb Haaland from New Mexico (now Secretary of Interior) supported Rep. Lee's 2020 bill, correlating the experiences of injustice for African American, Latinx and Indigenous communities, and stating that we, as a country, must "untangle the racist webs that are woven into our laws and policies." In particular, Rep. Haaland highlighted the intersection of health inequity with environmental injustice and police violence, and she noted the cumulative impacts of these injustices for African Americans and Native Americans, as well as undocumented youth. COVID-19 has demonstrated that we are all related and the pandemic affects everyone. Yet, the racial fault lines that dominate our society have accentuated the nature of injustice for these marginalized communities.

The idea that we are "all related" and that our well-being and survival is a product of collective interdependence is a cornerstone of many Indigenous philosophies, including those of the Navajo, Lakota, and Muscogee Creek Nations.[44] We might extend that ethical perspective to an intercultural context, as we recognize that the economic and physical well-being of all citizens is defined by how well our governments and institutions can coordinate the respective needs of the various groups and communities that comprise our pluralistic society. The process of healing from the pandemic, for example, requires attention to the artificial boundaries that we have constructed around access to healthcare, housing, and equal educational opportunity, all of which are current sites for racial inequity. As Nancy Fraser argues, the "identity model" of recognition often falls short in identifying the key patterns of social exclusion that require redress, perhaps through intentional redistribution or institutional restructuring.[45]

Finally, we must reconceptualize our notions of political status and civil rights to include human rights. In particular, Native peoples require acknowledgement of tribal sovereignty and the right of self-determination. Today, cities and counties share borders with Indian reservations, and many non-Indians live and work on or near the reservation. Similarly, tribal members often live or work in the cities and states that surround the reservation. The territorial and jurisdictional boundaries are intact, but the social boundaries are permeable, and tribal and state governments share common interests on issues of community health, education, environment, law enforcement and the administration of justice. Canada's movement to "Indigenize" public universities was an outgrowth of its Truth and Reconciliation Process designed to respond to the multiple harms of the residential boarding schools in Canada. The movement is particular to the needs of Native students and tribal governments, but the agency of transformation is more broadly applicable. One of the primary harms of racial injustice is continued subordination, and group autonomy can be expressed proactively to reclaim important aspects of group identity, whether constructed as "personhood" or "nationhood."

---

[44] See Deloria (1994, 1999).

[45] Fraser (2000).

The narrative about "inclusion" and American "citizenship" is incomplete because we have not yet crafted an ethics of inclusion that is founded on racial justice and moral recognition. Equal opportunity requires institutional restructuring and an active commitment to racial justice. Within that effort, open dialogue and multiple experiences should inform the understanding of "race" and equity within American democracy.

References

Bell D (1980) Brown v. Board of Education and the Interest Convergence Dilemma. Harv Law Rev 93:518

Brophy A (2006) Reparations: Pro & Con. Oxford University Press

Chin W (2015) The age of covert racism in the Era of the Roberts court during the waning of affirmative action. Rutgers Race Law Rev 16:1

Christie B, Cooper J (2021) Arizona Gov. Ducey signs bill banning critical race theory training in schools, governments. Arizona Politics, Fox 10 News (July 9)

Crenshaw KW et al (1995) Critical race theory: the key writings that formed the movement. The New Press, New York

Deloria V (1994) God is red: a native view of religion. Fulcrum Publishing

Deloria V (1999) Spirit and reason: the vine Deloria reader. Fulcrum Publishing

Dotson K (2011) Tracking epistemic violence, tracking practices of silencing. Hypatia 26(2)

Fraser N (2000) Rethinking Recognition. New Left Rev 3, May-June 2000

Kendi IX (2019) How to be an antiracist. Random House

McKellar K (2021) Utah Legislature approves resolutions banning 'harmful' critical race theory concepts. (Deseret.com, posted May 19. 2021)

Olsen J (2002) Whiteness and the participation-inclusion Dilemma. Polit Theory 30(3):384–409

Sandel MJ (2009) Justice: what's the right thing to do? Farrar, Straus and Giroux Publishers

Tsosie R (2016) The politics of inclusion: Indigenous Peoples and U.S. Citizenship. UCLA Law Rev 63:1692

Walker M (2002) Moral contexts. Rowman & Littlefield Publishers

Walker M (2006) Moral repair. Cambridge University Press

Yamamoto E et al (2007) American reparations theory and practice at the crossroads. Calif West Law Rev 44:1

Janus-Faced Affirmative Action: Restorative Justice and the Transition to a Just Society

Eric D. Smaw

Abstract In what follows, I argue in favor of backward-looking and forward-looking affirmative action policies in education and employment. In the course of doing so, I highlight and respond to objections to affirmative action offered by Richard Herrnstein and Charles Murray, Nicholas Capaldi, and Carl Cohen. In short, I argue that since there has been and continues to be state-based discrimination against African Americans affirmative action is warranted to redress discrimination and to assist us in transiting to a just society. I call this conception of affirmative action Janus-faced because it is backward-looking and forward-looking simultaneously.

1 Introduction

> The negroes, and in general all the other species of men (for there are four or five different kinds) are naturally inferior to the whites. Indeed, such a uniform and constant difference could not happen in so many countries and ages, if nature had not made an original distinction betwixt them. [In fact,] there never was a civilized nation of any other complexion than white, nor even any individual eminent either in action or speculation. No ingenious manufactures amongst them, no arts, no sciences.... [And yet] in Jamaica they talk of one Negro as a man of parts and learning... 'tis likely he is admired for very slender accomplishments, like a parrot, who speaks a few words plainly (Hume 1758, p. 629).

Some might be surprised to learn that the celebrated moral philosopher Immanuel Kant agrees with David Hume's claim that all "White" people are naturally, intellectually superior to all "Black" people. In fact, in the *Observations on the Feeling of the Beautiful and Sublime*, Kant tells us that "the Negroes of Africa have *by nature* no feeling that rises above the trifling" (Kant 1764, p. 110). In addition to this, he reminds us that "Mr. Hume challenges anyone to cite a single example in which a

E. D. Smaw (✉)
Rollins College, Winter Park, FL, USA

Florida State University, College of Medicine, Orlando Campus, Orlando, FL, USA
e-mail: ESMAW@Rollins.edu

© The Author(s), under exclusive license to Springer Nature Switzerland AG 2022   127
J. McGregor, M. C. Navin (eds.), *Education, Inclusion, and Justice*, Amintaphil:
The Philosophical Foundations of Law and Justice 11,
https://doi.org/10.1007/978-3-031-04013-9_9

Negro has shown talents... in arts or science or any other praiseworthy quality" (Kant 1764, p. 111). Since he believes that no one has or can meet Hume's challenge, he reaches a conclusion similar to that of David Hume. Kant writes: "so fundamental is the difference between these two races of man, and it appears to be as great in regards to mental capacities as in color" (Kant 1764, p. 111).

Today, few, if any, philosophers would defend Hume's and Kant's universal conclusion that all "White" people are naturally, intellectually superior to all "Black" people. For, such a claim would be undermined easily by the empirical facts that some "Black" people perform better in primary and secondary school than some "White" people; some "Black" people perform better on standardized tests than some "White" people; and some "Black" people have higher intelligence quotient scores (IQ scores) than some "White" people. For these reasons, those wishing to defend claims of "White" intellectual superiority would likely bend Hume's and Kant's racial intelligence hierarchy into a racial intelligence bell curve. This would allow them to reject the obviously false universal claim that all "White" people are naturally, intellectually superior to all "Black" people while accepting the particular claim that, *on average*, "White" people are naturally, intellectually superior to "Black" people.

Richard Herrnstein and Charles Murray employ this strategy in *Bell Curve: Intelligence and Class Structure in American Life*. They argue that, on average, European Americans have higher IQ scores than African Americans, and therefore, "White" people are naturally, that is, genetically, intellectually superior to "Black" people. They conclude that the differences in the average IQ scores between "White" and "Black" people account for the disparities we see in education, employment, incarceration, and crime rates. Thus, they conclude, in order to save the country from the decay that comes from promoting unintelligent people in education, industry, and government, the United States must abandon its affirmative action policies and redirect its resources toward gifted students instead (Herrnstein and Murray 1995, p. 442).

By contrast, Nicholas Capaldi and Carl Cohen avoid drawing conclusions about racial groups based on an intelligence hierarchy but they agree with Herrnstein's and Murray's conclusion that the United States must abandon its affirmative action policies. For example, in "Affirmative Action: Con," Nicolas Capaldi argues that African Americans do not lack opportunities, political rights, or educational resources, but rather, moral character. Therefore, he concludes that, if we are to see progress in the "Black" community, then we must abandon our affirmative action policies for moral character development. Additionally, in *Affirmative Action and Racial Preference: A Debate*, Carl Cohen argues that affirmative action policies are illegal and immoral because they violate the *Civil Rights Act* and run afoul of our moral commitment to the principle of equality. For these reasons, he concludes that the United States must abandon affirmative action.

In what follows, I respond to Herrnstein's and Murray's, Capaldi's, and Cohen's objections to affirmative action. In the course of doing so, I highlight past and continuing state-based discrimination against African Americans. I conclude that affirmative action initiatives are warranted, in part, to redress discrimination, and, in part, to help us transition to a just society. I call this conception of affirmative action Janus-faced because it is backward-looking and forward-looking simultaneously.

2 A Brief History of Affirmative Action in Education and Employment

Affirmative Action refers to a series of policies and initiatives that followed from the Executive Orders and administrative actions of Presidents Franklin D. Roosevelt, Harry Truman, John Kennedy, Lyndon Johnson, Richard Nixon, and Jimmy Carter. For example, in 1941, President Roosevelt signed *Executive Order 8802*, outlawing discrimination in the hiring practices of corporations that received federal defense contracts (Marable 1997, p. 4). Twelve years later, the Truman Administration directed the Bureau of Employment Security to act "affirmatively to implement policies of nondiscrimination" (Marable 1997, p. 4). Similarly, in 1961, President Kennedy issued *Executive Order 10925*, prohibiting government contractors from "discriminating against... applicants" for employment (J.F. Kennedy 1961, *Executive Order 10925*). Kennedy's *Executive Order* also required federal contractors to "take *affirmative action* to ensure that applicants and employees are treated [fairly]" in the hiring process (J.F. Kennedy 1961, *Executive Order 10925*).

While the Executive Orders and actions of Roosevelt, Truman, and Kennedy prohibited racial discrimination in the hiring practices of companies that received federal contracts, they did nothing to redress the discrimination that African Americans had experienced prior to 1941. It wasn't until the late 1960s that some colleges, universities, and the federal government sought to redress past discrimination through affirmative action initiatives. For example, in 1968, the admissions council at the University of California at Davis, School of Medicine, established a policy of reserving sixteen out of every one hundred seats in its entering class for minorities and other disadvantaged students. Similarly, in 1969, the Nixon Administration established the Philadelphia Plan, which set specific goals for hiring minorities to work under federal government construction contracts (Marable 1997, p. 7).

Not surprisingly, affirmative action was challenged in court. For example, in 1978, Allan Bakke sued UC Davis's medical school, claiming that its admissions policy violated the equal protection clause of the *Fourteenth Amendment* (*Regents of the University of California v Bakke* 438 US 265 (1978)). The Supreme Court agreed. It ruled that UC Davis Medical School's admissions policy was unconstitutional. However, the Court acknowledged that race could be used as one of several criteria for college admission. Consequently, the *Bakke* decision was only a partial win for those looking to overturn affirmative action. Affirmative Action detractors secured another victory in *Gratz v Bollinger*. In short, the office of undergraduate admissions at the University of Michigan adopted a points system for admitting students. Under UM's points system, minorities applicants received twenty points for simply applying. This prompted the Center for Individual Rights (CIR) to file a lawsuit against UM on behalf of students who had been denied admissions. The CIR claimed that UM's admissions policy violated the equal protection clause of the *14th Amendment*. The Supreme Court agreed. In 2003, it struck down UM's admissions policy as unconstitutional (*Gratz v Bollinger* 539 US 244 (2003)).

Of course, not all of the legal challenges to affirmative action prevailed. For example, in 1977 Congress passed the *Public Works Act*, which required that ten percent of federal funds for public works projects be set-aside to secure services from minority businesses. Henry E. Fullilove sued the U.S. Secretary of Commerce, Philip M. Klutznick, claiming that the set-asides provision of the *Public Works Act* violated the equal protection clause of the *14 Amendment* (*Fullilove v Klutznick* 448 US 448 (1980)). The Supreme Court disagreed. It ruled that "Congress has latitude to try new techniques such as the limited use of racial and ethnic criteria to accomplish remedial objectives," and therefore, its use of the spending power to pursue the objectives of the minority business enterprise provision of the *Public Works Act* was constitutional (*Fullilove v Klutznick* 448 US 448 (1980)).

In another case involving the University of Michigan, *Grutter v Bollinger*, Barbara Grutter challenged UM's law school admission policy on the grounds that it violated the equal protection clause of the *14 Amendment*. The Supreme Court disagreed. It found that the law school's use of race is part of a holistic approach to admission meets the legal criteria established in *Bakke* (*Grutter v Bollinger* 539 US 306 (2003)). Subsequent courts have ruled in similar ways. For example, the U.-S. Supreme Court affirmed its *Grutter* decision in the case of *Fisher v University of Texas at Austin* (*Fisher v University of Texas at Austin*, et al 579 US _ (2016)). Similarly, the United States District Court for Massachusetts relied on the *Grutter* ruling in upholding affirmative action in *Students for Fair Admissions v. Harvard* (*Students for Fair Admissions v. Harvard* 1:14-cv-14176-DJC United States District Court for the District of Massachusetts (2014)). In light of this mixed history, we can only conclude that affirmative action is legal when it is narrowly tailored to meet a compelling interest and illegal when it is defined broadly or fails to meet a compelling interest, at least for now. In the fall of 2022, the Supreme Court will hear two challenges to affirmative action in college admissions. One case involves Harvard University, and the other involves the University of North Carolina. Given the new composition of the Court, six conservatives and three liberals, many scholars believe that affirmative action will be struck down in the fall.

3   Challenges to Affirmative Action

3.1   *Bad Genes*

Although affirmative action is legal, not everyone thinks it is just. In *The Bell Curve: Intelligence and Class Structure in American Life*, Richard Herrnstein and Charles Murray argue that, in addition to the cognitive abilities that are necessary for performing tasks like reading, writing, and arithmetic, humans have a general intelligence that underlies all of their cognitive abilities (Herrnstein and Murray

1995, p. 3). General intelligence, according to Herrnstein and Murray, is measurable by IQ tests. On standard IQ tests the range for general intelligence is 50 to 150. Moreover, they estimate that IQ is 60% heritable, meaning that one's genetics are responsible for 60% of one's intelligence (Herrnstein and Murray 1995, p. 289). According to Herrnstein and Murray, on average, European Americans score 100 and African Americans score 85 on IQ tests (Herrnstein and Murray 1995, pp. 276–289). Consequently, they conclude that IQ tests demonstrate that, on average, European Americans are genetically, intellectually superior to African Americans.

More importantly, they argue that once we understand the relations between genes, intelligence, and social behaviors, we will be able to organize American society so as to maximize productivity and minimize social dysfunction. In fact, social engineering based on IQ scores is how Herrnstein and Murray propose to reorganize American society so, as they put it, "everyone has a place" (Herrnstein and Murray 1995, pp. 441–445). Towards this end, they examined the IQ scores of people in different professions and compiled a list of low IQ and high IQ professions. For Herrnstein and Murray, low IQ professions include ditch-diggers, farmers, and garbage collectors; medium IQ professions include police officers, mail carriers, and store clerks; and high IQ professions include college professors, doctors, and lawyers. After examining the distribution of African Americans and European Americans in high IQ professions, Herrnstein and Murray claim to have found that there are more African Americans working in high IQ careers than there should be based on their IQ scores (Herrnstein and Murray 1995, p. 321). They tell us that this is a consequence of affirmative action mandates that require minority representation in the workplace (Herrnstein and Murray 1995, pp. 479–508). They conclude that such mandates force companies to hire and promote less intelligent African Americans over more intelligent European Americans, which, in turn, costs companies billions of dollars in workplace inefficiency and under-productivity (Herrnstein and Murray 1995, pp. 71–85). To remedy this "problem," Herrnstein and Murray argue that the United States ought to abandon its affirmative action policies and redirect its resources toward gifted students. After all, they conclude, today's gifted students are tomorrow's leaders (Herrnstein and Murray 1995, p. 442).

3.2 Bad Character

Unlike Herrnstein and Murray, Nicholas Capaldi avoids drawing the conclusion that disparities in IQ scores between "White" and "Black" students illustrate that, on average, European Americans are genetically, intellectually superior to African Americans. Rather, he identifies the problem as bad character traits internalized by African Americans, such as a lack of self-discipline, a lack of personal responsibility, and a lack of self-respect (Capaldi 1996, pp. 99–100). These moral deficiencies, according to Capaldi, give rise to dysfunctional behaviors that lead African American youth to drop out of school and get involved in crime. This, he continues, is evidenced by FBI crime statistics which show that "Blacks make up approximately 12 percent of the nation's population and 39 percent of arrests for aggravated assault... 43 percent of arrests for rape, and 55 percent of arrests for murder" (Capaldi 1996, p. 97).

For Capaldi, what's worse is that too many people excuse the dysfunctional behavior of African Americans by pointing to poverty or racism (Capaldi 1996, p. 98). However, Capaldi maintains that, given the amount of government intervention that followed the Civil Rights Movement, we should not see large disparities in education, unemployment, incarceration, and crime rates between African Americans and European Americans, unless, of course, the real problem lies with African Americans. In light of this, he urges us to accept the facts that humans have self-destructive impulses that can only be controlled through self-discipline and that self-discipline comes from holding people responsible for their behavior (Capaldi 1996, p. 100). For this reason, he concludes that the United States ought to abandon its affirmative action policies and attempt to develop moral character in African Americans instead (Capaldi 1996, p. 102).

3.3   Bad Policy

Unlike Herrnstein and Murray, and Nicolas Capaldi, Carl Cohen refrains from attributing racial disparities in education, employment, incarceration, and crime rates to race-based genetics or bad character traits. Rather, he argues that affirmative action is illegal because it violates Title VI and Title VII of the *Civil Rights Act*, and immoral because it runs afoul of our commitment to the principle of equality. In *Affirmative Action and Racial Preference: A Debate*, he argues that Title VI and Title VII of the Civil Rights Act prohibit preferential treatment based on race. For example, he points out that Title VI makes it illegal to discriminate in industries that receive federal assistance, regardless of whether they are public or private (Cohen 2003, pp. 46–47). Similarly, Title VII makes it illegal to:

> fail or refuse to hire or to discharge any individual, or otherwise to discriminate against any individual with respect to his compensation, terms, conditions, or privileges of employment, because of such individual's race, color, religion, sex, or national origin. Or, to limit, segregate, or classify his employees or applicants for employment in any way which would deprive or tend to deprive any individual of employment opportunities or otherwise adversely affect his status as an employee, because of such individual's race, color, religion, sex, or national origin (Cohen 2003, p. 46).

Hence, in light of these sections of the Civil Rights Act, Cohen concludes that affirmative action violates U.S. law, and therefore, it ought to be abandoned (Cohen 2003, p. 48).

In a similar fashion, Cohen argues that affirmative action policies are immoral because they run afoul our commitment to the principle of equality. First, he reminds us that "treat like entities alike"—another formulation of the principle of equality—is a fundamental moral principle inherent in all western liberal democracies (Cohen 2003, p. 48). Secondly, he highlights the fact that the principle of treating like entities alike undergirds the founding documents of the United States of America, like the *Declaration of Independence*. In turn, these founding documents set the moral standard by which U.S. government policies are to be judged. Hence, since affirmative action violates the principle of equality that undergirds our most sacred founding documents, Cohen concludes that it ought to be abandoned.

4 Responding to the Challenges

4.1 The Genetic Superiority Argument

In 2012, the HMGA2 gene received a lot of attention because, while investigating the relation between genes and Alzheimer's disease, the Enigma Research Team—a group of two hundred scientists representing one hundred institutions from around the world—discovered that changes in the HMGA2 gene influence the overall size of the brain, and intelligence. According to the Enigma Research Team, "DNA is comprised of four bases: A, C, T and G. People whose HMGA2 gene held a letter "C" instead of "T" on a particular location of the gene possessed larger brains and scored 1.3 points higher on standardized IQ tests" (Brook 2012). Although 1.3 points is not a statistically significant difference on a standardized test, those who argue that European Americans are, on average, genetically intellectually superior to African Americans take it as definitive proof of their position.

In addition to the statistical insignificance of 1.3 points, there are many other problems with the claim that European Americans are genetically, intellectually superior to African Americans. First, scientists rarely associate intelligence or educational attainment with one gene. Usually, they associate them with many genes. In fact, in 2016, a study of the association between genes and educational attainment found that there are at least 74 genome-wide significant loci associated with educational attainment (Okbay et al. 2016, p. 539). More importantly, the scientists who conducted the study acknowledged that there is "genetic covariance between increased educational attainment and increased cognitive performance and intracranial volume," but they avoided drawing the conclusion that they have discovered the genes for educational attainment (Okbay et al. 2016, p. 540). In fact, they drew no connection between genes, educational attainment, and race. Moreover, they drew no connection between genes, intelligence, and race. Quite the opposite, they warned us against "characterizing the identified associated variants as 'genes for education'" because "(a) educational attainment is primarily determined by environmental factors, (b) the explanatory power of the individual SNP's is small, (c) the candidate genes may not be causal, and (d) the genetic associations with educational attainment are mediated by multiple intermediate phenotypes" (Okbay et al. 2016, p. 541).

For similar reasons, Professor Paul Thompson, the lead researcher on the Enigma Research Team, warned us against associating the HMGA2 gene study with intellectual determinism (Brook 2012). In fact, he argued that "if people want to change their genetic 'destiny,' they can either increase their exercise, or improve their diet and education" (Brook 2012). He continues: "Most other ways we know of improving brain function *more than outweigh the HMGA2 gene*" (Brook 2012). More importantly, however, like the researchers who studied the relation between genes and educational attainment, the Enigma Research Team drew no connection between genes, educational attainment, and race. Similarly, they drew no connection between genes, intelligence, and race.

Secondly, since the publication of the *Bell Curve*, many scientists and social scientists have rejected Herrnstein's and Murray's conclusions. For example, in "The Malleability of Intelligence is not Constrained by Heritability," Douglas Wahlsten argues that "Herrnstein and Murray claim high heritability of IQ means that improving the environment of a poor child a modest amount will be ineffective because such changes are limited in their potential consequences when heritability so constrains the limits of environmental effects" (Wahlsten 1997). He concludes, "they are simply wrong on this point. They commit... the vulgar error that confuses heritability and fixity" (Wahlsten 1997). Similarly, in *Not in Our Genes: Biology, Ideology, and Human Nature*, Lewontin, Rose, and Kamin argue that the "error of the biological determinists' view of mental ability is to suppose that the heritability of IQ within populations somehow explains the differences in test scores between races and classes" (Lewontin, Rose, and Kamin 2017). "What this ignores," they conclude, "is that the causes of the differences between groups tests are not the same as the sources of variation within them. There is, in fact, no valid way to reason from one to the other." (Lewontin, Rose, and Kamin 2017). Hence, in light of the findings of the two large-scale intercontinental scientific research studies of genes, educational attainment, and intelligence highlighted above, and the resounding rejections of Herrnstein's and Murray's conclusion by many scientists and social scientists, I conclude that, while genes influence intelligence and educational attainment, it is a mistake to conclude that genes determine intelligence or that they determine a measurable portion of intelligence that can be separated clearly from the effects of environmental factors like food, water, sleep, education, exercise, medicine, substance abuse, and so on.

Third, since 1969 there has been a dramatic decrease in the standardize test score gap between European Americans and African Americans. Hence, using genetics to explain the decrease in the standardized test score gap is problematic because it suggests that there has been genetic evolution in the brains of African Americans between 1969 and 1990 (years studied by Herrnstein and Murray), but no genetic evolution in the brains of European Americans over the same period of time. Given that twenty years is not enough time for evolution to occur, the genetic explanation is empirically and scientifically untenable. Even if twenty years were enough time for evolution to occur, we would see similar changes in the brains of African Americans and European Americans because both groups share the same environment, i.e. the United States. Even Herrnstein and Murray were forced to concede these points. They write:

> in the period as short as twenty years, environmental changes are likely to provide the main reason for the narrowing racial gap in scores. Real and important though the problems of the underclass are, and acknowledging that the underclass is disproportionately Black, living conditions have improved for most African Americans since the 1950's... assuming that

education affects cognitive capacity, the rising investment in education disproportionately benefits the cognitive levels at the lower end of the socioeconomic spectrum (Herrnstein and Murray 1995, p. 292).

Fourth, it's not clear what, if anything, I.Q. measures. For example, Herrnstein and Murray tell us that I.Q. tests measure general intelligence and that general intelligence underlies all specific cognitive processes. Here, Herrnstein and Murray accept Charles Spearman's explanation of general intelligence. That is, general intelligence is that which allows smart people to score well in unrelated fields of study, like reading and mathematics (Herrnstein and Murray 1995, p. 3). However, when we press experimental psychologist like Richard Herrnstein for an account of general intelligence they tell us it consists of cognitive capacities, like quantitative reasoning, visual-spatial processes, memorization, and so on. In other words, general intelligence underlies all specific cognitive processes like math and reading, and general intelligence is comprised of specific cognitive capacities like quantitative reasoning, i.e. mathematics, and memory and identification, i.e. reading. Here, Richard Herrnstein's reasoning is nauseatingly circular! More importantly, for me, it demonstrates that the very notion of general intelligence is specious.

Finally, the environmental explanation offers the best account of the decrease in the standardized test score gap between African Americans and European Americans. For example, in *The Bell Curve*, Herrnstein and Murray tell us that "Black progress in narrowing the test score discrepancy with Whites has been substantial on all three tests (science, mathematics, and reading) and in all age groups. For example, the overall average gap of .92 standard deviation in the 1969–1973 tests had shrunk to .64 standard deviation by the 1990's" (Herrnstein and Murray 1995, p. 291). To me, it's not surprising that there has been a decrease in the standardized test score gap since 1969. After all, the federal government began eliminating racial barriers to education and investing in education, healthcare, and nutritional resources in "Black" communities at the end of the Civil Rights Movement, i.e. in the late 1960's and early 1970's. Hence, the decrease in the standardized test score gap is a function of restorative justice, i.e. erasing racial barriers to education and opening up access to educational resources. More importantly, the fact that the standardize test score gap decreased when the government eliminated racial barriers to education and invested in education and other resources in "Black" communities explains why I am a proponent of backward-looking affirmative action initiatives.

4.2 The Bad Character Argument

I find Capaldi's bad character argument to be specious. First, it relies on statistics from the FBI's Uniform Crime Report which omits many of the mass murders of African Americans committed by European Americans prior to 1930. Secondly, the Uniform Crime Report is not adjusted to account for wrongful convictions. To be sure, the mass murders of African Americans during the Colfax Massacre of 1873 (Keith 2008), the Ocoee Massacre of 1920 (Fussell 2016), the Tulsa Massacre of

1921 (Brophy 2001) and others that occurred before 1930 do not appear in the FBI's Uniform Crime Report. After all, the FBI did not begin collecting crime statistics until 1930, and prior to the Civil Rights Movement many local law enforcement agencies allowed terrorist organizations like the Ku Klux Klan to murder "Black" people with impunity, particularly in the South. This, of course, is not meant to disparage the FBI. After all, it relies on local municipalities to forward it accurate crime information. However, this does illustrate that, even if the FBI had requested crime statistics regarding the mass murders of "Black" people prior to the 1930s, there would have been no arrests records or murder convictions to submit. For these reasons, the Uniform Crime Report is lacking information.

Secondly, in "Police Misconduct as a Cause of Wrongful Convictions," Russell Covey highlights jaw-dropping acts of police misconduct which have resulted in hundreds of wrongful convictions of African Americans in California, Texas, Louisiana, and New Jersey (Covey 2013, pp. 1138–1142). Similarly, police misconduct and wrongful convictions were investigated by the U.S. House of Representatives in *House Bill 46*. In *House Bill 46*, Congress found that some policing agencies operating under the federally funded Byrne Grant Program have engaged in false arrests, coercing witnesses, tampering with evidence, and wrongful convictions of African Americans in several states (See H.R. 46, Section 2). As a result of wrongful convictions, African Americans make up 13% of the U.S. population, but 62% of those exonerated for robbery, 59% of those exonerated for sexual assault, and 62% of those exonerated for robbery (Gross et al. 2017, p. 1). This illustrates that Capaldi's argument about "Black" criminality rests on statistics that underestimates crime committed by European Americans, because the FBI's Uniform Crime Report omits many massacres of African Americans committed by European Americans, and overestimates crime committed by African Americans, because the Uniform Crime Report is not adjusted to account for wrongful convictions.

Of course, there might be a charitable explanation for Capaldi's failure to notice these glaring problems with his argument, namely, American propaganda. After all, America has a long history of using propaganda to depict African Americans as criminals. For example, in 1915, D.W. Griffith released the film *The Birth of a Nation* which depicts "Black" men as criminals, prowling throughout neighborhoods looking to despoil the virtue of "White" women. There was great anticipation for the release of *The Birth of a Nation*, and it did not disappoint. President Woodrow Wilson reported that "it is like writing history with lightning" (Benbow 2010, p. 509). More importantly, millions of people across the nation viewed the film and believed that it was an accurate portrayal of the dangers of giving liberty to African American men.

Just fifty years later, President Richard Nixon unveiled his War on Drugs. Chief of Staff to President Nixon, H.R. Haldeman, told us that "President Nixon deliberately pursued a racist strategy" (Alexander 2010, p. 44). Haldeman continues: "Nixon emphasized that we have to face the fact that the whole problem is really the Blacks" and that "the key is to devise a system that recognizes this while not appearing to" (Alexander 2010, p. 44). The system "devised to recognize this without appearing to" was the War on Drugs. This was confirmed by John

Ehrlichman, former White House counsel and advisor to President Nixon, in an interview with *Harper's Magazine*. Ehrlichman confessed that

> the Nixon White House had two enemies: the anti-war left and black people. . . by getting the public to associate the hippies with marijuana and the blacks with heroin, and then criminalizing them both heavily, we could disrupt those communities. . . arrest their leaders, raid their homes, break up their meetings, and vilify them night after night on the evening news. Did we know that we were lying about the drugs? Of course, we did (Baum 2016).

Hence, in light of Haldeman's and Ehrlichman's revelations, it is clear that Capaldi's "Black" criminality argument is untenable, even on a charitable reading.

4.3   The Bad Policy Argument

I find Carl Cohen's argument that affirmative action is illegal to be problematic on jurisprudential grounds. Article III of the *U.S. Constitution* and the case of *Marbury v Madison* tell us that the U.S. Supreme Court is the final arbiter of U.S. law. In which case, Cohen can align his position with that of the Supreme Court, or he can reject the position of the Court and continue to maintain that affirmative action is illegal. If he aligns his position with that of the Court's then he must abandon his argument that affirmative action is illegal. After all, as I have illustrated above, the Supreme Court has ruled that limited uses of affirmative action are legal. If, however, Cohen continues to maintain the position that affirmative action is illegal then he must do so on grounds other than U.S. law. In which case, he would be guilty of committing a category mistake. For, as H.L.A. Hart teaches us, one must remember to distinguish "law as it is from law as it ought to be" (Hart 1958, p. 117). Hence, Cohen might argue that affirmative action *ought not* to be U.S. law on moral or political grounds, but he cannot argue that affirmative action *is not* U.S. law on moral or political grounds.

Lastly, I find Cohen's argument that affirmative action is immoral to be disingenuous. Obviously, we ought to treat like entities alike when their circumstances are similar. For example, we tax wealthy people at the same rate because they have similar amounts of money. However, when we have compelling reasons to treat like entities differently, then we are justified in doing so. For example, we tax wealthy people at higher rates than we tax middle-income people, even though they are both human beings with jobs and money. Similarly, the vast disparities that result from past and continuing discrimination against African Americans give us compelling reasons for treating African Americans differently, at least until we have substantially diminished or eliminated the disparities in question. This is perfectly consistent with our moral duty to act according to the principle of equality.

5   Janus-Faced Affirmative Action: Restorative Justice and Transitions to a Just Society

While the Supreme Court has struck-down many affirmative action initiatives, it has upheld many others. In fact, as I have illustrated above, the Supreme Court has ruled that backward-looking affirmative action initiatives are warranted as redress for past practices of racial discrimination. After all, there would have been greater "Black" representation in all areas of education and employment if it were not for Jim Crow Segregation. This is evidenced by the fact that the percentages of African Americans entering all levels of colleges and universities, and advancing in various areas of employment, have been increasing steadily since the end of segregation. Of course, the standard objection to backward-looking affirmative action is that those who benefit from affirmative action today were not harmed by segregation of the past. After all, the vast majority of college applicants and those seeking employment today were born after the passage of the *Civil Rights Act* and the *Voting Rights Act*. Therefore, it looks like affirmative action gives an unjustified advantage to many African Americans.

Of course, the objection that backward-looking affirmative action gives an unjustified advantage to many African Americans ignores the continued racial discrimination against African Americans, like the discrimination in policing that I have highlighted above. Affirmative action initiatives are excellent ways to reintegrate those falsely accused and wrongly convicted back into American society. Moreover, as Kenneth Karst puts it in "Forward-Looking Affirmative Action,"

> structures of advantage and disadvantage tend to replicate themselves. Consider the causal connections in the cycle that lead from advantages in jobs to increased affordability in housing, and on to access to the better schools, and back to qualifications for the better jobs, and so on, and on, in a cycle of advantage. Justice Ginsberg [reminds] us that similar cycles reinforce disadvantage (Karst 2004, p. 65).

Hence, those of us who argue for forward-looking affirmative action initiatives take seriously the fact that access and denial are often reproduced subtly, even unconsciously, in the norms and customary practices of people within communities, states, and the nation, despite the passage of laws like the Civil Rights Act and the Voting Rights Act.

Even more, we have notice that subtle behaviors can have huge impacts on different racial groups. In fact, my discussion of Capaldi's "Black" criminality argument above is an excellent example of this. I suspect that Capaldi did not articulate a racially biased argument intentionally. Rather, probably, he has internalized American propaganda about African Americans and crime, and therefore, it never even occurred to him to question the statistics in the Uniform Crime Report. More importantly, Capaldi's oversight gives us a small window into his racial consciousness. When police officers in various parts of the country exhibit a racial consciousness similar to that of Capaldi's, it can have serious negative consequences on the lives of African Americans, like false arrest and wrongful convictions, which, in turn, perpetuate the stereotype of "Black" criminality. When employers exhibit a racial consciousness similar to that of Capaldi's, it can have serious negative consequences on the opportunities of African Americans, like being overlooked for employment, promotion, and leadership positions. For this reason, I conclude that forward-looking affirmative action initiatives are warranted because they will help us arrive at a just society. That is, a society in which everyone has equal access and opportunity to participate in the institutions of the state without having to overcome explicit or subtle barriers because of their race.

Finally, I imagine that backward-looking and forward-looking affirmative action initiatives will not be needed in perpetuity. In fact, it would be prudent to monitor the outcomes of affirmative action initiatives, make adjustments, and scale them back as colleges, universities, and industries achieve greater diversity, inclusivity, and belonging, provided that we also make adjustments to and scale back other forms of preferential treatment that has nothing to do with academic performance in college or performance in the workplace, including preferential treatment for athletes, children of wealthy donors, children of alumni, children of Hollywood elites, and the children of college faculty and staff. While these kinds of preferential treatment initiatives are not categorized as affirmative action, usually, they have the same, and sometimes a greater, impact on college admissions. For example, the National Bureau of Economic Research found that those applying to Harvard University between the years of 2009 and 2014 had a 14 times greater chance of being admitted if they were athletes and a 5.7 times greater chance of being admitted if their parents were alumni of Harvard (National Bureau of Economic Research 2019, p. 14).

As for how we will know when we have achieved a just society, and affirmative action initiatives are no longer needed, some argue that we might simply defer to demographic data as our guide. For example, in "Affirmative Action: Pro," Albert Mosely proposes that we use a proportionality standard (Mosley 1996a, b, p. 41). That is, we might make the percentages of racial groups in education and employment roughly proportional to their demographic make-ups of society. Thus, he concludes, we will know that we have achieved a just society when we have proportional representation of the races in education and employment. While I do not have an objection to Mosely's proposal, I advocate for a slightly different way of using racial demographic data. We should not try to achieve an exact match between the racial make-up of colleges, universities, and industries and the racial make-up of society because we might inadvertently restrict the free choices of individuals. Rather, we ought to establish a range within which it is acceptable to have college admission and employment data deviate from demographic data. The range should be wide enough to account for free choice but not so wide that it is useless for identifying discrimination.

6 Conclusion

In this article, I have responded to Herrnstein's and Murray's, Capaldi's, and Cohen's objections to affirmative action. In doing so, I have argued that backward-looking affirmative action initiatives are warranted to redress past discrimination against African Americans and that forward-looking affirmative action initiatives are warranted to help us transition to a just society. I have called this conception of affirmative action Janus-faced because it is backward-looking and forward-looking simultaneously.

References

Alexander M (2010) New Jim Crow. The New Press, New York
Baum D (2016) Legalize It All: How to Win the War on Drugs. Harper's Magazine. https://harpers. org/archive/2016/04/legalize-it-all/
Benbow M (2010) Birth of a quotation: woodrow wilson and "like writing history with lightning". J Gilded Age Progr Era 9(4):509–533
Brook H (2012) Big Brains and High IQs linked to small gene. BioNews https://www.bionews.org. uk/page_93542
Brophy A (2001) Tulsa Race Riots of 1921 in the Oklahoma Supreme Court. Oklahoma Law Rev 54(1):67–148
Capaldi N (1996) Affirmative action: con. In: Affirmative action. Rowman & Littlefield, New York, pp 65–110
Cohen C (2003) Race preference is morally wrong. In: Affirmative action and racial preference: a debate. Oxford University Press, Oxford, pp 23–45
Covey R (2013) Police misconduct as a cause of wrongful convictions. Wash Univ Law Rev 90(4): 1133–1186. https://openscholarship.wustl.edu/cgi/viewcontent.cgi?article=6013& context=law_lawreview
Fisher v University of Texas at Austin, et al. 579 US (2016). https://www.oyez.org/cases/201 5/14-981
Fullilove v Klutznick 448 US 448 (1980). https://www.oyez.org/cases/1979/78-1007
Fussell M (2016) Dead men bring no claims: how takings claims can bring redress to real property-owning victims of Jim Crow Race Riots. William Mary Law Rev 57(5):1913–1948
Gratz v Bollinger 539 US 244 (2003). https://www.oyez.org/search/gratz%20v%20bollinger
Griggs v. Duke Power Co., 401 U.S. 424 (1971). https://supreme.justia.com/cases/federal/ us/401/424/#tab-opinion-1949186
Gross S, Possley M, and Stephens K (2017) Race and wrongful convictions in the United States. National Registry of Exonerations. http://www.law.umich.edu/special/exoneration/Documents/ Race_and_Wrongful_Convictions.pdf
Grutter v Bollinger 539 US 306 (2003). https://www.oyez.org/cases/2002/02-241
Hart HLA (1958) Positivism and the separation of law and morals. Harv Law Rev 71(4):593–629
Herrnstein R, Murray C (1995) The bell curve: intelligence and class structure in American life. Simon and Schuster, New York
Hume D. Original date (1758) Of national character. In: Miller E (ed) Essays moral, political and literary. Liberty Fund, Indianapolis
Kant I. Original date (1764) Observations on the Feeling of the Beautiful and Sublime (Goldthwait J. trans). University of California Press, Berkeley
Karst K (2004) Forward-looking affirmative action. Columbia Law Rev 104(1):60–74
Keith L (2008) The Colfax Massacre: the untold story of black power, white terror, and the death of reconstruction. Oxford University Press, Oxford
Kennedy JF (1961) Executive Order 10925, Part III, subpart A, section 301-1. https://www. presidency.ucsb.edu/documents/executive-order-10925-establishing-the-presidents-committee-equal-employment-opportunity
Lewontin RC, Rose S, Leon K (2017) Not in our genes: biology, ideology, and human nature. Haymarket Books, Chicago

Marable M (1997) Staying the path to racial equality. In: The affirmative action debate. Addison-Wesley Publishing Co., New York, pp 3–15

Mosley A (1996a) Affirmative action: pro. In: Affirmative action. Rowman & Littlefield, New York, pp 1–63

Mosley A (1996b) Response to capaldi. In: Affirmative action. Rowman & Littlefield, New York, pp 1–63

National Bureau of Economic Research (2019) Legacy and Athlete Preferences at Harvard. https://www.nber.org/system/files/working_papers/w26316/w26316.pdf

Okbay A, Beaucamp JP, Fontana MA, Lee JJ et al (2016) Genome-wide association study identifies 74 loci associated with education attainment. Nature 533:539–542

Regents of the University of California v Bakke 438 US 265 (1978). https://www.oyez.org/cases/1979/76-811

See H.R. 46, Section 2, Findings of Congress. https://www.congress.gov/bill/114th-congress/house-bill/46/text

Students for Fair Admissions, Inc. v. President & Fellows of Harvard College 980 F.3d 157 (1st Cir. 2020). DISTRICT OF MASSACHUSETTS BOSTON DIVISION, docket # 1:14-cv-14176-DJC. https://www.clearinghouse.net/chDocs/public/ED-MA-0002-0001.pdf

United States H.R. 46, Section 2, Findings of Congress. 2016. https://www.congress.gov/bill/114th-congress/house-bill/46/text

Wahlsten D (1997) The malleability of intelligence is not constrained by heritability. In: Devlin B, Fienberg S, Resnick D, Roeder K (eds) Intelligence, genes, and success: scientists respond to the bell curve. Springer Press, New York

Three Responses to Racism and Systemic Racism: Therapy, Punishment, and Education

Laurence Houlgate

Abstract What roles should the responses of therapy, punishment and education to racism play in a pluralistic democracy that has a long history of bigotry, racism and systemic (institutional) racism? What does justice require of any public response to racism and systemic racism? The first step toward an answer to these questions begins with a discussion of therapy. In recent years therapy has been by far the most popular U.S. response to racism, touted by hundreds of legislators, governors, and mayors, under the banner, "Systemic racism is a public health crisis". But an analysis of the concept of therapy shows that it has implications that are unacceptable in a liberal-democratic society. Racism is not a disease nor is it a symptom of a disease. It does not make racists candidates for cures created and administered by public health therapists. Punishment as a response to racism is seen to do no better. The concept of punishment implies the existence of a transgressor who violates the law. But racist thoughts and expressions do not violate valid laws in constitutional democracies. It is not a crime to be a racist unless the racist behavior is harmful to others. At the same time, it is acknowledged that punishment is a justifiable response to *systemic* racism because such institutional systems can and often do violate contemporary valid laws. The concept of education avoids the unacceptable implications of therapy and punishment. Education does not assume that racism is a symptom of a disease nor does it assume that racism violates valid laws. An analysis of the concept of education shows it to be a voluntary relationship between student and teacher in which students are at liberty to retain or give up their prejudicial opinions. If responsive education succeeds in an effort to eliminate or mitigate racism, then this might eventually have the side effect of abolishing all systemic racism.

L. Houlgate (✉)
Emeritus Professor of Philosophy, California Polytechnic State University, San Luis Obispo, California, USA
e-mail: lhoulgat@calpoly.edu

© The Author(s), under exclusive license to Springer Nature Switzerland AG 2022   143
J. McGregor, M. C. Navin (eds.), *Education, Inclusion, and Justice*, Amintaphil:
The Philosophical Foundations of Law and Justice 11,
https://doi.org/10.1007/978-3-031-04013-9_10

1 Introduction

On August 7, 2020 Michigan governor Gretchen Whitmer declared that racism is a public health crisis and signed a bill requiring state employees to undergo "bias training" as a corrective (Detroit Free Press 2020). Governor Whitmer is not the first to use the words "public health crisis" when discussing racism and systemic racism. Several other state governors, public health organizations, city councils, state legislators, news reporters and opinion columnists have used the same or similar words (Pew Trusts 2020). I believe that this is a mistake. Racism and, by extension, systemic racism are not public health crises to be dealt with by public health professionals and organizations.

I do not deny that racism and systemic racism have severely harmed large minority populations for hundreds of years. Minority communities targeted by racist attitudes and behavior have long been "in crisis." They have experienced and continue to experience long, unbroken periods of great difficulty, danger, and suffering. If what Governor Whitmer means by the words "racism is a public health crisis," is "racism *creates* public health crises," then I have no grounds to disagree.

But the latter interpretation does not imply that the racism and racist institutions should also be classified as public health problems. If the primary charge of public health organizations is to prevent the spread of disease and deliver therapy to those who are ill, then I argue that there are no good reasons for saying that what racists need is therapy or that systemic racism should be rooted out and "cured" by public health officials.

I also contend that punishment is an unjustifiable response to racism, where this word refers only to racist beliefs or racist speech about the inferior status of persons of a particular race. At the same time, I will also argue that *systemic* or *institutional* racism is a clear candidate for both abolition and punishment under the law.

In the final section, I argue that education is a justifiable response both to racism and, by extension to systemic racism, both because education (properly defined) escapes assumptions that burden both therapy and punishment responses to racism itself.

Finally, implicit in this discussion are the moral principles that guided the framers of the U.S. Constitution and the philosophers who argued for what J.S. Mill called "freedom of thought and expression" (Mill 1859; Houlgate 2018).

2 Therapy

Since the question is whether racism and systemic racism *ought* to be classified as public health crises, the first step is to suggest a few relevant definitions, followed by an attempt to provide an analogical argument for the conclusion that racism is a suitable candidate for a therapeutic response.

2.1 Definitions

A "health intervention" or response to a public health crisis is a response to illness, sickness, disease, unhealthiness, or unsoundness. If the health crisis is "public" then the illness affects humans in one or more geographic areas, confined to one locale, a particular state or country, or all areas on earth. Public health crises in the past include Spanish flu (1918), H5N1 (bird flu, 2004), HIV/AIDS (1981-), SARS (Severe Acute Respiratory Syndrome, 2002), and several diseases (such as cancer) caused by ingestion of, use of or exposure to toxic products (for example, Thalidomide, DDT, asbestos, nicotine).

"Racism" means "a belief that race is the primary determinant of human traits and capacities *and* that racial differences produce an inherent superiority of a particular race." A second, simpler definition is "racial prejudice or discrimination" (Merriam Webster 2020).

"Systemic racism" is "a doctrine or political program based on the assumption of racism and designed to execute its principles" (Merriam Webster 2020). A stronger definition recently offered to Merriam Webster by a graduate student says that systemic racism is "prejudice *combined* with social and institutional *power*. It is a *system of advantage* based on skin color" (Hauser 2020).

"Public health" is "the science of protecting and improving the health of people and their communities. This work is achieved by promoting healthy lifestyles, researching disease and injury prevention, and detecting, preventing, and responding to infectious diseases" (CDC Foundation 2020). Unlike private practice physicians who are primarily interested in treating patients who are sick, "those who work in public health try to *prevent* people from getting sick or injured in the first place" (American Public Health Association 2020).

2.2 Framing an Analogical Argument

As everyone reading this essay well knows, we have a contemporary (2020) example of a non- controversial public health crisis that is now having a devastating effect on almost all countries on earth. The official name is *Novel Coronavirus Disease, COVID-19*, which was declared a "pandemic" by the World Health Organization on March 11, 2020. I will use this disease as a model for creating an analogy between a known public health crisis (COVID-19) and racism. Here is the first part of the analogy.

(a) *Disease name*: COVID-19
(b) *Symptoms*: Fever or chills, cough, shortness of breath or difficulty breathing, fatigue, muscle, and body aches, etc.
(c) *Cause* of the symptoms: SARS-cv2 (severe acute respiratory syndrome-coronavirus 2).

(d) *Preventative measures*: Social distancing, face masks, testing, contact tracing, self- quarantining, vaccination (when available). In extreme circumstances, these measures might be required by law, subject to fines.

If racism is a candidate for public therapy, then we should be able to transfer these classifications to the alleged "disease" of racism. But this is not an easy task. Using (a)–(d) as my guide, here is the best I can offer:

(a^1) *Disease name*: Racism (see preceding definition).

(b^1) *Symptoms:* Racist speech, hate speech, hate crimes, systemic (institutional) racism, promotion of biased legislation, practices and protocols detrimentally affecting minority communities (e.g., creating laws that require public schools to be segregated by race; sentencing Black persons to longer jail terms than White persons for committing identical offenses).

(c^1) *Cause(s)* of the symptoms: Prejudiced beliefs of individuals and an ideological and dominant culture which rationalizes and justifies their superior position (Zatz et al. 1999).

(d^1) *Preventative measures*: Avoid contact with known racists and racist communities; remove young children from racist parents; prohibit racist speech on social media; prohibit the publication and distribution of racist literature and all other means of distribution of pro-racist opinions; quarantine known racists; administer anti-racist vaccines or drugs when available, even if the racist objects to the medication.

2.3 Problems with the Analogy

There are at least three problems with the proposed analogy.

First, the symptoms named in (b) are involuntary. The sick persons who suffer from COVID-19 do *not choose* to have a fever and shortness of breath. Fatigue and fever are physical conditions that one *undergoes,* not something one *does.* The person who suffers cannot control the causal connection between disease and symptoms of the disease. Attempts can be made by a medical staff to mitigate the severity of the symptoms but the symptoms themselves are beyond the control of the patient.

But the so-called symptoms named in (b^1) are voluntary. Legislators in the southern states who created and voted for Jim Crow laws in the early twentieth century did not do so because they had *no control* over their prejudices. We do not think of these racist legislators as "sufferers" or "victims" of a disease.

Second, it is a category mistake to classify racist conduct or the public expression of a racist belief or opinion as symptomatic of an underlying cause (c^1). The relationship between a disease and the symptoms of the disease is that of cause and effect. As argued by Plato 2400 years ago, the relationship between beliefs and behavior is *not* one of cause and effect, but a relationship of reason to action

(Plato, *Phaedo*, 95a – 105a; Houlgate 2017).[1] If it is believed by White racists that Black persons are inferior to White persons, this a *reason for* not a *cause of* their racist behavior. A prejudiced opinion about the natural superiority of White people is a *reason for* creating and voting for a Jim Crow law, not a *cause of* this act. If legislators are asked "Why did you vote for that bill?" they would answer "Because it prohibits Black people and other inferior minorities from using public toilets designated for their superiors." They would not say "I couldn't help it. My beliefs made me do it."[2]

Third, the proposed preventative measures (d^1) are unjust. Although the concept of injustice has several different meanings or uses, one meaning relevant to accusations of racism is in the context of what a person *deserves*. Thus, when we say that it is unjust to deny Black people access to public toilets designated for Whites Only, we mean that they *do not deserve* this kind of treatment. And if asked "Why kind of treatment do they deserve?" one response might be: "They deserve to be treated as persons."

We treat human beings as persons when we permit them to make the choices that will determine what happens to them; and second, when our responses to them are responses respecting their choices. The obvious examples are cases of coercion. If I ask you for a loan of $1000, and you agree to loan this amount at an annual rate of 7%, then you are determining what happens to you. If you refuse to loan me this amount, then I will respect your choice and walk away. But if I point a gun at you and say, "Give me $1,000 or I will kill you," and you hand over the money, you have not "determined" to give me this amount and I have certainly not respected your choice to defer.

If we imagine a public system of response in which racists are coercively treated with therapy, then the analogy with the gunman example is obvious. Racists would have no more of a choice to receive therapy than has the victim of the gunman a choice to hand over her money. In both cases, the right to be treated as a person has been violated.

Suppose that racists are not coercively treated with therapy, but therapy is the only response offered to those who have been identified as racists. It is their choice to accept or deny the offer. But these options do not avoid the criticism that racists are not being treated as persons. If therapy is the only public response available, then it still remains that racists are believed to be candidates for therapy. They need therapy because racism is believed to be symptomatic of an underlying condition that racists cannot help having. If this belief is dominant, then racists are not being treated as

---

[1] Socrates is portrayed by Plato as sitting in jail waiting for the executioner to appear. Socrates tells his friend Cebes that if the philosopher Anaxagoras were asked "Why is Socrates sitting in jail?" he would give a mechanistic account of the position of Socrates' bones and muscles. Anaxagoras mistakenly takes the question to be about the cause of Socrates' sitting position instead of being about Socrates' reason for sitting, which has already been answered ("I am waiting for the executioner to appear").

[2] A possible objection to this is that racism might be a mental disease in which racist beliefs are one of the symptoms (not the cause) of the disease. See Sect. 2.5 below for a response to this objection.

persons. Their "choice" not to be treated for the underlying condition is like the choice of a schizophrenic not to receive treatment for her brain disorder. Moreover, her choice not to be treated will probably be construed as further evidence of her illness.

What we are looking for here is a response to racism that is not unjust. The injustice of therapy is that it is not what racists *deserve*. They deserve a response that recognizes their ability to make their own choices about what to think, what to say and how to behave, so long as these choices do not harm others. In other words, what they deserve is to be treated as persons.

2.4   Five Unwelcome Consequences of Classifying Racism as a Disease

If we insist on using the disease model for racism and its offspring (systemic racism), then the institutions of social control will respond with therapy as the appropriate response to these so- called diseases. "The logic of sickness implies the logic of therapy" (Morris 1968, p. 382).[3] Here are five more unwelcome implications of using the disease model as a public response to racism.

No Fault Responses   If racists and the cultures in which they reside are believed to be sick, then therapists will say that they are *not at fault* for their racist behavior. Their behavior is only a manifestation of an illness that is beyond their control. We do not blame corona-virus victims for being fatigued, running a high fever and coughing, so we *must not* blame racists for their overt racist behavior, including their manipulation of institutions to gain power over those whom they believe to be inferior (systemic racism).

Compassionate and Beneficent Responses   Therapy implies that one must make a compassionate response to racism, not anger or accusations. Therapists only see people as suffering—and their response is to do whatever will relieve the pain. Hence, a compassionate response to the so-called disease of racism would be to quarantine racists when there is a threat that they might spread the disease to others. Therapists would also attempt to find and administer a cure of the disease from which the racist is suffering.

No Proportionality of Cure to Behavior   "With therapy, attempts at proportionality make no sense." (*id.*, 484) Proportionality of a response belongs to the logic of punishment, not the logic of therapy. The doctors who treat corona-virus victims might treat identical patients for a week or several months before they dismiss them, depending on the status of their health, not on how much they might have harmed

---

[3]Most of the observations in this section about the definition and implications of therapeutic interventions are taken from Herbert Morris' groundbreaking article "Persons and Punishment" (1978).

others by infecting them. By analogy, it would be permissible to force feed one racist with anti-racist pills and let him go home after one week while confining another racist to an insane asylum for a lifetime.

No Reason to Wait for Therapeutic Intervention   "In a system motivated solely by a preventive and curative ideology there would be less reason to wait until symptoms manifest themselves in socially harmful conduct" (*id.*, 485). If a person has symptoms of COVID-19, then the strong desire of therapists is to prevent that person from spreading the virus to others and to treat the disease with hospitalization, if necessary. By analogy, if racist conduct is construed as a symptom of an underlying disease, then there is no good reason to wait until the racist harms others. Steps should be taken *now* to eliminate the underlying disease (c^1), by whatever means are available.

Derogation in Status of Protests Not to be Treated   Those persons who are found to have COVID-19 might not want to submit to a cure, if and when a cure is available. When a vaccine is made available for immunizing persons from the corona virus, there will be many people who will refuse to be vaccinated. By analogy, if a preventative to racist behavior is developed in the form of a pill or vaccine, then some with the so-called racist disease might not want to take it. Their protest might be listened to, but it might also be regarded as signs of a selfish concern for themselves rather than a concern for the health of others who they might "infect" when they express their racist opinions.

2.5   Objections and Replies

It might be objected that the criticism of the analogy (at 1.3) fails because therapeutic interventions in Western democracies are almost always voluntary. Therapy is not forced on anyone unless they have a serious mental illness (e.g., Schizophrenia) and they pose a threat to themselves or others (Wikipedia 2020)[4] Hence, even if racism is classified as a disease and a cure for racism existed, it would still be the choice of the afflicted person or persons to seek a cure—unless they posed a threat to themselves or others.

The answer to this objection is that it commits the straw man fallacy. It is true that under existing law, it is the free choice of racists to retain or discard their racist beliefs. But this is not what is being disputed. My argument is for the quite different

---

[4]Further involuntary treatment requires a court order based on proof that the individual poses a continuing threat to public safety. Since the late 1990s, a growing number of states have adopted Assisted Outpatient Commitment (AOC) laws. Under assisted outpatient commitment, people committed involuntarily can live outside the psychiatric hospital, sometimes under strict conditions including reporting to mandatory psychiatric appointments, taking psychiatric drugs in the presence of a nursing team, and testing medication blood levels. Forty-five states presently allow for outpatient commitment. (Wikipedia 2020).

claim that the therapeutic model mistakenly assumes that *having* a false belief is like having a virus or some other disease that can somehow be cured through therapeutic intervention.

Hence, the analogy is false for reasons already cited. To say that the beliefs of a racist can be cured is to wrongly assume that the relationship of a belief to action is like the relationship of a virus to a symptom, in which case we would have to declare that any harm to others motivated by racist hatred would not be the fault of the person who had the alleged disease of racism. To repeat: a belief is a *reason for* not a *cause of* action.

The objector might respond with the claim that racism *is* a disease in the same way that the coronavirus is a disease: the only difference between them is that racism is a *mental* disease. Therefore, the straw man fallacy is irrelevant. A racist is not just a person with a set of false beliefs. Racists are like schizophrenics. Racists suffer from a chronic brain disorder that has a causal relationship to their false beliefs. When the brain disorder is active in schizophrenics, they have "delusions, hallucinations, disorganized speech, trouble with thinking and lack of motivation." (American Psychiatric Association 2000). Racists also suffer from a brain disorder, but with different symptoms: false beliefs about the physical and moral inferiority of persons of a different skin color or ethnicity, resulting in derogatory speech and behavior that targets these groups.

There are two responses to this objection. First, the *Diagnostic and Statistical Manual of Mental Disorders (DSM)*, does not include racism, prejudice, or bigotry in its text or index. One of the reasons given for this omission is that so many Americans are racist. "Even extreme racism in this country is normative—a cultural problem rather than an indication of psychopathology is mainly a product of learned behavior" (Poussaint 2002).

Second, "research informs us that a majority of explicitly racist persons do not have any psychopathology" (Bell 2004). Hence, it would be of no use to attempt to find the causes of racism by studying genetics or "use advanced imaging to look at the brain structure and function" of racist people.

Those on both sides of the debate about classifying racism as a mental disorder agree that "extreme racist delusions can also occur as a major symptom in other psychotic disorders, such as schizophrenia and bipolar disorder" (Poussaint 2002). But this implies only that some racists have a mental disorder. It does not prove that racism *is* a mental disorder.

3   Punishment

Punishing racists who are a part of or who encourage and enable systemic racism is an alternative and possible solution for ridding the country of a scourge that has caused considerable damage to minority communities.

But there are problems with using the punishment model as a justifiable response to racism.

3.1 The Concept of Punishment

Thomas Hobbes declared in *Leviathan* that "a punishment is an evil inflicted by public authority on him that has done or omitted that which is judged by the same authority to be a transgression of the law" (Leviathan, ch. 14; Houlgate 2020). Hobbes adds that "the end" of inflicting evil on transgressors is to dispose others to obedience.[5]

Although punishment may have other ends than general deterrence (for example, incapacitation of the transgressor), the first part of Hobbes' definition is adequate as a definition. It contains the necessary conditions for an act to be an act of punishment. It must be: (a) an evil inflicted on a person or persons; (b) by a public authority; (c) for transgression of the law; and (d) judged [to have transgressed the law] by the same public authority.

3.2 Punishing Racist Beliefs and Behavior

There are existing criminal laws prohibiting racist behavior. Relevant examples are laws prohibiting hate crimes (bias crimes) committed on the basis of a person's race.[6] For example, in a 2020 federal conviction, two white men were convicted of conspiring to—and committing—hate crimes against black men in Maine. They had brutally assaulted these men only because they were black. One of the conspirators has already pleaded guilty. His punishment is life in prison (U.S. Department of Justice 2020).

All four criteria of Hobbes' definition of punishment (a)–(d) have been met in this case. A public law was transgressed, as determined by a judge or jury, and an evil (life in prison) was inflicted on the transgressor by the judge.

Unlike therapy, punishment is also consistent with the right a transgressor to be treated as a person. The assumption is that transgressors *made their own choice* to violate the law. They were not forced by another to do the illegal act, nor were they suffering from a physical or mental disease that caused them to do what they did. Hence, punishment is a public response that they deserve.

---

[5]Hobbes was one of the first philosophers to distinguish between the definition or meaning of "punishment" and the general justification for punishment (Hobbes 1651; Houlgate 2020).

[6]Title 1 of the Civil Rights Act of 1965 permits federal prosecution of anyone who "willfully injures, intimidates or interferes with, or attempts to injure, intimidate or interfere with ... any person because of his race, color, religion or national origin" or because of the victim's attempt to engage in one of six types of federally protected activities, such as attending school, patronizing a public place/facility, applying for employment, acting as a juror in a state court or voting." Those who are found guilty will "face a fine or imprisonment of up to one year, or both. If bodily injury results or if such acts of intimidation involve the use of firearms, explosives or fire, individuals can receive prison terms of up to 10 years, while crimes involving kidnapping, sexual assault, or murder can be punishable by life in prison or the death penalty."

However, there is no indication in Hobbes' definition of punishment about the *content* of the existing laws that have been transgressed. If the transgressors, like Socrates, had been found guilty and sentenced to death for violating a law prohibiting the teaching of philosophy, this would also satisfy the four criteria for punishment.

There are limits to who can be justifiably punished because there are limits to the *kind* of conduct that can be legally prohibited. Punishment as a response to racism would have to meet the conditions for illegality set out in U.S. Constitution and its amendments. In the particular case of punishing persons for racist thought and expression, this would involve the provisions set out in the First Amendment. If Congress can *"make no law... abridging the freedom of speech, or of the press"*, then Congress can make no law abridging an individual's freedom to express their racist beliefs, even when the expression rises to the level of hate speech (speech that vilifies, humiliates, or incites hatred against a group or a class of persons on the basis of race).

3.3 Justifiable Limits of the Criminal Law Concerning Systemic Racism

Although racist beliefs and expressions of beliefs cannot be punished, there are provisions in the law that make systemic (institutional) racism punishable. The historic instances of punishable systemic racism include slavery, Jim Crow laws, and the banking and real estate industry practice of redlining.[7]

Slavery is now a federal crime, punishable by 20 years in prison. Jim Crow laws have long been struck down by the courts. Federal civil rights laws have made it punishable for any person or group to interfere with any of several different kinds of activity once prohibited by Jim Crow, including attempts to prevent any eligible voter from casting a vote during an election. Finally, federal law put a stop to red lining under the 1968 Fair Housing Act and the 1977 Community Reinvestment Act (Brooks 2020).

Recent examples of systemic racism include calling back job applications with white-sounding names fifty percent more of the time than applicants with black-sounding names, even when they have identical resumes as all other college graduates (Bertrand and Mullainathan 2003). The Civil Rights Act of 1991 provides monetary damages in cases of intentional employment discrimination.

Systemic inequality in education has had bad consequences, some of them on-going. For example, when all age groups are combined, black students are three times more likely to be suspended from school than white students, even

---

[7] The banks and real estate agents outlined in red ink maps of neighborhoods where people of color lived. If you lived inside the red lines, loans were considered risky and banks were less likely to give loans or invest.

when their infractions are similar (U.S. Department of Education Office for Civil Rights 2014). There appears to be no threat of punishing anyone for this disparity. The only recourse that the family of a suspended student has is to bring a lawsuit against the school district.

4 Education

Education is "all the processes that affect people's beliefs, commitments, capabilities, and actions" (Crittenden and Levine 2018). This definition is too broad. A person's beliefs can be affected by processes as simple as watching the movements of a butterfly. A person's actions can be affected by processes as complex as assembling a computer.

'Being educated' does not imply the existence of another intelligent human being in the guise of an educator or teacher. Many people are self-educated. And these days, one can be educated by a robot. Nor do the words 'being educated' imply a set of restrictions in the content of what one has learned. You can be educated by reading material that others would regard as morally offensive, irreligious, or in violation of other social norms.

4.1 Civic Education

'Civic education' is a narrower term denoting processes affecting people "as members or prospective members of communities" (*Ibid.*) When people hear the words 'civic education' they understandably think of the processes that take place in public schools. But there are many other ways of giving and getting a civic education within small communities. The beliefs, commitments, capabilities, and actions of children are shaped and altered by teachers, parents and close relatives, friends, peers, and religious instructors.

Restrictions on the content of what is taught depend on the type of community. Schools sponsored by the Catholic Church have an agenda that is noticeably different than the liberal agendas of public schools required by federal and state regulations. A school sponsored by the Ku Klux Klan or the Nazi Party can (logically) use the word 'educating' to refer to what their teachers do in the classroom when they hold discussions about the alleged inferiority of non-white races.

4.2   Comparing Education and Therapy

Unlike therapy, the person who is being educated is referred to as a *student* not a patient, and the fact that students need to be taught the details of a particular subject (e.g., geometry) or a wide range of subjects (e.g., history) does not imply that they are ill or sick.

Although the process of educating does not assume illness of those who are being educated, it does assume *ignorance* in some form or other, for example, a lack of propositional knowledge ("knowing that") or the lack of a skill ("knowing how"). The student who is being taught U.S. history may not know *that* slavery was introduced in America over 400 years ago. The student who is being taught automobile repair does not know *how* to repair and replace a carburetor. The student who is being taught logic does not know *that* modus ponens is a valid argument form and may not know *how* to think critically about the problems of philosophy.

There is no guarantee that students who are taught theoretical ethics will use what they have learned in everyday life. The student who has studied Kant's *Grounding of the Metaphysics of Morals* might show a perfect understanding of the Categorical Imperative on his final examination but continue to hold and act on racist beliefs.

There are limits to the *methods* that can be used to educate. There is a contemporary event that stands as a powerful example of how some 'therapists' are attempting to cure their patients by changing the beliefs and attitudes of the entire cultural group to which they belong, with the aim of wiping out their identity. The cultural group is the Muslim Uighurs of Xinjiang and the therapists are agents of the Chinese government. A leaked memo obtained by BBC News says that thousands of Uighurs are being detained in prison camps and are "subject at least to psychological torture because they literally don't know how long they're going to be there... Detainees will only be released when they can demonstrate they have transformed their behavior, beliefs and language." (BBC News 2020).

The Chinese government refers to their harsh methods as 'education'. But their methods are probably better classified as 'brainwashing', a term defined as "*a method for systematically changing attitudes or altering beliefs, originated in totalitarian countries, especially through the use of torture, drugs, or psychological-stress techniques*" (Merriam Webster 2020). The difference between education and brainwashing is cited at end of the preceding quote: *torture, drugs, psychological stress*. Students are learners, not victims. Their beliefs are not the product or effects of threats or fear; their opinions are arrived at voluntarily, by choice, even if they seem mistaken and even absurd to others. There is a distinction between "She said that her religion is false because she knew they would kill her unless she said it," and "She re-examined her religious beliefs and concluded that they are false."

Although education assumes that the person being educated has a choice about what to believe, this tells us nothing about the *effect* of education as a tool to deter racist attitudes and behavior. If young racist students have a choice to make, will they opt to give up their racist beliefs after a lesson on the moral equality of the races? This is an empirical question, still being investigated and debated. Philosophers can and will debate the foundations of morals for the next 2,000 years but once they reach agreement, they will still be left with the empirical question about how to *motivate* people to do what is generally agreed to be morally right.

4.3 Comparing Education and Punishment

Unlike the concept of punishment, the idea of education does not imply that the person who is being educated has done something morally or legally wrong. Students are not regarded as suspects or criminals; education is not regarded as a deprivation for wrongdoing and teachers are not seen as the agents of the deprivation.

Punishment has been used to change beliefs by punishing persons merely for *having* what are regarded as wrongful beliefs. The plight of the Uighurs is a sad example of this tactic. Punishment for beliefs is unjustifiable because the person who has what is regarded as a wrongful belief may not want to change her mind or behavior. A just system of law would accommodate this and therefore ought not to make racist beliefs punishable offenses.

Although a desire to educate others does not imply wrongdoing, education can be used to mitigate future wrongdoing by bringing about changes in personal beliefs and attitudes. In this respect, education bears some slight resemblance to therapy.[8] If a student is ignorant about facts that belie her racist beliefs, her teacher might want to correct the student's lack of knowledge and the student *might* regard the teacher's attempt to help as an act of beneficence.

4.4 Education as a Just Response to Systemic Racism

An important difference between education, therapy and punishment is that education can justifiably be used to alter or change beliefs. If a teacher gives a racist student an argument that explains why racism is morally wrong and as a result the student changes her mind about the immorality of what she has previously thought about communities of color, then her change of mind is something *she has done*. She has been persuaded, not bullied, or forced to change her mind. Unlike the public responses of therapy and punishment, education of those who are or might harbor racist beliefs and attitudes is morally justified by the moral principles inherent in liberal democracy. It treats those who are educated *as persons*; as ends in

---

[8] This is probably what Governor Whitmer meant by "bias training" for Michigan police officers (supra., 1).

themselves, not merely as means to an end (Kant 1781). And, by implication, civic education treats all persons as moral equals.

The counterargument to this is that "prescribing education as the cure for racism often confuses individual bigotry with a system of domination" (Ray and Aja 2020). If we see systemic racism as a system of *domination*, "racism can be manipulated, *because* it is bigger than any individual." It is systemic and "highly educated people, who sometimes know better, contribute to systems of racial harm on a regular basis" (*id.*) Here is the rest of the quote:

The architecture of American racism is not an unfortunate accident: It was created intentionally to acquire and keep power. The highly educated designed America's system of segregation and America's prison system. Highly educated lawyers devise arguments to protect police who kill black and brown folks, highly educated prosecutors decline to bring charges, and highly educated judges assign light sentences. There is no good evidence that educating police about implicit bias works to lessen harm. And whites with high cognitive ability are no more likely to support practical policies that lessen racial inequality. But their education does allow them to offer more sophisticated justifications for privilege.

5 Conclusion

I am a philosopher, not a social scientist. Despite the powerful condemnation of the 'highly educated' in the preceding quote, education is, I believe, the best response to both personal racism and punishment is the best response to systemic racism. By 'best' I do not mean 'most effective' because the empirical data cited in the quoted passage does not support this. I mean 'morally best' because education is consistent with the right to be treated as a person. Education has the potential to change personal racist behavior by changing minds without the use of force or threats of force and without the presumption that racism is a mental disorder. Punishment has the potential to dismantle systemic racism by making illegal the practices of the highly educated folks mentioned in the quote.

But the road ahead is rough. If a child grows up in a racist culture where there are few opportunities to be educated by anti-racist teachers and not allowed the experience of interacting with children of other races, then sociologists and other social scientists predict that there will be little change in beliefs and attitudes.[9] It might be

---

[9] As an example of the frustration felt about biased White parents in the mid-twentieth century, here are the lyrics of "You've Got to be Carefully Taught" (South Pacific, Rodgers and Hammerstein, 1958). The song and the award-winning musical itself were banned in most southern states of the U.S. But the bans were lifted many years ago. The song can now be heard without restriction on a multitude of audio and visual media.

You've got to be taught to hate and fear

You've got to be taught from year to year

another one hundred years until the original ideals of universal equality will be finally achieved after a long transition to true union of all races and ethnicities.

References

American Psychiatric Association (2000) Diagnostic and Statistical Manual of Mental Disorders, 4th edn. American Psychiatric Press, Washington, DC

American Public Health Association (2020) What is Public Health? https://www.apha.org/what-is-public-health

BBC News (17 September 2020) Xinjiang: China Defends 'Education' Camps. https://www.bbc.com/news/world-asia-china-54195325

Bell C (1 December 2004) Racism: A Mental Illness? Psychiatric Services. 55(12), http://ps.psychiatryonline.org

Bertrand M, Mullainathan L (2003) Are Emily and Greg More Employable than Lakisha and Jamal? A Field Experiment on Labor Market Discrimination. National Bureau of Economic Research. Working Paper 9873 http://www.nber.org/papers/w9873

Brooks KJ (12 June 2020) Redlining's legacy: Maps are gone, but the problem hasn't disappeared. CBS News. https://www.cbsnews.com/news/redlining-what-is-history-mike-bloomberg-comments/

CDC Foundation (2020) What is Public Health? https://www.cdcfoundation.org/what-public-health

Crittenden J, Levine P (2018) Civic Education. The Stanford Encyclopedia of Philosophy (Fall 2018 Edition), Edward N. Zalta (ed) URL = https://plato.stanford.edu/archives/fall2018/entries/civic-education/

Detroit Free Press (8 August 2020) Governor Gretchen Whitmer on Public Health Crisis. https://www.freep.com/story/news/local/michigan/2020/08/05/racism-michigan-governor-gretchen-whitmer-public-health-crisis/3297123001/

Hauser C (10 June 2020) Merriam-Webster Revises 'Racism' Entry After Missouri Woman Asks for Changes. New York Times

History.com. American Slavery Before Jamestown https://www.history.com/news/american-slavery-before-jamestown-1619

Hobbes T (1958 [1651]) Leviathan: Parts I and II. In: Schneider HW (ed) Macmillan, New York

Houlgate L (2017) Understanding Immanuel Kant: The Smart Student's Guide to Grounding for the Metaphysics of Morals, (Amazon Kindle)

Houlgate L (2018) Understanding John Stuart Mill: The Smart Student's Guide to Utilitarianism and On Liberty, (Amazon Kindle)

Houlgate L (2020) Understanding Thomas Hobbes: The Smart Student's Guide to Leviathan, (Amazon Kindle)

It's got to be drummed in your dear little ear

You've got to be carefully taught

You've got to be taught to be afraid Of people whose eyes are oddly made

And people whose skin is a different shade You've got to be carefully taught

You've got to be taught before it's too late Before you are six or seven or eight

To hate all the people your relatives hate You've got to be carefully taught

Kant I (1781) Critique of Pure Reason. A51/B76. (Several editions and translations) Kerstein, Samuel, "Treating Persons as Means", The Stanford Encyclopedia of Philosophy (Summer 2019 Edition), Edward N. Zalta (ed) https://plato.stanford.edu/archives/sum2019/entries/persons-means/

Merriam Webster (2020) Racism. https://www.merriam-webster.com/dictionary/racism

Mill JS (1978 [1859]) On Liberty. Ed. Elizabeth Rapaport. Hackett Publishing

Morris H (1968) Persons and punishment. The Monist 52(4):475–501

Pew Trusts (15 June 2020). Racism is a Public Health Crisis. https://www.pewtrusts.org/en/research-and-analysis/blogs/stateline/2020/06/15/racism-is-a-	public-health-crisis-say-cities-and-counties

Plato. 427/428 – 347/348 BCE. Phaedo. (Several editions and translations)

Poussaint AF (2002) Racism can be a delusional symptom of psychotic disorders. West J Med 176(1):4. https://doi.org/10.1136/ewjm.176.1.4

Ray V, Aja A (18 June 2020) Racism isn't about ignorance. Some highly educated people have upheld systemic inequality. Washington Post. https://www.washingtonpost.com/nation/2020/06/18/racism-isnt-about-ignorance-some-smartest-minds-have-upheld-systemic-inequality/

U.S. Department of Education Office of Civil Rights (2014) Civil Rights Data Collection. Issue Brief No. 1. www.ocrdata.ed.gov

U.S. Department of Justice (2020) Hate Crimes Case Examples. https://www.justice.gov/hatecrimes/hate-crimes-case-examples

Wikipedia (2020) Involuntary Treatment. https://en.wikipedia.org/wiki/Involuntary_treatment

Zatz MS, Mann R, Coramae GL (eds) (1999) Images of color, images of crime: readings. Crime Law Soc Change 32:279–281. https://doi.org/10.1023/A:1008328019994

Part V
Civility, Incivility and Civic Learning

Three Arguments for Incivility

Robert G. Boatright

Abstract The idea that we should be civil to each other has become controversial in the current American political climate, and in particular in higher education. Some argue that calls for civility are a means of stifling dissent, while others contend that uncivil acts by political leaders necessitate an uncivil response. In this chapter I argue that much of the contemporary debate over civility rests on a disagreement about what civility is. To support my argument, I draw upon Michael Oakeshott's *On Human Conduct.* Oakeshott defines civil association as a state of voluntary equality within a particular group or society. This theory holds that civility is not a moral condition or imperative—that is, it is not something we "should" be. Instead, it is something that we are under certain circumstances. Accordingly, incivility is a denial that we are engaged in any sort of shared enterprise or have a shared set of facts or reference points. Civility is best achieved not when we call for it, but when we refer to community or to other values.

1 Making Space for Incivility

American colleges and universities face a challenge today in balancing calls for inclusion and diversity, on the one hand, and efforts to create a sense of community and shared purpose on the other. How does one build a community out of calls for disruption or radical change to that community itself? How does one make a virtue out of pluralism when the very institutions that are supposed to foster pluralism are increasingly looked upon with suspicion by so many? These are not solely questions about higher education. But conflicts are particularly stark in higher education

---

All page references are to Michael Oakeshott's *On Human Conduct* (1975) unless otherwise indicated.

R. G. Boatright (✉)
Clark University, Department of Political Science, Worcester, MA, USA
e-mail: rboatright@clarku.edu

© The Author(s), under exclusive license to Springer Nature Switzerland AG 2022   161
J. McGregor, M. C. Navin (eds.), *Education, Inclusion, and Justice*, Amintaphil:
The Philosophical Foundations of Law and Justice 11,
https://doi.org/10.1007/978-3-031-04013-9_11

because of colleges' emphasis on cultivating the ability to speak freely and, I would contend, because of the natural inclination of young adults to seek out opportunities to challenge authority. American colleges, in addition, aspire both to be inclusive communities in their own right and to be agents of change in the broader society. These pairings make it inevitable that societal norms about civil engagement will be contested.

In this chapter I address this problem with reference to civil and uncivil political discourse. I seek to make the case that efforts at categorizing modes of incivility can actually help us to understand one of the core questions facing educators or civic leaders today: how can a pluralist community include some of those who are hostile toward that community? When does rebellion or dissent strengthen the community and when does it harm it? Can a civil community, construed in one way, presume or even value a certain level, or certain types, of incivility? It is all a matter of definition, but these definitions, as I shall argue, are important to us if we want to understand the motives of those with whom we disagree.

This chapter proceeds in three parts. First, I explore three arguments for incivility, and I discuss the consequences of these definitions for our understanding of community. There are few instances where incivility is directly defined in any detail; rather, calls for incivility tend to be presented within political calls to action, so the effort to define incivility here amounts to a bit of rhetorical detective work on my part. Second, I review some of the standard definitions philosophers and political theorists have presented of civility; I pay particular attention here to one definition, offered by the British philosopher Michael Oakeshott, because I find this definition to be the most useful in thinking about how to develop and nurture communities, be they educational ones or larger political entities. And third, I close with some thoughts on the practical problems our schools and our society will face in encouraging open discussion of our differences in the current political climate.

2 Three Arguments in Favor of Incivility

Detailed explanations of what civility is have been common for centuries, and are certainly having a bit of a moment today (e.g. Mason 2018; Bejan 2017). It is rare, however, to see a theoretical defense of incivility. Most arguments for incivility, however, contain within them a definition of civility. That is, it is sometimes easier to say what one is arguing against than what one is arguing for. There are, I would contend, three major types of arguments in favor of incivility.

2.1 Performative or Strategic Incivility

First, some scholars argue that civility is a tool that has historically been used to silence people who aren't part of the "in group"—racial minorities, women, immigrants, and so forth. Gaye Theresa Johnson, a professor of African American Studies at the University of California, Los Angeles, argues that "people of color don't get to orchestrate the terms of civility. Instead, we're always responding to what civility is supposed to be" (Bates 2019). There is substantial historical evidence to support Johnson's claim, and it is easy to find contemporary examples where claims about incivility seem linked to sexism, misogyny, racial animus, and so forth – one need look only at the back-and-forth between Senators Mitch McConnell and Elizabeth Warren about Warren's "persistence" in speaking on the Senate floor (Flegenheimer 2017); the conflict between Representatives Alexandria Ocasio-Cortez and Ted Yoho (Broadwater 2020); or controversies regarding whether athletes' practice of "taking a knee" in support of the Black Lives Matter movement is civil.

Protest movements are often criticized for being uncivil, but these groups often respond that incivility—as exemplified, perhaps, by groups like ACT UP in the 1980s and 1990s—tends to get things done (see, e.g., France 2020; Lerner 2020). One could argue, furthermore, that uncivil protests can become mainstreamed just as social movements gradually take on the institutional features of organized interests (McAdam 1982), and that they are therefore a precursor to establishing durable and equitable forms of representation.

Even when "uncivil" groups are not ultimately successful, however, interviews with the leaders of such actions tend to reveal that incivility is a strategic choice. It is performative. In this sense, incivility is not a denial of social rules; rather, it is a choice meant to demonstrate that the goals of the actors are so important that they override rules of civility *in this instance*. The rules do matter, otherwise the uncivil action itself would be meaningless. When the action is taken by actors who are otherwise known for their civility—as in the case of the "wall of mothers" and "leaf blower dads" in the Portland, Oregon protests during the summer of 2020 (Lang 2020)—the transgression becomes more notable.

Another way to think about performative incivility is not in terms of the time or circumstance, but in the creation of identity. Consider, for instance, the rituals that go into the establishment of particular subcultures. Gatherings of heavy metal or hardcore punk fans, for instance, have rules and rituals of their own, but can be oriented toward the expression of "uncivil" sentiments about organized religion, contemporary politics, or other features of society. In this instance, again, statements which might be construed as "uncivil" by outsiders are the point of the endeavor, but the very identity of everyone participating in these concerts is rooted in an agreement to engage with each other in a civil fashion. One need not be part of the subculture in question to recognize—or, perhaps more importantly, appreciate and support—performative incivility. One need only be able to understand that the performance is not necessarily reality. Virtually all sorts of provocative music, comedy, or other performances rely upon our willingness as an audience to ourselves to be shocked in this limited, temporary way before returning to our regular lives.

There is, then, no moral reason to object to incivility in this sense. It is hard to imagine a healthy, pluralistic or multicultural society which does not include or encourage some instances of strategic incivility. We can only know what the rules are when we are able to understand when they have been transgressed, and the only way to have a democratic society is to discuss when, where, and why transgressions happen. Furthermore, given the organized nature of some of these performative efforts, it is plausible to argue that these are not instances of incivility after all. If we conceive of civility as a set of culturally defined rituals, then things that might seem uncivil to an observer may in fact merely be observing the norms of a different culture. They call attention, as well, to our own norms—we can better understand our own culture if we can distinguish it from others.

2.2   Incivility as Bluntness

Second, one might view civil discussion as a form of moral equivocation, a decision not to say clearly what one wants or believes is right. To discuss matters in a reasoned, civil fashion presupposes that one is open to having one's opinion challenged, or that one is willing to soften the blow of ideas in order to placate one's real or imagined foes. Yet sometimes things are not really up for debate; furthermore, sometimes it is important to say what we think without having to debate. We have more important things to do, and the feelings of those who might be easily offended by our uncivil statements should not stand in the way.

There is no clear partisan or ideological angle to such arguments. One sees them, for instance, in objections from the left to toning down criticisms of George W. Bush; the progressive news magazine *In These Times* regularly attacks moderate Democrats for calling for civil discussion, using headlines such as "The Year in 'Civility': The 6 Worst Appeals to Norms and Good Manners" (Cartolano and Lazare 2018) or "Rehabilitating a Monster: George W. Bush and the Bankruptcy of Civility Politics" (Chamseddine 2018). Similarly, Joe Biden was criticized by some on the left for speaking of his cordial relationships with segregationist Southern Democrats ("Civility is Overrated" ran one headline on the topic (Serwer 2019)). Yet such claims are also common on the right, as in, for instance, arguments that "civility is used as a pretext to shut down debate" (Steller 2017) or that civility and "political correctness" are one and the same. Both sides' arguments frame civility in a shallow manner—as a set of manners or an agreement not to use certain words or phrases. If we limit our speech, the argument goes, we lose our ability to condemn awful people, or we turn the other cheek when confronted by things that require a direct response.

There is, again, some truth to these claims. As Mark Kingwell (2012, p. 149) points out, civility can be inefficient. Yet perhaps there is a difference between bluntness and incivility. If we speak in direct terms to children, to those who do not speak our language well, or to our dogs, we do not do so because we wish to be uncivil. Rather, we assume before making our statement that our effective vocabulary is limited, and the various forms of social etiquette that we might offer someone else do not apply here.

Yet claims about bluntness are just as often a means of establishing difference, a performative way of wielding power over discussions in which we are not actually participating. During his 2016 campaign, Donald Trump often railed against "political correctness," equating it with the policies of his predecessors in both parties. In one speech alleging that immigrants are responsible for gun violence, Trump claimed that past Democratic leaders "have put political correctness above common sense, above your safety, and above all else. I refuse to be politically correct" (quoted in Weigel 2016). Here, Trump is preparing the audience for "uncivil" claims by emphasizing the importance of speaking directly and urgently, by claiming that the stakes are too high to engage in polite discussion or to avoid potentially hurting people's feelings.

Arguments about bluntness, then, may pose only a limited threat to serious discussion. In some circumstances they may be necessary (as in my instructions to my dog) because other conversations are not possible. In others, they at worst pose the threat of showing the speaker to be an insensitive boor. Even here, though, they are limited in nature because they presuppose that it is only sometimes, or to some audiences, that we must speak directly, without niceties. They only harm this particular conversation. And by limiting civility to an issue of manners or etiquette, such critiques may not really presume to question broader societal ideas about civility and community.

The boor's argument here, as well, is not something that can be entirely discarded. If I violate the etiquette rules of a dinner party, it may well suggest that I don't belong, but I did not mean to offend. Similarly, when my dog does something she's not supposed to do, it may well be because she doesn't know any better. Protestations about political correctness are somewhat like this—the speaker may really not know that a term is offensive. Such claims can ring shallow when they are accompanied by the claim (implicit in the Trump statement above) that the speaker has no time or motivation to learn how to stop giving offense. But we can still imagine some circumstances where this is true—where, for instance, learning the niceties of communicating in a foreign tongue, or arranging the table for a formal dinner do in fact get in the way of other legitimate aims.

There is, however, a more troubling implication of the bluntness argument. It is not the uncivil statement that matters here as much as it is the pretense. The person who speaks bluntly seeks to exercise power over those whose thoughts he does not fully understand—in some of the examples I have given, as when one speaks to a child, a pet, a person with limited language skills, the speaker has the advantage of being able to modify his language. He chooses not to because we face some sort of emergency, and it is urgent to speak directly.

Are we in an emergency situation? Who is to decide? In day-to-day life, we may easily identify such emergency moments. If a speeding car is headed your way, perhaps I can be forgiven for not bothering with pleasantries when I yell at you. But a social or political state of emergency requires a declaration of sorts, and is often subject to dispute. There are two implications here.

First, in *On the Social Contract*, Rousseau (1978, Book 4, ch. 6) explores the circumstances under which a democratically governed state might temporarily grant dictatorial power to one person. Laws, he argues, can accrete over time and become inflexible, unable to allow a government to respond to a crisis in a timely fashion. In these circumstances, it may be wise to suspend the laws and appoint a dictator. This dictator, says Rousseau, cannot legislate but can rule by fiat for the duration of the crisis. One might, similarly, see an accretion of norms governing proper behavior or speech as inhibiting our ability to say necessary things. Because these are norms, not laws, however, we cannot expect an orderly process of suspension (and it is perhaps unrealistic to expect the process Rousseau describes as being orderly, either). All we can do, then, is abrogate this power to ourselves. He who declares that there is an emergency, an urgent need to speak bluntly right now, is in effect doing this.

Second, one might argue that the declaration of some sort of emergency is what power is about. In *Political Theology*, Carl Schmitt equates sovereignty with the declaration that one is the exception, that one can (or must) stand outside of norms and rules. For Schmitt, any constitutional government tends toward this moment. This declaration of exception is the moment when "the power of real life breaks through the crust of a mechanism that has become torpid by repetition" (Schmitt 1985, p. 15).

In both of these instances, we might contend that a declaration of any sort of emergency might be an assertion of power. It does not have to be only about power (in contrast to our third case below), but it might be. It may be (as in the case of Trump) that the speaker does not benefit from clarifying what the motivation is. So, incivility may pose a threat, but the threat does not lie in the incivility itself but in what it represents. It alerts us to other problems. A response to incivility in this sense requires a determination of whether the invocation of the reason to speak uncivilly is justified.

2.3 Incivility Claims as Assertions of Power

And third, one might present a Thrasymachean critique, contending that the rules of civility are constantly changing and are merely a function of power. This is in many ways the current critique by some on the right. Whenever anyone gains power, as some argue that people on the left have, those who are empowered redefine what is legitimate to discuss and brand previously acceptable modes of discourse as uncivil. Ruth Braunstein (2018) refers to such conflicts as "civility contests" in which competing factions seek to define their mode of expression as "civil" and that of their opponents as "uncivil."

On its face, this type of incivility seems to be little different than the first type. This framing assumes, again, that rules are used to limit the expression of out-groups. However, in this framing, the identity of the out-groups is irrelevant— that is, racial minorities or women do not risk having their speech or actions branded "uncivil" because of bias or a history of oppression; rather, they simply have the misfortune of being on the losing side. Were they in power, they would similarly hold the speech or action of their opponents to be uncivil. This may be what makes this approach attractive to some conservatives (see, for instance, critiques of Senator Ben Sasse's calls for civility, such as in Allen (2018). This is at its heart an argument about identity politics, but it is not an argument about any particular sort of identity.

This critique is ultimately of more consequence than the two previous critiques because it denies any special status to any norms about discourse. Norms about how one addresses one's antagonists, about how votes are taken, or about acceptable forms of evidence have no greater status than the actual issues being contested. In Lilliana Mason's (2018) framing of contemporary identity politics, the goal of winning becomes more important than the preservation of norms or rules. Here, political polarization has reached the point that any conflict over policy becomes a conflict over rules and norms, and vice versa, and a loss on one issue is a sign of impending losses on a wide range of issues and of a threat to the losing group's identity or status. It doesn't matter what you win as long as you win.

As with the first two types, one can find instances where this critique is justified. There are, to be certain, instances where democratic communities have systematically limited the rights of minorities, and the rhetoric surrounding their disenfranchisement often makes reference to their incivility, vulgarity, or lack of acceptance of democratic norms. Morgan Kousser's (1974) discussion of how black voters were removed from the southern electorate in the 1890s is replete with whites' arguments that a white electorate would resolve conflicts in a more civil fashion—while still, somehow, looking out for the interests of African-Americans. This cynical framing was an effort to present disfranchisement as a matter of improving governance, of linking it to the ambitions of the Progressive movement. It is not clear that anyone outside of the South was persuaded by this argument, but it should alert us that disingenuous calls for civility have a long history.

Yet ultimately this argument presumes a much more comprehensive understanding of what civility is, and it thus requires a more detailed response. The reader will note that above I have not made a moral case for civility. This is the case in part because I do not see contemporary arguments for what gets termed "incivility" to be a challenge to norms of civility, and I see the claims here as being eminently reasonable and worthy of inclusion in any sort of democratic discourse. The idea of civility as power, however, requires a much more elaborate response, to which I now turn.

3   A Moral Case for Civility

Michael Oakeshott argues in *On Human Conduct* (1975) that it is hard to justify civility on its own terms. We should not be civil in order to achieve any higher-level goals, although civil conduct can facilitate the pursuit of such goals. When we break civility into its component parts or practices we find that each of these is arbitrary. Because we cannot make a moral case for any of its component parts, we cannot make the case for civility as a whole. We can, however, observe civil conduct or its absence. And when civility disappears or changes, we can ask why this has happened. Such questions may lead us to an inquiry into morals. Once civility is gone, however, we have no obvious way to reconstruct it.

To understand Oakeshott's theory of civility, we must first understand what it is not. Civility, Oakeshott argues, is not social, largely because there is no such thing as "the social." Nor is it possible to talk about human "behavior" or any other forward- or backward-looking attribute to the things we do. There is only "conduct." People sometimes choose to work cooperatively, but this choice does not suggest that there are social wants or goals (pp. 87–89). When we are together, we remain distinct individuals. Similarly, then, civility is also not goal-oriented. Oakeshott describes what he calls "enterprise associations" which form because of a shared goal, but these associations are only valid when there is an explicit agreement about what that goal is and what the discrete steps are by which the association will do to achieve that goal (114, 174). The association has no standing apart from these agreed-upon steps, and it dissolves once the goal is reached or once individual pursuits are introduced that deviate from that agreement. Civility also has nothing to do with rationality, then, as rational behavior is by definition goal-oriented (89). To whatever extent we engage each other civilly, it is a matter of enjoying the trip, not the destination.

Civility is also distinct from friendship. Friendship, for Oakeshott, is not strictly goal-oriented—we do not make friends for the explicit purpose of achieving a shared goal. We might also see friendship as a matter of enjoying the trip, not the destination. Yet friendship is a distinctly moral orientation because we do have some sort of commitment to the future. Friendships, or romantic relationships, develop and deepen over time. We develop a shared store of memories or in jokes. They require a past and they anticipate some sort of a future, while civil conduct does not. We do not set out to make our friends better, but when friendships work out, we generally do.

Oakeshott describes civility, then, as a condition. In this regard, his categorization fits solidly into the sort of postmodern camp that Hannah Arendt (1958) defines when she speaks of the "human condition." Oakeshott describes this condition as the "Respublica" (147)—not to be confused with the "republic." He is not interested in whether civil conduct has anything to do with human nature—it is merely a mode of conduct in which we sometimes find ourselves. We do not even notice the components of civil conduct, although we do notice distinctly uncivil things. In Oakeshott's (1996, p. xi) posthumously published book *The Politics of Faith and Scepticism*, his editor, Timothy Fuller, likens this mode of human conduct to the use of garlic in cooking—we don't really notice the garlic when properly used, but we do notice it absence or its excess.

What, then, does this condition entail? At a minimum, it entails a voluntary equality of participants (112, 121). This does not assume any sort of broad commitment to equality as a social feature—there are, after all, plenty of human endeavors where all are not equal. A musical performance, for instance, may well include an audience, which is not equal to the participants in its musical ability, as well as a set of finer gradations of talent or role in regard to who will play what. There are many other analogies—a pickup basketball game (as opposed to a basketball league), an ad hoc faculty lunch, an impromptu meeting of neighbors. Some might involve action, some might require some sort of specialized knowledge, but these things come about after the decision to engage. Civility also is distinct from preestablished hierarchies—Oakeshott presents the civil condition as being distinct from religious, military, or political relationships (110).

Civility also requires rules: not formal ones, but rules which are generally accepted. Rules of civility are distinct from admonitions, predictions, or advice (124). They exist because we accept them, not because we have engaged in a process of justification. One set of rules is not necessarily better or worse than another, but we have the rules that we have. We can and do change the rules over time, but we do not necessarily engage in deliberation or any sort of formal democratic or other political process when this happens. These are rules of engagement—they do not prescribe any particular outcome, action, or performance, but they do make these things possible.

It is easy to see, then, why civility cannot be justified. We do not have to engage in the aforementioned musical performance, or any other shared activity. There are many other things we could be doing, and it would be a matter of taste, and nothing else, to posit that our engagement here, or the choice to play basketball, is a moral one. The civil condition allows for the performance of moral acts, however (175). Suppose that an injury occurs in that pickup basketball game, and one of the participants steps forward to cauterize the wound. Some distinctly uncivil things might occur as well, as might some immoral ones. And this civil engagement might bring about a host of behaviors that are simply interesting. We cannot prescribe these, we cannot expect them, and we have no ready means to distinguish among them by drawing upon any characteristic of civil conduct. And these rules or activities are also, finally, not justified with reference to elites—those who stand outside of the relationship we have established (153).

Despite the modesty of Oakeshott's political examples, he speaks in somewhat grand terms about civility. The point of *On Human Conduct* is to explain "the European state" (part 3). Civility is not a prerequisite of the state, let alone of democratic states. It can exist in a variety of contexts. Yet there is such a thing as "civil conduct"—or as people other than Oakeshott might say, "civil society"—that exists within states. When we are together, we have opportunities to develop rules of civility to engage in civil conduct, and one way in which we are together is as citizens of a state.

At the same time, many of those who have written on civility have emphasized the little things that are components of civil conduct. Montesquieu (1989, 1271) describes the relationship between civility and manners. Walter Lippmann (1955, p. 132) characterizes it as an openness to different beliefs. In his essay "Two Concepts of Civility" Anthony Laden (2018) explores the moral status of the disappearance of the fish fork from table settings. Patrick Deneen (2016, p. 104) notes that the terms "civility" and "politeness" are both etymologically related to the existence of cities—from *cives* and *politeia*. The little things imply bigger things. Yet these little things can seem either innocuous or, more ominously, like status markers imposed upon us by elites.

This is the problem brought about by changes in what is civil. Rules of civility get broken, and we notice this. Sometimes, their disappearance may mean nothing, as is the case, perhaps, for the fish fork. But their disappearance is cause for investigation, at least for those whose activities are affected by the change. Why did they disappear? Some breaches of civility may be a consequence of immoral acts, or of a greater loss. A vulgar tweet from our president, for instance, may only be a violation of civility, but it may also say something about institutional breakdown or something more sinister. Changes to the rules of civility can have "ripple effects," bringing conflicts and tensions to the surface that merit inquiry (180).

The problem then becomes how we understand our role in such breaches. For Oakeshott, one possibility stands above all others—we may have ceased to engage each other as equals, to have improperly understood what civil conduct is (168). We may have too expansive an understanding of our condition. Civil rules are corrupted, he argues, when they are confused with wants or with substantive agreements about what is to be done. We may have become nakedly self-interested, seeking to use the rules for our immediate advantage. Or we may have become self-interested in a more philosophical sense, in our efforts to define ourselves or create ourselves through our engagement with others. Oakeshott refers to this as the disposition to "self-employment," to recognize one's self and others in one's actions (324).

Because the individual components of civility cannot be justified, however, we cannot simply recreate them. We can't be authoritarians of civility, forcing everyone to use fish forks. Nor can the state legitimately develop ways to formally legislate civility. One is reminded here of Rousseau's (1969, Part 2) account in the *Second Discourse* of the complicated and contingent way in which human society developed. If we abandon all of that, we can't just simply put it back. One can't really go back and add garlic to the meal after it has been cooked.

In the end, Oakeshott concludes that there is a sort of second-order morality to civility—we can have a commitment to being civil, but faithfulness to it can be seen as a sort of moral position even if the individual rules don't have moral import (175). This is a weak case in that one's commitment to civility does not require faithfulness to any particular component of civil behavior.

4   Applying Oakeshott's Definition

Oakeshott helps us put the various arguments for incivility in context. Civility is not a first order goal, and calls for civility are likely to be taken poorly. They are, furthermore, not always necessary. Many attention-grabbing instances of confrontational or unconventional behavior can actually strengthen community if they become subject for discussion. They are performative or strategic, designed to foster conversations which can be conducted in an open fashion.

4.1 Civility on Campus

Oakeshott's understanding of civility suggests that we can appeal to some of the things we value most in having a civil community without making the appeal *about* civility. We can emphasize the importance of community, or shared values that the community holds or should hold. We can emphasize continuity—the traditions that schools have, the connections students establish to prior students simply by being there. When colleges and universities talk about this, they are talking about civility without using it as a term to silence. Such suggestions, furthermore, can often lend themselves to questions about what in the tradition is of value, or of how to think about different pieces of a school's tradition.

Oakeshott also calls our attention to different roles within the community. At the level of higher education, it suggests that transparency about the imperatives faced by faculty, staff, administration, alumni, benefactors, and students can enhance conversation. An openness about how each is evaluated, what right each has to make determinations about, for instance, the curriculum, grading, hiring, and so on can help to structure conversation while also helping to understand why each participant has different limits on his or her ability to make changes or address problems.

In today's political climate, this approach may well frustrate many people. The appeal of populism, particularly on the right today, has been its rejection of such discussions. The rules will always be made by elites, with malign or selfish intent. Institutions, including the norms associated with civil discourse, are impediments to action. At a minimum, such an approach sounds like a way to put off decisions—create a task force, make some recommendations, and hope that the unrest dies down in the meantime. Yet such an approach is perhaps a way for colleges to serve as correctives to such societal trends. It is hard to create true disagreement or deliberation on college campuses today because so many of them—or, at least, so many of our elite private colleges and universities—are relatively homogeneous in ideological terms. Spending some time teaching about the role of institutions, about norms, about deliberation can create a modicum of disagreement without creating debates just to have debates. It can enhance free expression while subtly orienting that expression towards articulation of what the civic community is or should be.

4.2 Civility in American Political Discourse

We can easily see the same confusions and conflicts in our broader society as well. To take the most obvious example, that of our former president, it makes a difference how we think about a presidential tweet. We might consider it to be a performance—an effort to draw attention by criticizing one's antagonists. We might consider it to be an effort to convey a policy idea, and the brevity of the medium might require that its author dispense with social niceties. Or we might take it to be an effort to sow discord or to delegitimize the endeavor of having reasoned conversation.

I note Donald Trump's tweets here not so much to blame him for uncivil discourse in America today, but to point out the problem of discerning intent within a given community. One might argue that the resolution to the problem of classifying any or all of the president's statements might be to determine what he means—does he mean his statement to be a statement of policy? Was there a master plan behind the statement, or was it merely a passing thought? We as a nation have been debating such things since the beginning of the 2016 presidential race.

Yet ultimately perhaps resolving the question of intent does not rely so much upon the speaker as on the audience. Given that we cannot know what Trump meant, might we decide to treat these statements as if they are an instance of one type of incivility and not another? If we consider them as performance, we could perhaps choose simply to ignore them and move on with other business. Certainly, we do not treat provocative statements by, say, professional comedians with the same concern we treat those by professional politicians. We choose, then, to ascribe intent to people when we do not or cannot actually know what they are thinking.

There is no clear answer to how we should treat incivility, then, but the campus example suggests that if we believe we have a community, or if we are willing to extend a presumption of positive intent to those who are part of our community, we might benefit from seeing how such presumptions work in a broader content. That is, we might work to assume that we do share a community and values with people whose statements might at first glance strike us as being uncivil or harmful to community. And we might consider how the community-building efforts that are the mark of a successful college or university might be expanded—we might consider how efforts to encourage speech and dialogue on campus can be expanded upon and applied elsewhere in order to improve the quality and openness of American political discourse.

References

Allen C (2018) Another Sasse Treatment on What Ails us. Law & Liberty Blog, December 17. https://lawliberty.org/another-sasse-treatise-on-what-ails-us/

Arendt H (1958) The human condition. University of Chicago Press, Chicago

Bates KG (2019) When Civility is Used as a Cudgel against People of Color. National Public Radio, March 14. https://www.npr.org/sections/codeswitch/2019/03/14/700897826/when-civility-is-used-as-a-cudgel-against-people-of-color

Bejan TM (2017) Mere civility: disagreement and the limits of toleration. Harvard University Press, Cambridge MA

Braunstein R (2018) Boundary-work and the demarcation of civil from uncivil protest in the United States: control, legitimacy, and political inequality. Theory Soc 47(2):603–633

Broadwater L (2020) Ocasio-Cortez Embraces a Republican's Insult. New York Times, July 21

Cartolano M, Lazare S (2018) The Year in 'Civility.' In These Times, December 17

Chamseddine R (2018) Rehabilitating a Monster: George W. Bush and the Bankruptcy of Civility Politics. In These Times, September 6

Deneen PJ (2016) Conserving America? Essays on present discontents. St. Augustine's Press, South Bend IN

Flegenheimer M (2017) Republican senators vote to formally silence Elizabeth Warren. New York Times, February 7

France DP (2020) The activists. New York Times Magazine, April 13

Kingwell M (2012) Unruly voices. Biblioasis, Toronto

Kousser JM (1974) The shaping of Southern politics: suffrage restriction and the establishment of the One-Party South, 1880-1910. Yale University Press, New Haven

Laden A (2018) Two concepts of civility. In: Boatright RG, Sobieraj S, Young DG, Shaffer TJ (eds) A crisis of civility?: Political discourse and its discontents. Routledge, New York, pp 9–30

Lang M (2020) Leaf Blower Wars. Washington Post, July 26

Lerner B (2020) Activism Doesn't Need to be Peaceful. Larry Kramer Taught us That. LGBTQ Nation, June 7. https://www.lgbtqnation.com/2020/06/activism-doesnt-need-peaceful-larry-kramer-taught-us/

Lippmann W (1955) The public philosophy. Mentor, New York

Mason L (2018) Uncivil agreement: how politics became our identity. University of Chicago Press, Chicago

McAdam D (1982) Political process and the development of black insurgency, 1930-1970. University of Chicago Press, Chicago

Montesquieu C (1989) The spirit of the laws. In: Cohler A, Miller B, Stone H (eds) Cambridge University Press, New York

Oakeshott M (1975) On human conduct. Clarendon Press, Oxford

Oakeshott M (1996) The politics of faith and the politics of scepticism. Yale University Press, New Haven

Rousseau JJ (1969) The first and second discourses. In: Masters J, Masters R (eds) Bedford St. Martins, Boston

Rousseau JJ (1978) On the social contract. In: Masters J, Masters R (eds) Bedford St. Martins, Boston

Schmitt C (1985) Political theology. In: Schwab G (ed) University of Chicago Press, Chicago

Serwer A (2019) Civility is Overrated. The Atlantic, December 1

Steller T (2017) Danger of 'Civility" Being Used as Pretext to Shut Down Debate." Arizona Daily Star, June 19

Weigel M (2016) Political correctness: how the right invented a phantom enemy. The Guardian, November 30

Moral Capital, Civic Grace, and the Role of Education

Joan McGregor

Abstract Moral capital is the set of shared norms and values in a society. The question of this chapter is what is the role of moral capital in the smooth running of society but particularly in times of crisis? Even before pandemic of 2020–2021 and racial reckoning in America, we found ourselves in a place where social norms are flaunted by our leaders, by television and radio personalities, on social media, and generally deteriorating throughout the society. This paper explores the notion of moral capital, what it is and the role it plays in flourishing societies. And finally, I will argue for the important role that higher education plays in supporting moral capital mostly through cultivating the virtues of civility, civic grace, and the epistemic virtues.

> What we learn in time of pestilence: that there are more things to admire in men than to despise. Albert Camus *The Plague*

> Before we went on any protest, whether it was sit-ins or the freedom rides or any march, we prepared ourselves, and we were disciplined. We were committed to the way of peace - the way of non-violence - the way of love - the way of life as the way of living. John Lewis

The global pandemic brought with it an urgent summons to observe and reflect on the role of moral capital in times of crisis. We have seen signs both of partisan divides giving way in the face of our shared fragility, and of continued suspicion and mistrust, often organized along party lines. We observe that expertise is unavailing when mistrust of experts dictates personal and collective choices. We see large-scale cooperation for the public good and indifference to the plight of the most vulnerable,

---

This work on moral capital was generously supported by a grant from the National Institute on Civil Discourse.

J. McGregor (✉)
School of Historical, Philosophical, and Religious Studies, Arizona State University, Tempe, AZ, USA
e-mail: j.mcgregor@asu.edu

both wearing masks in public and keeping one's distance and not doing so. Furthermore, we see different societies faring unevenly in face of a common threat—Germany's death rate remained far lower than other nations' as a percentage of cases, for example—and we wonder what we can learn from their successes and failures, as a function of the relative health of their civic cultures. Attention to the moral capital of society may be more important than ever as to whether a state emerges safe and strong during an emergent national and international crisis. The COVID-19 epidemic, beyond its general devastation, exposed to the world the racial disparities in the U.S. health care system, the impact of many minorities being essential workers, and revealed the underlying underinvestment in minority neighborhoods, making minorities more susceptible to the virus's worst outcomes. On top of that national disgrace, the taping of the latest public acts of murder of black men and women often at the hands of police, exposes yet again not only the structural injustices but overt injustices against people of color. Those injustices have for too long been invisible to much of white America, but these epidemics, the COVID one and the police brutality one, are making them impossible to ignore. What is the role of moral capital in these times of crisis? Even before COVID and George Floyd, we found ourselves in a place where social norms are flaunted by our leaders, television, and radio personalities on social media and generally deteriorating throughout the society. This paper explores the notion of moral capital, what it is and the role it plays in flourishing societies. And finally, I will argue for the important role that higher education plays in supporting moral capital mostly through cultivating the virtues of civic grace and civility.

1   What Is Moral Capital?

David Brooks of the *New York Times* defines moral capital as "the set of shared habits, norms, institutions and values that make common life possible" (Brooks 2016). Lamenting evidence of America's loss of moral capital, Brooks observed that "human beings have an impressive capacity for selfishness" and that "the struggle for power tends to become barbaric." For this reason, "people in decent societies agree on a million informal restraints" that "girdle selfishness and steer us toward reconciliation." Historically social and political thinkers, notably Adam Smith, John Locke, David Hume and Edmond Burke, among many others, acknowledged the importance of moral capital (although they didn't use that expression) for a well-functioning society. Though most of the attention of Adam Smith is on his work on political economy, in particular his observation that individuals acting on their own self-interest in the market could almost miraculously through the invisible hand create wealth, he was well aware of the importance of morality and social practices in making a functioning society, including the market (Smith 2014).[1] Self-interest must be reined in by morality since morality is about "mutual understanding and habitable ways of life" (Walker 1998, p. 6). John Stuart Mill argued for another notion for cultivating sympathy and concern among a citizenry he called "religion of humanity." For Mill, the idea of the religion was to squash narrow-minded self-interest and greed and encourage promotion of sympathy for the common good (Mill 1933). Jean-Jacques Rousseau in *The Social Contract* (1762) discussed the notion of "civil religion", a similar concept to moral capital, and a requirement of a healthy body politic. "The object of civil religion for Rousseau is to foster sentiments of sociability and a love of public duties among citizens, extending those bonds throughout a citizenry and its membership" (https://www.britannica.com/topic/civil-religion).

In the view of cultural critics across the political spectrum, moral capital is currently in high demand and low supply. According to social psychologist Jonathan Haidt, moral capital captures "the degree to which a community possesses interlocking sets of values, virtues, norms, practices, identities, institutions, and technologies that mesh well with evolved psychological mechanisms and thereby enable the community to suppress or regulate selfishness and make cooperation possible" (Haidt 2012, p. 292). Haidt's notion of moral capital builds upon what political scientist Robert Putnam describes more broadly as social capital, those "features of social organization such as networks, norms, and social trust that facilitate coordination and cooperation for mutual benefit" (Putnam 1994, p. 67). In his influential book *Bowling Alone,* he defines social capital as: "connections among individuals – social networks and the norms of reciprocity and trustworthiness that arise from them" (Putman 2000, p. 19).

Societies to be well functioning need to have high levels of social and moral capital. Moral capital is that set of shared social practices embodying norms, standards, values, and virtues which are largely unarticulated in a society that bind and sustain a moral community. Those shared practices play out in civil society through voluntary associations with different individuals and groups whether they be religious associations, unions, fraternal clubs, identity groups or political ones but also in the marketplace at large. Citizens count upon others behaving according to these shared social practices that account for our responsibilities to one another. Of course, the social practices are more complex than everyone having the same responsibilities; responsibilities often depend on one's identity, the context, and other factors. Nevertheless, we can leave the understanding of social practices fairly broad at this stage. To achieve the goods associated with civil society individuals must restrain themselves from acting on self-interest at every turn and abide by these shared norms and standards or understandings—or generally social practices (Haslanger 2018). We have social practices regarding cooperation, trust, listening to one another, not exploiting others and so on. The social practices are experienced

---

[1] Looking at Adam Smith's work in totality, *The Wealth of Nations* and *The Theory of the Moral Sentiments* it is clear that Smith thought that both what he called sympathy (the basis for him of public morality) and self-interest work together for a well-functioning society.

at large and small scales—for example, queuing up in an orderly manner at the movie theater and not calling people names are small scale social practices that shape our everyday social lives. Large scale social practices involve basic trust in and fidelity to government. These social practices are based as Margaret Walker argued on our shared moral understandings, "about what people are supposed to do, expect, and understand...Particular understandings are revealed in the daily rounds of interaction that show how people make sense of their own and others' responsibilities in terms of the identities, relationships, and values" (Walker 10).

The use of the term 'capital' might be thought problematic. 'Capital' conjures notions of financial resources and not moral ones. But if we think of "moral capital" as a resource or property or treasure that we share as a society, and that we can have more or less of it, then the term capital makes sense. Think of the use of 'natural capital' in the sustainability literature meaning the world's or nation's stock of natural resources, including the soils, air, water, and living organisms. Ecologists are now discussing the services we get from nature that we don't pay for, so-called 'ecosystem services.' Having these ecosystem services is to have natural capital. The use of the nomenclature of 'capital' in this case is meant to show the valuable resources and services we get and share of that natural capital.

Moral capital is valuable for members of society. It is not, however, something that any one of us has individually: it is something that the group has. The social practices that make up our moral capital, for example practices of civility, are a public good.[2] The goods of moral capital are of mutual benefit to citizens in a given society. Civility benefits everyone by maintaining a social practice of respect for one another, even those you disagree with, listening to arguments but not necessarily agreeing. Public goods according to economists have the characteristic of "nonrivalrous consumption," that is, any one person's consumption of the good does not diminish others' enjoyment of it. Also, like other public goods, the benefits of moral capital can be shared whether one contributes or not. There are some costs to contributing to the moral capital of society—sacrificing self-interest—but the benefits of everyone complying results in mutual benefit to members of society. But like other public goods in the strict sense, free riders cannot be excluded from the benefits (nonexcludability). This can lead to another problem of public goods: prisoners' dilemma problems. It might be rational for each actor to follow their own self-interest, non-compliance by being uncivil, but the net effect, if enough people defect from the social practices of civility, is that we are worse off than if we complied. This is the situation we find ourselves in today, where individuals are not abiding by the social practices, for instance, of civility, and since there are enough people doing so the practice of civility is eroding, and consequently we are not sharing the benefits.

How much moral capital a society has could presumably be determined. Think of a failed state where there aren't social practices of trust, reciprocity or cooperation,

---

[2]https://www.econlib.org/library/Enc/PublicGoods.html; see *Civility in Politics and Education* ed by Deborah Mower and Wade Robison where they discuss this idea.

and no constraint on selfishness, etc. at one end, and at the other a highly homogeneous society where all norms are shared. The first society has a deficit of moral capital and cannot function efficiently as a society, the citizens cannot pursue their projects without great difficulty. The second society has an abundance of moral capital and might be highly efficient. This is not to say that a society in which all the norms are shared is the best society all things considered—it depends on which norms are shared. Traditional liberals suppose that we need to have shared norms, particularly norms for the democratic functioning of the society, including civility, norms for coordinating behavior. However, liberals don't believe that everyone in the society has to share the same values about what is the good life. The shared values for liberals are focused among other things on how we interact and engage with one another and even how we define general values about the common good of the society. For example, a society might agree that everyone ought to have high-quality education and healthcare, and have equal opportunity to live whatever is their own conception of the good life. Having a shared infrastructure of social practices doesn't guarantee that the allocation of responsibilities and burdens is fair or appropriate; they are always open to normative critical reflection and revision (Chambers and Kopstein 2001). Many societies' moral understandings of responsibilities place extra burden on some identities than others; for example, women are thought to be primarily responsible for child and elder care. That moral understanding of our social practices disadvantages women by placing an extra burden on them and permitting men to deflect the responsibility for those activities. Having an abundance of moral capital does entail that the moral understandings of who is responsible for what and to whom are justified. Some practices of responsibility may be based on unjustified allocations of power and privilege.

2   The Importance of Moral Capital

The current social climate in the United States compels us to address the decline of moral capital. There have been daily reports of norm busting by former President Donald Trump and other populist and autocratic leaders around the world. Trump relishes the disruptive antics that come with ignoring the social practices of responsibility that come with our democracy. Trump is not fully responsible for the decline of moral capital in the United States although his presidency has escalated its decline. Trump has disregarded and openly broken the traditional norms and standards that politicians and other public officials usually obey. The results of his behavior have compromised and made many question our shared understanding about norms and standards. These deflections of responsibilities are big and small: they include, not releasing his taxes, publicly commenting on an opponent's spouse's looks, calling facts fake news, firing government oversight officials, publicly berating journalists doing their jobs, tweeting conspiracy theories, pardoning his friends, and on and on. Many of those around Trump and other major political leaders encouraged by his disregard of norms have acted in similar ways. The former

President's willingness to countenance white supremacists and the flying of the Confederate flag, permits followers to suppose that it is publicly acceptable to express those views openly. Rather than being the only one, the former President's actions are amplified when others take his lead.

Because not everyone has given up our moral understandings of our social practices, Trump and his allies gained further advantage by disregarding norms while others followed social practices. For example, top military and government officials traditionally do not openly criticize sitting Presidents. This practice prevented many from speaking out against former President Trump's actions and thereby, without public criticism from high level officials, credence was given to Trump's actions. That social practice of not criticizing a sitting President was made visible when someone like General Mattis, pushed to his limits when former President Trump ordered the military to clear the streets of peaceful protesters in Washington so he could take a photo in front of a church, speaks out against the President's behavior (Goldberg 2020). What all this shows is how these invisible social practices function in our society to maintain a structure that permits the society to work for everyone. And how when enough of the norms are broken with impunity the system starts to deteriorate (note there are times, such as in the case of General Mattis, where social practices should be broken). Shared social practices hold our civil society and our system of democracy together. As mentioned earlier, this does not mean that we shouldn't engage in normative critical reflection on our social practices and advocate for change as a result when they are not working. Not all social practices are good ones and some perhaps ought to be changed to ensure that some are not burdened or excluded based on their identities, for example. Nevertheless, it would be inaccurate to describe former President's Trump's flouting social norms such as taking seriously his responsibilities as the President of the United States to lead the country through a crisis, such as a pandemic, as attempting a normative critique of those practices. The former president was more clearly acting on the basis of his perceived self- interest.

The deterioration of our nation's moral capital, which includes disregarding social practices that make a democracy work, e. g., tolerance of differences of opinions, open rational discussion and debate, reliance on empirical data is exhibited on both the right and the left. Some of the instances which have become common-place, include "cancel culture", namely, attempting to publicly shame and "cancel" someone, often on social media who expresses views that others believe are offensive (The Guardian 2019). Cancel culture not only means to publicly humiliate the offender, it has a chilling effect on speech and has led to firing of people with the offending viewpoints. Concerned about saying something "wrong" results in stifling speech in classrooms, meetings, newsrooms and other settings where it is important to hear various views. Other recent occurrences that are eroding our social practices of toleration and civility have come with some students and faculty around the country stopping speaking appearances on college campuses because the ideas are offensive, and they don't want to give them a "platform." This cancelling or calling out and trying stop the person from speaking undermines traditional liberal values of free speech and tolerance. This of course is a complex issue and just pointing out some on the left as wrongdoers because of "cancelling" is too facile. Right wing politicians, notably Trump himself, regularly and viciously go after people, in effect canceling them. Additionally, much the free speech debate leaves out the role of power in getting heard and how some voices have historically and systemically not had access to channels of getting heard. Social media has provided the less powerful with a larger platform for getting legitimate grievances hears. Needless to say, this is a complex issue that cannot be fully and judiciously addressed here.

Another aspect of the deterioration of our moral capital is the outrage expressed over even minor offenses. We have a society that seems to express "righteous outrage" and anger over minor infractions. The former President's allies are often wallowing in their racial grievances, saying that they are victims. Requirements to wear a mask in public during the pandemic was met with a deep sense of grievance about taking away individuals' rights—including their purported Constitutional rights to go maskless. Without fitting objects for outrage and anger it loses its potency,—as Etzioni has recently argued, if every infraction is treated the same, as an outrageous act—then "outrage" loses its power, plus it's exhausting (Etzioni 2019).

For a society to function well and citizens to live flourishing lives there needs to be enough moral capital so that people don't have to expend all their energy and resources trying to determine what their interlocutors or their bargainers or their government officials are going to do. Moral understandings that ground expectations and foster basic trust and cooperation are essential. Imagine a society where you can't rely on anyone you're dealing with to do anything they say they are going to do. You cannot trust anyone and do not have reliable expectations about the behavior of others. Others in your society do not try to speak the truth and there are not agreed upon standards of facts and evidence. That type of society is not only inefficient but one where it is impossible for most individuals to flourish. The practices of responsibility have broken down with agents not sharing understandings about who is responsible to whom and for what. Nations where there isn't wide-spread trust, loyalty, reciprocity, solidarity, respect, and justice, for example, nations where there is distrust of government and others, a lack of a sense of the common good or willingness to sacrifice anything for anyone, no reciprocity just exploitation of others, and so on, cannot at the minimum function efficiently; and they certainly don't have the basic requirements to function as a democracy. Governments that abuse power, foment or tolerate corruption, and sow the seeds of distrust and animosity against others in society degrade the moral and social capital of the society. Loyalty to the nation and a shared sense of the common good are eroded. In democracy, what constitutes facts and truth, where expertise about various topics can be found, arguably are also essential aspects of the moral capital that make the democracy function. At its core, keeping self-interest in check is fundamental to the scaffolding of moral capital and taking responsibility for the social practices of your society.

3 Civility

Norms of civility play a central role in the moral capital of society and to some large extent the complaints about the demise of moral capital in our society revolve around the loss of civility (Mower and Robison 2012). Consider the social media ecosystem flaunting norms of civility; even what the former President regularly did on Twitter. The social practice of civility was constantly disregarded by former President Trump where he, among other things, name-calls his opponents and doesn't adhere to standards of factfinding and truth telling.

Questions about the importance of civility have been raised from feminist, critical race, and postcolonial theorists (Zerilli 2014; Hernández 2015). Critics of the social practice of civility (Trump doesn't provide a critique of civility but just disregards the norms of civility—those are different) argue that calls for "civility" have been used as weapons against those who are least powerful when they are making claims for equality (Bates 2019). Martin Luther King was implored by white clergymen to back off of the direct action of boycott and sit-ins in Birmingham and act more civilly. Dr King responded "Frankly, I have never yet engaged in a direct-action movement that was 'well-timed' according to the timetable of those who have not suffered unduly from the disease of segregation. For years now, I have heard the word 'wait.'...This 'wait' has almost always meant 'never.'" MLK's critiques of civility make the point that the loudest most privileged voices get heard, and entrenched norms of civility lockout those less positioned to get their voices heard. Incivility it is argued is necessary for the less powerful to get their viewpoints and justice claims heard. The experience of the colonized find antipathy with the calls for civility when their lives and cultures were destroyed. That colonization process drove out different notions of civility. Women's claims of sexual harassment and assault were often silenced as being impolite and that they were troublemakers, another way of ensuring that the dominant voices and perspective stays dominant.

Though it is true that "behave civility" has been used as a weapon by the powerful, privileged, against those seeking to rectify injustices and get their civil rights protected, it does not follow that civility, that is, a normatively justified practice of civility, has no value. The concepts of 'justice' or 'rights' have historically been used as means of exclusion as well, but it doesn't follow that those concepts aren't worthwhile. Civility has been deployed in terrible ways, but its value is still central to human well-being and certainly critical to democracy. Civility, meaning respecting others equally in your society, listening to their views, disagreeing without anger and rancor, relying of facts, is the foundation of democratic processes. Furthermore, listening to differing views is what makes knowledge possible by permitting individuals to advance ideas even unfavorable ones without being silenced or cancelled. Civility is not just being polite, civility is a disposition towards your fellow citizens, to treat them with respect, not necessarily to agree with them on issues. Protests, such as the Black Lives Matter protests are civil protests, done civilly, just as is "taking a knee" to express disgust against police brutality. Threats and bombing abortion clinics are not civil protests. The fact that calls of "civility" has been used insidiously to exclude and perpetuate domination doesn't mean that we shouldn't critically reflect on the practice to develop an understanding that doesn't exclude certain people and holds everyone to account for that respect for others.

4 "Civic Grace"

Then presidential hopeful Senator Cory Booker argued that what we need in this society [to recapture our moral capital] is the resurgence of "civic grace." What Booker was encouraging is that we should stop dividing ourselves into rival groups, treating each other as less than, and start treating each other with grace as a way to rebuild our moral capital. Civic grace is an intriguing idea. What the Christian notion of grace means was nicely explicated by Peter Wehner of *The New York Times* in 2018. He said:

> It is the unmerited favor of God, unconditional love given to the undeserving. It's a difficult concept to understand because it isn't entirely rational. "Grace defies reason and logic," as Bono, the lead singer of U2, put it. "Love interrupts, if you like, the consequences of your actions."

> There's a radical equality at the core of grace. None of us are deserving of God's grace, so it's not dependent on social status, wealth or intelligence. There is equality between kings and peasants, the prominent and the unheralded, rule followers and rule breakers.

> If you find yourself in the company of people whose hearts have been captured by grace, count yourself lucky. They love us despite our messy lives, stay connected to us through our struggles, always holding out the hope of redemption.

Grace is associated with unmerited benefits, love, and equality. Though grace is connected with Christian theology it actually has an earlier meaning or life articulated in the works of Cicero and Seneca. Seneca in particular wrote extensively about the ethics of grace (Seneca 2011). For Seneca, the qualities of grace and what makes something an act of grace are as follows. First of all, an act of grace has to be something that's an unmerited favor, not something that is deserved. Bestowing upon others acts of kindness whether they are worthy or not is the condition of grace. It's unmerited in the sense that it's not grounds for desert; grace exceeds what's owed or what could be demanded. In other words, it is not a duty of justice or a claim of justice. Second, the act of grace has to be beneficial to the recipient, that is, it has to be something that's thought to be good for them. It doesn't have to in fact be good for them, but it has to be given in a spirit that it's thought to be a favor to them. Being beneficial and unmerited are essential to gracious acts but they're not themselves sufficient for something to be a gracious act. Something might in fact be beneficial to somebody and be unmerited but if it's not done with intention to do that then it's not a gracious act. The definition put forward by Glen Pettigrove is "an act of grace is an intentional act of unmerited favor" (Pettigrove 2012, p. 127). Expanding on that definition: something can only be a gracious act when it's done solely for the benefit of whom it's being bestowed on—it can't be transactional, that is, the giver can't expect to get something for doing the act of grace.

There are two things we can talk about: acts of grace and the character trait of grace. A gracious person is somebody who is inclined and spontaneously ready to promote others' interests. They take delight in benefiting them. The spontaneous readiness to promote others' interests is a defining feature of a gracious person. The value of grace, both acts of grace and the character trait of grace are significant to all our lives. Clearly when we're young we're recipients of lots of acts of grace from our parents and other adults around us. Doing things for us that are not merited but just for our own benefit define childhood. But the importance of acts of grace extends beyond childhood and into our adult lives. As adults we are dependent upon the unmerited favors from others particularly when we are vulnerable to calamity. We must, as Seneca reminds us, rely upon the grace, the generosity of others, for aid in our time of adversity. When there is a natural disaster, for instance, we rely upon others for their unmerited assistance. We rely on others acts of kindness to help us out, Seneca says, since we're vulnerable creatures and often need others' help in small and large ways. Pettigrove elaborates by adding "[Th]us our existence and well-being depend in a real way on our being the recipients of acts of grace" (Pettigrove 136).

> Our safety depends on the fact that we have mutual acts of kindness to help us. What alone equips us in life and fortifies us against sudden attack is our exchange of favours. . . . God has given that vulnerable creature [i.e., the human being] two things that make him strongest of all, reason and fellowship. That is how, no match for anything if he lived in isolation, he comes to be master of all things (Seneca, vi.18).

Everyone requires unmerited acts of kindness or favors for our existence. Acts of grace are fundamental, therefore, for human existence. Taking this notion of grace and putting it in the public square, that is, in civil society it is the bestowing upon our fellow citizens those unmerited favors for their benefit. Civic grace commands us to cultivate dispositions so that our attitudes toward others, even strangers, are to bestow upon them kindness. We should create relationships with others, even our political opponents in society, based on grace. Not doing it for our own benefit but doing it for the benefit of others. Not doing so because others deserve it, can claim it as a right, but because they will be benefited by it. Civic grace makes a better society for everyone. Civic grace is the disposition which animates civility in contexts where one's interlocutor doesn't deserve it. In the political sphere it is listening to others' views, trying to understand their point of view. Ultimately one does not have to agree but one has to listen and engage with them. Encouraging the disposition to engage in civic grace would bolster our moral capital.

5   Universities Developing Civic Grace

What role do universities play in developing and sustaining the moral capital of society? In the 20th century there was widespread skepticism about universities teaching virtues. Some of that skepticism was drawn from the idea that universities should not be inculcating religious values in their students. Currently there is widespread criticism that university faculty indoctrinate their students in liberal values. The critique is that universities should not be teaching moral values (particularly liberal values) to their students. Even Stanley Fish entered the debate arguing that universities should not teach values but should focus on the methodologies of the disciplines. Outside of religious schools there continue to be serious skepticism about universities teaching values.

The skepticism is misplaced. First, universities clearly see their mission to develop in students intellectual or epistemic virtues, viz. love of wisdom, openness to ideas, perseverance, ability to reason, epistemic humility, and so on. Cultivating an atmosphere where students really listen to different perspectives, explore a variety of different ideas, try to understand the views of others, act graciously towards those who they differ with makes them competent learners and knowledge producers. Students need to be able to try out ideas, make mistakes, and redeem themselves. Group think or dogmatism is dangerous for creativity and knowledge production. This is particularly important for universities where we want students to get out of their comfort zone, try out ideas and discover the truth. Students should be encouraged to have epistemic hygiene, that is, understand what are reputable sources of information, how to assess data, and how to argue for positions. All of this entails cultivating epistemic virtues.

Universities should see as their mission cultivating two moral virtues and the intellectual virtues: the virtue of civic grace both as the basis of the virtue of civility and as for the basis of epistemic virtues. Developing the virtue of civic grace in students is cultivating the disposition to grant unmerited favors on their interlocutors, further fostering elements of the virtue of civility, namely active listening, trying to understand others' perspectives, rational debate and deliberation, and generally giving respect to others, even those we disagree with. The virtue of civility, then, is necessary for the epistemic virtues. Like Aristotle, I believe that the intellectual virtues and the virtues of civic grace and civility are not taught but developed through trial and error. Universities need to create opportunities throughout the curriculum and outside the classroom for students to exercise their abilities and develop these dispositions. Faculty without knowing they are doing so are often exhibiting the intellectual virtues (and we hope the moral ones as well) when teaching. Universities acknowledging their role in cultivating these virtues in students will not only make their students better learners but also prepare them to be decent citizens for our democracy (Schwartz and Sharpe 2012).

6 Summing Up

Moral capital is essential for individuals to live well in society. Our shared moral understandings of who is responsible to whom for what provide the infrastructure of civic life. That is not to say that all of our social practices are good ones and shouldn't be normatively assessed. They aren't and they should be. Nevertheless, purposely disregarding norms, based on self-interest, can erode the social practices that make to a robust society and particularly when democratic norms are flaunted put democracy jeopardy. I have argued that universities should acknowledge their roles in developing some of the virtues, particularly the epistemic virtues and the virtues of civic grace and civility. Not only will these virtues make for better knowledge seekers and producers but will also ready our students for their entry into civil society and democratic citizenry.

References

Bates KG (2019) When Civility Is Used as A Cudgel Against People of Color. All Things Considered
Brooks D (2016) How to Repair Moral Capital. New York Times.
Chambers S, Kopstein J (2001) Bad civil society. Polit Theory 29(6)
Cowan, Tyler Public Goods in The Library of Economics and Liberty. https://www.econlib.org/library/Enc/PublicGoods.html; Accessed 04/2021
Etzioni A (2019) America Must Learn to Deal with Moral Outrage. Available at SSRN: https://ssrn.com/abstract=3493390
Goldberg J (2020) James Mattis Denounces President Trump, Describes Him as a Threat to the Constitution. https://www.theatlantic.com/politics/archive/2020/06/james-mattis-denounces-trump-protests-militarization/612640/. Accessed 10/2020
Haidt J (2012) The righteous mind: why good people are divided by politics and religion. Vintage Books, New York
Haslanger S (2018) What is a social practice? Royal Institute of Philosophy Supplement 82
Hernández RD (2015) The World Turned on its Head: Coloniality, Civility and the Decolonial Imperative. NACCS Annual Conference Proceedings. 2
Mill JS (1933) The Collected Works of John Stuart Mill, Volume X - Essays on Ethics, Religion, and Society ed. John M. Robson, Introduction by F.E.L. Priestley. Toronto: University of Toronto Press, London: Routledge and Kegan Paul
Mower D, Robison W (2012) Civility in politics and education. Routledge
Pettigrove G (2012) Forgiveness and love. Oxford University Press
Putman R (2000) Bowling alone: the collapse and revival of American community. Simon & Schuster, New York
Putnam R (1994) Social capital and public affairs. Bull Am Acad Arts Sci 47(8):5–19. https://doi.org/10.2307/3824796
Schwartz B, Sharpe K (2012) Colleges should teach intellectual virtues. Chronicle of Higher Education
Seneca LA (2011) On benefits (trans. Miriam Griffin and Brad Inwood). University of Chicago Press, Chicago

Smith A (2014) The wealth of nations shine classics; the theory of the moral sentiments (1802). George Bell and Sons. York St. Covent Garden and New York, London

The Guardian 2019 Barack Obama takes on 'woke' call-out culture: 'That's not activism' – video. https://www.theguardian.com/us-news/video/2019/oct/30/barack-obama-calls-out-politically-woke-social-media-generation-video

Walker M (1998) Moral understandings: a feminist study in ethics. Routledge, New York

Zerilli L (2014) Against civility: a feminist perspective. In: Civility, legality, and Justice in America, 4 edn. Austin Sarat. Cambridge University Press, Cambridge, pp 107–131

Part VI
Justice in University Admissions

"Merit" in University Admissions

Ann E. Cudd

Abstract Most institutions of higher education apply some criteria for admission and the most elite institutions use individual merit-based criteria to select from among large numbers of applicants for admission. Since institutions of higher education are publicly subsidized almost without exception, and higher education offers significant social and financial benefits, we should question the system of distribution of these benefits. In this essay I ask whether the individual merit standard for university admissions is a fair and just system. I argue that it is not but that does not mean that we should abandon the whole idea of pursuing excellence. Rather I shall argue that a different conception of collective merit that suggests a different filter for university admissions would better meet the social goals we have for higher education.

1 Introduction

Universities exist primarily to create new knowledge, educate individuals, and serve society through related activities and products, and are almost without exception, highly subsidized by their state and national governments.[1] A higher education confers great benefits on students, especially those who attain credentials through

---

[1] The US federal government subsidies to institutions of higher education through student aid, research grants, and contracts total over $1 trillion according to DataLab (2019) and this funding goes to every university and college, including so-called private ones, though to varying degrees. For example, Harvard University received $1.18 billion in federal funding in 2018 according to DataLab (2019). State and local governmental support for higher education, which varies greatly from state to state, totals over $100 billion (see Whitford 2021) and also supports both public and private universities and colleges. There may be a few rare, small institutions that accept no public funding and are not 501c3 nonprofits, but the vast majority receive significant funding and are subsidized by tax benefits that accrue to students who pay tuition and donors.

A. E. Cudd (✉)
University of Pittsburgh, Department of Philosophy, Pittsburgh, PA, USA
e-mail: acudd@pitt.edu

© The Author(s), under exclusive license to Springer Nature Switzerland AG 2022
J. McGregor, M. C. Navin (eds.), *Education, Inclusion, and Justice*, Amintaphil:
The Philosophical Foundations of Law and Justice 11,
https://doi.org/10.1007/978-3-031-04013-9_13

the completion of degree and certificate programs. Beyond the intrinsic rewards of education, attaining a degree from an accredited university unlocks economic opportunity and enhances social status. Universities themselves are highly stratified by their status and quality, and the more elite the institution, the greater the social benefits that are conferred with its degree, both to society and to individuals.

Although higher education also serves public purposes, it is not strictly a public good in the economists' sense of being non-excludable and non-rival. People can be excluded from consuming a university education and it is "rival" in that the expert teaching and mentoring of the faculty is a scarce good that can be consumed by only so many. Those who are admitted, who can access higher education are benefitted much more than those who are not admitted. And those who are admitted to a higher quality institution are benefitted more than those who are only admitted to lower quality ones. Let us call this inequality "access inequality". Because not everyone can attain a higher education and because of the stratification of institutions and their unequal benefits, higher education is a source of inequality in society. Thus, it is important to ask if access inequality, which is imposed by publicly subsidized institutions, serves society in ways that are fair and just.

Let me begin by stipulating that ability to pay is not a fair and just means of distributing higher education. Unless there is adequate financial support to enable low-income students to attend university, the system reinforces class and racial inequality by differentially benefitting the better off. There is no justification for this source and reinforcement of inequality, although there is no question that ability to pay is currently a source of inequality of access to higher education.

Ability to benefit from higher education or succeed in completing a degree, on the other hand, is a legitimate justification of access inequality. After all, we don't want to waste scarce resources on those who cannot be benefitted if that excludes others who would benefit. However, ability to benefit only provides a necessary condition for a claim on access to some higher education and not necessarily an equal claim to admission to any university. Many persons are able to benefit only from some educational opportunities—few of us can benefit from advanced seminars in highly abstract, esoteric subject areas—and some persons are able to derive far greater benefit from educational opportunities than others. Furthermore, education is a collective endeavor and the members of the group benefit each other differentially. It is educationally better to be in a group of more motivated, talented, enthusiastic, critically engaged, and cooperative fellow students, for instance. These differences in ability to benefit from and to confer benefits on others are arguably legitimate reasons for differential access to universities. Thus, an important way that access inequality can be justified is by appeal to one's ability to learn, create, and collaborate with and inspire others as the entrance criterion for selecting students to admit to universities.

Universities see themselves and promote themselves as offering admission based on individual merit. The resulting merit system is supposed to justify access inequality and to benefit society. As a system, higher education often purports to be a meritocracy, although that has come into serious question in recent years.[2] The questions that have been raised have to do with ways in which the admissions system is corrupted by money and power. There have been fewer critiques of the whole idea of individual merit as the justification for access inequality. Leaders in higher education tend to focus on the opportunity it provides for those who are able to access it to live flourishing lives and become better citizens, and rarely consider how it creates inequality by denying access to others or by producing a hierarchy of status in society.

In this essay I ask whether the individual merit standard for university admissions is a fair and just system. My answer is that it is not but that does not mean that we should abandon the whole idea of pursuing excellence. Rather I shall argue that a different conception of collective merit that suggests a different filter for university admissions would better meet the social goals we have for higher education.

2 Merit in University Admissions: Measurement Problems

Universities typically assess merit by evaluating and ranking individuals on the basis of a few forms of evidence: standardized test scores, high school transcripts, grades, and class rank are the most common, supplemented sometimes by prompted essays, resumes of extracurricular activities, letters of recommendation, especially by high school guidance counselors, portfolios of creative work, and personal interviews. For most universities, test scores and high school grade point average (gpa) dominate the evidential basis for admission, with minimal scores often forming a cutoff below which admission is extremely improbable.[3] While test scores are rapidly becoming optional at many universities in this Covid-19 pandemic era, they remain a dominant criterion for admission at many others. Merit-based scholarships are even more often tied to high test scores, as universities compete to enroll high scoring students in order to attain higher national rankings, as well as because universities take high scoring students to be more meritorious for admission.

These predominant criteria are especially problematic, both from the perspective of equity and justice and as a measure of individual ability or potential. First, they are

---

[2]Consider the "Varsity Blues" admissions scandal, in which a private college counselor bribed athletics coaches and found ways to cheat on SAT exams in order to sell positions in elite institutions for wealthy students who would not otherwise have gained admission to them. See Jaschik (2019). Or consider the fact that many of the most elite universities practice "legacy admissions," which prioritizes children of alumni in admissions. Some universities will also prioritize children of high dollar donors.

[3]Legacy status, athletic talent, and direct donations by an applicant's family sometimes circumvents the merit system, allowing students who would otherwise fall below the cutoff for admissions to be pre-emptively offered admission. I am ignoring these cases for now in the interest of addressing the more common means of gaining entrance to most universities. However, in some very elite universities these pre-emptions of merit admissions form a very significant proportion, if not quite a majority, of the admitted class.

manipulatable through coaching and careful planning, but that requires financial and social resources that are not available to all students. Test scores often correlate with the quality of one's high school education. The quality of a student's high school and its offerings are obviously quite variable and very much a function of family income and geographic locale. Both test scores and gpa's are susceptible to being coached, which is fine if high test scores and gpa's are meritorious in themselves. No one argues that. Rather, they are taken to indicate that a student has a higher ability to learn or has learned more in high school and thus is capable of benefitting from a university education and benefitting others with whom they are learning to a higher degree. But if anyone can increase test scores through a short, intensive course or practice, then it is not much of an indication of either of these desirable qualities.

Furthermore, test scores are not fully predictive of future academic success. It is somewhat controversial how predictive of academic success test scores are, though they are better predictors when combined with high school gpa.[4] The biggest problem with using this correlation to justify use of test scores in admissions and financial aid decisions is that it presupposes that college grades are independently measuring the proper thing. Yet there is reason to question that claim. Grades given by professors in an institution have to be assessed relative to the curriculum and the student body that they have—after all, not all or most students can fail without the institution failing. They are therefore to some degree relative to the inputs. While the movement to specify and assess learning objectives for degrees has changed this somewhat, faculty have largely resisted attempts to objectively assess the outcomes of their teaching efforts.

University curricula and assessments of student learning also reflect the cultural expectations of majority white professors and institutions, which are biased toward the majority forms of expression and the status quo of disciplinary knowledge creation. If we believe that being innovative or original has merit, then we are systematically biasing against that form of merit when we take prediction of higher gpa in university to be the ultimate goal of admissions judgements. This warrants a deeper interrogation of our teaching methods to be truly inclusive of diverse expression, but for now I simply wish to draw out the implication that that test scores correlate with college grades is not determinative in favor of using test scores for admissions and as the ultimate measure of merit.

Test scores and high school grades are not suited to revealing special talents. The most talented are often misfits and don't score well in high school because they are bored by it, and may not take or do well on exams as a result. Furthermore, there are many special talents and competencies that we want in our students and that allow them to benefit from and benefit

others that are not accounted for by these tests and grades, such as intuition, creativity, emotional intelligence, and leadership abilities. These can be revealed by essays, interviews, and letters of recommendation, but those are not as heavily

---

[4]The most optimistic think that test scores plus high school gpa correlates with college grades at .35 level (Sackett and Kuncel 2018), which is significant but still leaves plenty of room for error.

weighted by most admissions committees if they are considered at all, and they rely on subjective judgment that is susceptible to bias.

Finally, scores and high school gpa are not conducive to building a diverse student body that is inclusive of racial minorities or low-income students. Whatever one thinks about the predictiveness of test scores and in some cases gpa, the fact is that there are clear racial disparities as well as disparities by family income level in test scores and gpa, as well as in the resulting university attendance patterns.[5] If we rely on them to populate our student bodies, especially if we are not allowed by law to explicitly take race into account, our universities will continue to reflect and reinforce racial inequality and socioeconomic inequality. Thus, our current system for measuring and rewarding merit in university admissions is an obstacle to social mobility on a society-wide scale, since more individuals who get to participate in and benefit from higher education are already largely affluent and majority white students.

3 Merit in University Admissions: Psychological Problems

The individual merit-based admissions system creates significant psychological problems that are also unjust. First, high stakes testing creates a high level of student anxiety. The competitive nature of the current system and its link to status for students and their parents has created an epidemic of anxiety and stress.[6] This generation of students is under enormous pressure (and was even before the Covid-19 pandemic). There are now more students competing for roughly the same numbers of slots in elite universities. The elite universities really are harder to get into than in past generations, if by hard we mean requiring higher test scores and grades.[7] Furthermore, a college-level education is even more important now for attaining a middle- or upper-class standard of living, which applies ever more pressure on students to get that education. Finally, universities compete for students with merit-based scholarships that have in turn become a source of competition among affluent students and their parents. Thus, the individual merit system in university admissions subjects students to psychological harms.

Another psychological problem with this merit system for university admissions is that it creates a false sense of desert within those who attain admission to or merit scholarships for more or less competitive universities. Since the merit system is biased in favor of affluent and white students, those students who take their admissions or scholarship offers as deserved are misled. They in fact were not competing on a fair basis with others and their false beliefs create a sense of entitlement and

---

[5] See Reeves and Halikias (2017).

[6] See Hurley (2020).

[7] See Petrilli and Enamorado (2020) for evidence.

arrogance.[8] Their interactions with the less fortunate are likely to be distorted and to create a false and unhealthy status hierarchy. Meanwhile, those who are not privileged by the individual merit system tend to see themselves as unworthy and lesser, feelings which can thwart their confidence and undermine their sense of belonging and well being. This is not only psychologically damaging for the less fortunate, but also harms the ability of the entitled and arrogant to interact success-fully with broader society. Witness the rise of populism and Trumpism, which pits the educated elite against the strange coalition that includes the very wealthy who can buy their way into elite universities and those who have been shut out of the benefits of an elite university education.

There is a further problem with so-called "merit" scholarships, which are really nothing more than a means to drive net tuition revenue on the part of the schools that give them out. Merit scholarships are a palatable and flattering way for universities to price discriminate, by offering students who have likewise competing offers from other universities a discount on their tuition. One indication of how much "merit" scholarships are misnamed is that the most elite universities give out no merit scholarships at all. The elite universities need not compete for highly capable and motivated students; there are many more than they need to fill their classes. Since they do not need to compete for the very most desired students, they offer only financial aid to meet the financial needs of the low- and middle-income students they desire to admit. The measure of affordability is based on a federally determined standard level of ability to pay based on family income and wealth. Since this measure is fixed independent of universities, such financial need awards are not typically reasons for students to select among them based on competing awards.

Perhaps the most widely damaging psychological effect of the individual merit system is that it encourages a fixed mindset. A serious problem with the emphasis on tests is that it encourages the high scorers to think that they are innately intelligent while implying for low scorers that they lack innate intellectual talent, and that nothing they do will change that. Yet there are far too many counterexamples of persons who are very successful in almost any field who did not perform well on these tests but succeeded because of motivation, interest, encouragement, and practice. Those who score highly on these exams are misled into thinking that it is their innate talent that made them succeed. This is damaging to them in that it makes them believe that when they do face difficulties or failure, it is due to not having enough of that special talent rather than realizing the truth: intellectual breakthroughs are difficult for everyone and they require practice and persistence to achieve. For almost any university-level skill or topic, these are the attributes needed to succeed, not some innate specific talent. Belief in this view that almost anyone can succeed in almost any skill given dedication, practice, and good coaching is the idea of the growth mindset.[9] Basic academic skills like algebra, calculus, and critical reading can be learned through practice and study; students just need the right role models,

---

[8] This is a point emphasized throughout Sandel (2020).

[9] See Dweck (2006).

encouragement, motivation, and guidance to master them. If we want to build a society of educated, self-directed people, then we want to encourage a growth mindset in everyone.

The individual merit system discourages socially disadvantaged and minoritized students. Since minority students know about the disparities, they are discouraged and feel that the odds are stacked against them. This creates and exacerbates the conditions for creating stereotype threat, which occurs when a person's identity is highlighted for them in connection with a task on which that identity is stereotypically connected with underperformance on that task. (Steele 2010) Being the 'only one' of a certain identity in a group highlights that identity, and in a class in a subject where one's identity is typically minority, there is the almost automatic stereotype of underperformance of that identity in that subject area. Think of women in engineering classes. Minority students are likely to find themselves as the only one in many situations at elite universities, surrounded by people who adhere to, and even themselves believing in, the myth of the fixed mindset. The doubt and anxiety created by stereotype threat actually depresses the ability to learn and achieve at a high level.

As it is used in university admissions, merit judgments are highly problematic psychologically—both individually and socially. University admissions should not be based on mistaken and biased notions of innate talent that create unjust social inequalities and psychological harm. To fix university admissions, we need to go back to first principles. In particular, what is the point of university admissions?

4   University Admissions to Achieve Social Purposes

The goal of university admissions at each university is to enroll classes of students to achieve the mission of the university. Before I discuss the missions of universities, let's be clear about what university admission is not for or not about. First, it is not for rewarding individual desert, let alone for compounding privilege. Universities do not exist to reward individuals, although they may think of their admission to a university as their reward for working hard or having certain talents. That's not what universities are for or do. No one individual has any claim on university admissions except insofar as their inclusion among the enrolled students would demonstrably better serve the university's legitimate mission than those who were admitted and their exclusion from the university was due to some unfairness or injustice. One has a right to be judged fairly but not to admission to any particular university. Second, the point of university admissions is not about marketing a commodity for individual consumption. Universities compete for students based on price and on something we call "brand", which is the way we try to appeal to students' non-price interests in their college educations. Such branding can be seen as an attempt to communicate the vision and mission of the university to prospective students in order to attract those who will best benefit and be benefitted by attending said university. Branding can also create false or misleading impressions, however, when it focuses on maximizing revenue for the university. That can lead to a mismatch between faculty and students that does not serve the university's mission. I won't have much to say about this aspect of university admissions processes here, but just flag it as an issue to address in a broader study of admissions.

Third, admissions does not aim at maximizing revenue per se. While it is true that universities must bring in revenue to balance their budgets, the budget is set in order to achieve the mission of the university. That is, the budget serves the mission, not the reverse, as is true in all non-profit institutions. The mission has to be specified relative to the market conditions, such as the number of students who are likely to demand the kinds of degrees and educational experiences that the university seeks to offer, as well as the available outside support from government and private sources.

University admissions at any given institution is for assembling a student body that will best achieve the university's mission. Missions vary in the degree to which a university supports research, community outreach, economic development, and teaching at various degree levels and in various disciplines or professional preparation. Some specialize in undergraduate teaching, others in medical and health related research, still others in adult continuing education. Because (and to the degree that) they are highly socially supported, universities' missions must and do include social purposes. These include supporting research and innovation to create sustainable economic growth in society, but also social justice and democratic equality. Thus, we should see university admissions as aiming to convene groups of students with faculty and facilities to optimally educate and inspire creative, innovative research in an equitable and democratic environment, with special focus on the areas of education, research, and civic engagement that the particular university's mission emphasizes.

While university education contributes to flourishing lives for individuals who consume it, there are equally important goals that are social goals and that we all benefit from and therefore justify the public funding of higher education. One goal is economic, namely to improve the productivity of members of society. This goal is furthered greatly by mass higher education, but also by elite higher education that brings together the most motivated, interested, and accomplished students and faculty to study and collaborate together to take on important problems and challenges that hold great value to solve. The other goal is a political, republican goal, and that is to nurture democratic habits and values that promote democratic equality. I take this to be the value of seeing all of our fellow citizens as equally worthy of dignity and respect. Becoming educated and informed is one important way of being seen as worthy of respect, while being excluded from higher education is surely a sign of disrespect. Democratic equality does not require that everyone, even all who can benefit, have an equal chance to be admitted to every institution. Fair equality of opportunity has to be upheld and seen to be so in university admissions in order to meet the goal of democratic equality. Given the economic goals just described, there is a clear social value to creating student and faculty groups that will be able best to develop solutions to difficult problems. Earlier I argued that the current university admissions system does not optimally attain these social goals because it uses individual merit criteria that are not well suited to identifying those most able to benefit from university education and to benefit others by their collaborative presence, and because the individual merit criteria create individual and social psychological harm. Thus, we should reinvent our admissions system to better meet the goals we have for higher education.

5   The Case for Maximizing Inclusive Diversity in University Admissions

One crucial goal in our reinvention of university admissions is to improve its ability to admit a diverse set of students. Diversity serves both the economic productivity and democratic equality goals of universities. Although it is sometimes criticized as an expedient political or even ideological commitment, diversity can, when properly nurtured, demonstrably improve creativity, innovation, and productivity. We do our very best work collaboratively, and groups that are diverse and that encourage different perspectives are most effective. Complex problems and challenges require groups with multiple tools and perspectives to solve. Inclusively diverse groups are more innovative, productive, and responsive to a wider range of social issues and needs. Diversity brings different ideas, ways of thinking and analyzing problems together. Diverse individuals have different senses of what the right questions and problems are, as well. Inclusivity is critical to being able to achieve these benefits from diversity because groups need to be able to hear and learn from all the diverse voices within the group. The learning environment for all is improved by bringing together diverse groups of students. Inclusively diverse groups are better educational contexts for students who will live in a globally interconnected world and join and lead diverse teams in future. Students cannot learn to interact sensitively and competently with persons from other cultural and class backgrounds without practice in an environment that is open to new experiences and critical questioning. This argument for diversity builds on the previous one about diversity and productivity: if diversity is important for teams and groups to be productive, then it's important to teach students how to benefit from interacting in and leading such groups. Inclusively diverse groups are better able to attract diverse talent to join them and then to benefit from that diversity. A group can fail to be inclusively diverse either by lacking diversity or by lacking inclusivity. If a group is not very diverse, it is hard for someone who brings the only diversity to a group to be able to see themselves and thrive in such an environment because they worry that they will be perceived as different and lesser, or as having to prove themselves. This is how stereotype threat takes hold and undermines the performance of minoritized members of groups. They may not contribute at all to discussion or not bring their unique insights to bear. Furthermore, a false sense of privilege and superiority on the part of the majority causes them not to take a critical attitude toward their ideas, and group-think takes hold. This can happen as well if the minority is suppressed by the majority members who dominate and exclude.

Finally, inclusive diversity is required by democratic equality because demonstrating diversity symbolizes and communicates respect across difference, whereas a lack of diversity, particularly in a group that has high status, projects a lack of respect for minoritized or excluded groups. Exclusionary behavior towards minorities also projects this lack of respect.

These are all important arguments in favor of admitting a diverse group. Despite the appeal of these arguments, however, two objections arise in the context of arguing for prioritizing diversity in university admissions. First is the claim that there is a trade-off between merit and diversity, that if we promote diversity as a qualification for admission we will necessarily sacrifice merit or student quality. To counter this objection, it is important to emphasize the first argument I gave for diversity in university admissions. If it is true that diverse groups achieve more than non-diverse groups, then the merit or excellence of a group is linked to its collective diversity. Notice I said: "diverse groups". I think an important insight into refuting the idea that there is a tradeoff between diversity and merit is to look at how individuals improve the excellence of the group as a whole, rather than seeing merit as measurable individually in isolation from the group. That is, a group can accomplish more when it is composed of diverse individuals.

The second objection is that it is impossible to judge merit in the holistic way that achieves the goal of group excellence without discriminating against individuals. To respond to this objection we need to see how to assemble these groups that achieve more through inclusive excellence.

I want to look at a model that helps to understand why and how diverse groups are more innovative and productive. Scott Page has developed a model of what he calls "diversity bonuses" that explains when and how diverse groups are more productive than groups with homogeneous background and experiences.[10] He argues that there are only certain kinds of problems where diversity bonuses are possible, these are the non-routine, cognitive challenges that we might call open-ended or complex problems—the kinds of issues that universities tackle.[11] Complex problems and challenges require groups of scholars with multiple tools and perspectives to solve. Each individual brings to a problem or questions a cognitive repertoire, which Page's model represents as a toolbox full of tools that we use to solve problems. Our tools consist in different ways of looking at and analyzing a problem: different lenses, metaphors that help to understand things in different ways, analogies to other experiences, analytical or computational strategies that break problems down, simplify, and point towards solutions. In some cases these tools are gained through cultural constructs and linguistic conventions that we learn through our upbringing and our social interactions, in other cases through explicit learning about modeling

---

[10] See Page (2018).

[11] Not all creative or innovative achievements are made by groups, but few individuals can achieve breakthroughs at high levels without the support of others who serve as critics, confidantes, sounding boards, collaborators, or mentors.

techniques or of approaches to critical analysis, and still others from experience in facing similar problems in our past.

When faced with a really hard problem that resists an intuitive or rote strategy for solving, the more different, relevant tools one has, the more likely one is to come up with a good solution. Individuals add problem solving value to a group on this model if the tools that they bring to the problem are different and if the tools are relevant to the problem. If the individual's toolbox overlaps with that of others in group, or if the tools are not relevant, then there are no additional tools and the group will be no more likely to solve the problem than the individual with the most finely-honed tools. But if individuals bring different tools, they add new problem-solving strategies to bear on a problem and makes solving it more likely. Thus, diversity in the toolboxes results in bonuses, that is, in more, better, more innovative and creative solutions.

An important implication of the diversity bonus model is that any given individual's contribution to the group effort depends on the composition of the group as a whole, and not only on the tools that the individual brings to the group. One individual may have very few relevant tools while another has far more, but the contribution that each makes to a group depends on how many new and different tools they bring, which depends on the toolboxes of the other members of the group. The individual with fewer tools may contribute more if their tools are different from the existing tools in the group while the individual with more tools brings only redundant ones.

It is important to note that on this model, just introducing diversity is not sufficient. Quality of one's tools matters too; having a deeper knowledge of statistical modeling, or a better facility with a given language can of course help in problem-solving. Page's model assumes that new tools are relevant to the problem area and that diverse voices who bring new and different tools are included and valued. The first point suggests that not all forms of diversity are useful or relevant, which is surely true. But we often don't know what will be relevant until it is brought to bear and tried out. Barbara McClintock, for example, insisted on taking a holistic view of the organism, which Evelyn Fox Keller called a "feeling for the organism," and this led her to hypothesize and discover transposition of genes.[12] Whether this is a feminine approach to genetics or just an outsider approach, it was McClintock's diverse perspective that allowed her to make this important discovery. And its very diversity might have been seen as making it irrelevant, which may explain why her discovery took so long to receive any uptake.

This points to Page's second assumption, which is that diversity is only useful if it is welcomed. Otherwise, the opportunity to gain from diversity is wasted; the additional tools are not brought to bear on the problem.

Of course, there are other problems with exclusion of diverse voices other than failure to achieve diversity bonuses. Recall that I gave four arguments in favor of diversity and inclusion. I have focused on this very instrumental value of creative

---

[12] See Fox Keller (1983).

productivity that diversity serves in order to consider how diversity serves the purpose of building and assessing the collective merit or excellence of a group. Insofar as the mission of universities is to teach skills needed to participate in and lead diverse groups, as well as civic participation and democratic values for a multicultural society, cultural diversity and the inclusion of oppressed and minoritized persons among the student body also has a very direct connection to those aspects of the mission.

6   Collective Merit and University Admissions

Given this argument for diversity bonuses, how can we apply it to our understanding of merit in university admissions? Since diversity bonuses accrue to the group based on the diversity of the group, there is no single individual merit scale that we can rank applicants on without considering how they relate to the group. Thus, we cannot simply rank order all the individuals on a single scale of ability and take the top n ranked students to get the ideal class. Rather, we should assemble the group holistically, composing it of individuals who we believe bring diverse tools, including perspectives and experiences that come from their upbringing, culture, and background.

We should view the goal of as optimizing the collective merit of the whole, not as assembling a set of individuals with the highest merit in and of themselves. In the context of university admissions and isolated from the group, individual merit is not measurable. A person's contribution to the group depends on what talents and abilities the others bring to the group. That is not to say that we do not want to include special talents, unique perspectives, or natural leaders in our group. Rather, the question of merit in the context of admissions is fundamentally about the collective. In pursuing the admissions goal of crafting the class, we should ask ourselves what constitutes the ideal university student body as a collective and this precludes looking at each individual in isolation from the whole. Selecting students in this holistic way is a hard problem to solve in itself, and I can't lay out the solution here, but the solution is clearly not a method that results in a group of mainly white, affluent students.

One might object that given my emphasis on democratic values of democratic equality, equality of opportunity, and fairness, the idea of merit completely antithetical to this. Should we abandon the whole notion of meritocracy? Or to ask the question another way, is there a legitimate social role for elite, publicly supported, higher education in a democracy? I believe the answer is yes. First, excellence as an important value. There is nothing wrong with and many things good about people striving to do better: to think more logically, creatively, with greater appeal to evidence, aiming to create a broader impact. Excellence advances innovation and discovery, leading to economic benefits. We need competence and evidence-based policy in our public bureaucracy. Both science and creative expression benefit from nurtured talent. And there is no denying that talent and drive are not uniform or ubiquitous. Furthermore, if we do not aim for excellence in university admissions, then we will fall back on some other way of distributing scarce education resources, such as what we are actually doing now, which is according to economic and white skin privilege.

Finally, it is sometimes argued that meritocracy undermines democratic equality.[13] Michael Sandel argues that merit inevitably creates social discord by causing elites to look down on those who are considered to have less merit. But if the measure of merit in the context of admissions is fundamentally about how the individual contributes to the collective, not the individual's abilities as measured apart from all the others, that undermines the claim that the individual who is admitted deserves admission through their individual talents alone. Admission is offered due to their contribution to the collective merits of the group that the admitted individual will join. In this way no one can say "I deserve admission to University A because of my individual talents and abilities." Rather one could say "I gained admission to University A because, in the presence of these other individuals in the student body, we can productively contribute to achieving the university's mission." Furthermore, students are admitted only when it appears that they are committed to bringing out the best in others to achieve that collective merit. This encourages us to think of the good of the whole and not only our individual good. It encourages individuals to nurture their talents as well as their appreciation for the talents and contributions of others.

Selecting students according to the collective merit their presence co-creates with others justifies access inequality. First collective merit meets the benefit from and benefit others by criterion. Second, collective merit meets the requirement of fair equality of opportunity by selecting only based on contributions to collective benefit and by embracing diversity and focusing on and democratic equality. Collective merit in university admissions would be a transformation to achieve the true promise of publicly supported higher education.

References

DataLab (2019) Federal Investment in Higher Education. https://datalab.usaspending.gov/colleges-and-universities/

Dweck C (2006) Mindset: The new psychology of success. Ballantine Books, New York

Fox Keller E (1983) A feeling for the organism, the life and work of Barbara McClintock. Henry Holt, New York

Guinier L (2015) The Tyranny of the meritocracy: democratizing higher education in America. Beacon Press, Boston

Hurley K (2020) College Admission Anxiety: How to Navigate It in the Wake of the Scandal. https://www.psycom.net/college-admission-anxiety-scandal

---

[13] This is argued by both Guinier (2015) and Sandel (2020), for example.

Jaschik S (2019) Massive Admissions Scandal. Inside Higher Ed, March 13. https://www. insidehighered.com/admissions/article/2019/03/13/dozens-indicted-allegedmassive-case-admis sions-fraud

Page S (2018) The diversity bonus. Princeton University Press, Princeton

Petrilli M, Enamorado P (2020) Yes, it really is harder to get into highly selective colleges today comparison of SAT scores over time tells a story. EducationNext.org, 24 March 2020

Reeves R, Halikias D (2017) Race gaps in SAT scores highlight inequality and hinder upward mobility. Brookings Social Mobility Papers. https://www.brookings.edu/research/race-gaps-in sat-scores-highlight-inequality-and-hinder-upward-mobility/

Sackett P, Kuncel N (2018) Eight myths about standardized admissions testing. In: Buckley J, Letukas L, Wildavsky B (eds) Measuring success: testing, grades, and the future of college admissions. Johns Hopkins University Press, Baltimore, pp 13–39

Sandel M (2020) The Tyranny of Merit. Farrar, Straus and Giroux, New York

Steele C (2010) Whistling Vivaldi and other clues to how stereotypes affect us. WW Norton & Company, New York

Whitford E (2021) State Higher Ed Funding Increases for 8th Straight Year. Inside Higher Ed, May 26, 2021. https://www.insidehighered.com/news/2021/05/26/state-higher-ed-funding increased-29-last-year

An Alternative to "Merit" in University Admissions a Comment on the Paper of Ann E. Cudd

Richard Barron Parker

Abstract Richard Barron Parker raises a number of challenges to Ann Cudd article "Merit". Cudd's suggests that addmissions to elite universities should seek diversity and ask what applicants can contribute to the group. To this suggestion, Parker argues that policy is just another type of "merit". He argues that a better policy would be a lottery system.

1. I agree with Cudd that "access inequality" to higher education in America is so severe that higher education itself "is a source of inequality in America". Indeed, the United States is in danger of going the way of Japan, England, and France where admission to the University of Tokyo, Oxford or Cambridge, or the École nationale d'administration is a prerequisite for holding high political office.

I also agree with Cudd that any individual merit standard for university admission cannot be the basis for a fair and just system of university admissions. Cudd suggests instead a system which emphasizes diversity and looks at what the applicant can contribute to the group rather than whether or not the applicant's individual talents merit admission. That is: "...look at how individuals improve the excellence of the group as a whole, rather than seeing merit as measurable individually in isolation from the group."

A problem with Cudd's proposal is that the ability to contribute to the group is just another sort of individual "merit." Sorting out the individuals who have the ability to "improve the excellence of the group as a whole" would require the same huge cast of admissions officers and consequent expense that now burden universities. It is easy to foresee disputes about how to determine which applicants deserve

---

Richard Barron Parker passed away in the Spring of 2021 and was unable to complete a final revision of his chapter. His wife gave us permission to publish this piece.

R. B. Parker (✉)
Portland, ME, USA
e-mail: j.mcgregor@asu.edu

"diversity bonuses" similar to disputes over which tests should be used to determine individual "merit" under the old systems.

I do agree with Cudd that an ability to benefit from and succeed in completing a degree is a necessary requirement for an individual's admission to a particular university, even if this results in "access inequality" for others.

Finally, I agree with Cudd that excellence of education is the major goal in university admissions. America still ranks as #1 in the world in the quality of its universities. We do not want to give that up.

Given all of the above, can we come up with an alternative that (1) allows elite universities to not continue to make judgements of "merit" in deciding whom to admit, and (2) ensures that all those admitted can in fact benefit from their education or succeed in completing a degree and thus (3) preserves the excellence of our elite universities?

2. One answer to the above question is some sort of lottery system. A lottery system for college admission has been a frequent topic for discussion in recent years, especially since the lawsuit against Harvard University by Asian students, which Harvard won in early 2021, and the numerous criminal convictions of parents cheating to get their children into elite universities. (See Google under the search words "lotteries for college admission" for a large number of links to various articles pro and con.)

I would like to suggest a lottery system that avoids many of the common criticisms of lottery systems and yet satisfies conditions (1), (2), and (3) above. I have chosen the University of Chicago for my model because unlike Harvard, Stanford, or most other American elite universities in the United States, the College at the University of Chicago is not the heart of the University. The University of Chicago is centered on its graduate and professional schools. Thus, it might be more amenable to try the lottery system suggested below for its College. And the University of Chicago has a long history of being adventurous compared to its more conventional competitors.

The class of 2024 in the College of the University of Chicago had 34,372 applications, of which 2511 were accepted and 1848 enrolled, an acceptance rate of just over 7%, after the laborious processes described and condemned by Cudd of who has the most individual "merit."

In my suggested system, we need first to establish an outside boundary which ensures that each person accepted into the lottery can in fact benefit from a University of Chicago education, that is, condition (2) above. Do the winners of the lottery have the intelligence and discipline to do the work required of a University of Chicago student? One possible boundary would be to make any valedictorian or salutatorian from any high school in the United States eligible for the lottery. Prospective students could enter the lottery multiple times up to the age of 30. There are roughly 24,000 public high schools and 2000 private high schools in the United States. With two students eligible from each school, that would mean that roughly 52,000 high school graduates would be eligible for the University of Chicago lottery in any given year. Students from prior years would swell the numbers eligible for the lottery. To enter the lottery to enter the University of

Chicago, all that would be necessary would be to send the University of Chicago your name, contact information, and some certification from your high school that you were either the salutatorian or valedictorian of your high school class.

Would Chicago be able to attract enough students to enter its lottery? Probably, especially if people up to the age of 30 could enter the lottery and people could enter again and again until they were 30 years old. The requirement of being a salutatorian or a valedictorian severely restricts the number that could apply from any given high school or prep school. However, the requirement to be a valedictorian or salutatorian ensures that the student will have the ability to benefit and be able to do the work. No matter what the sort of high school, small and rural or large and urban, it is highly likely that a student with the discipline and intelligence to be one of the two best students in their high school class would be able to benefit from a University of Chicago education.

There is some movement among American high schools for doing away with valedictorians and salutatorians on the grounds that such awards generate unhealthy competition among students. Such high schools might be willing to certify one or two students as the best students who graduated in any given year. Any high school teaching staff would have a better sense of who was remarkable in any given graduating class than any admissions committee at a remote university. Such certification could provide entrance into the University of Chicago's lottery. If a high school refused to so certify any students, then students from those high schools would be ineligible for the lottery. Some such certification might also be needed for international students from other systems of secondary education.

Note that the diversity in race and culture would be ensured by the diversity of high schools in the United States. Excellent public high schools, such as the Bronx High School of Science or wealthy suburban high schools, could enter only two students in the lottery in any given year. Excellent private high schools such as Phillips Exeter Academy or St. Paul's School could also enter only two students in the lottery in any given year. Many of the students entering the lottery would be coming from high schools that were often not very good, but they would be the very best students from those not very good high schools.

The actual distribution of students in the Class of 2024 at Chicago is:

Asian	25%
Black or African American	10%
Hispanic or Latino	15%
International	14%
Other categories:	??

Well less than 50% of the Class of 2024 at Chicago are White. Something like the same distribution would result under this proposal for entrance to the lottery, perhaps a bit lower for Asian students and higher for Black and Hispanic students. The sheer diversity of high schools in the United States would ensure diversity in the winners of the lottery.

3. Cudd makes the point that easier admission for the children of faculty, alumni or high-income donors undermines the current system of admission on individual

"merit." We are not interested in sustaining any system of individual "merit" so we can admit some students to the lottery or to the University directly without being "unfair."

Any elite private university needs strong alumni backing and a rich donor class. We need to modify our lottery system to allow for a small percentage of special admissions. There must be some special admissions that can be handled either by admission to the lottery without being a valedictorian or salutatorian or by simply granting a place without going through the lottery at all. For example, the University of Chicago might grant admission to the lottery to any faculty child, or to any one generation legacy. These children would not need to be a salutatorian or valedictorian to enter the lottery. In all of these cases, an independent individual assessment of whether the student could actually benefit from a Chicago education would have to be made. These students would be a small part of the lottery pool.

The greater benefit of a place regardless of the lottery might go to the child of a donor giving $1,000,000 or to a two-generation legacy. Places might also be granted to the extraordinary student who was an Olympic athlete, a world-famous pianist, the author of a prize-winning novel, or a mathematical genius at the Bronx High School of Science with terrible grades in anything but mathematics. In all these cases, an independent individual assessment of whether the student could actually benefit from a Chicago education would have to be made. These students would also be a small percentage of those admitted to the University.

4. Some of the best parts of Cudd's paper are where she details the psychological costs of the current system, fostering an arrogant elite with a false sense of entitlement. Perhaps the major advantage of a lottery system is that it reduces those psychological costs. Instead of people priding themselves on having gotten into the University of Chicago on their individual merit, or feeling terrible because they have not measured up by not getting in, everyone would have to say, "I was just lucky." Or "I was just unlucky."

Collective Merit in University Admissions

Richard T. De George

Abstract This paper argues that Ann Cudd's proposal to replace individual student merit in college admission with her version of collective merit does not succeed in making the procedure more morally justifiable or socially desirable than current procedures. It is not possible to implement it without introducing arguably arbitrary criteria. Her proposal, moreover, involves changing the traditional notion and purpose of the university with insufficient evidence, argument or specification to justify the change.

1   Introduction

In her paper, "Merit in University Admissions," Ann Cudd's main stated thesis is that the current individual merit standard for university admissions" is not "a fair and just system." She does not want to "abandon the whole idea of pursuing excellence" but she argues "that a different conception of collective merit that suggests a different filter for university admissions would better meet the social goals we have for higher education" (Cudd, in this volume, p. 193). In the paper she goes far beyond the issue of fairness in admissions, and proposes a purpose of the university different from the traditional one and a radical change in the nature of the university in order to achieve more inclusive diversity. Access equality is to be achieved by building inclusive diversity into the outcome of the admissions process. Equal results replace equal access, and the change, I shall argue, leads to a very different, vague and questionable notion of excellence from the one of individual merit.

R. T. De George (✉)
University of Kansas, Department of Philosophy, Lawrence, KS, USA
e-mail: degeorge@ku.edu

© The Author(s), under exclusive license to Springer Nature Switzerland AG 2022
J. McGregor, M. C. Navin (eds.), *Education, Inclusion, and Justice*, Amintaphil:
The Philosophical Foundations of Law and Justice 11,
https://doi.org/10.1007/978-3-031-04013-9_15

2 University Admissions

Cudd's paper starts with measurement problems in university admissions. As she correctly points out, individual student applications typically include standardized test score, high school transcripts (GPAs), class rank and sometimes essays, letters of recommendation, extracurricular activities and other similar documentation. Each, taken by itself, is limited and in some ways defective. The logic of her implied argument seems to be that since each of the parts is defective, all of them together must be defective. More importantly, Cudd argues, the notion of individual merit is the wrong notion to use. Those who would like to correct the defects of present criteria to make the entrance requirement fairer are simply trying to find ways to preserve the status quo. Probable success in college, as presently conceived, is probable success in meeting the "cultural expectations of majority white professors and institutions, which are biased toward the majority forms of expression and the status quo of disciplinary knowledge creation" (Cudd, in this volume, p. 194). This seemingly off-hand characterization seems to be an indictment of the whole university tradition. If the aim of the university is to create and transmit knowledge, but all it has done since its inception in the thirteenth century is reflect the cultural expectations of white professors, and that is not knowledge, then what is knowledge, and what is it that universities have been creating and transmitting? What kind of knowledge is the university supposed to create and transmit? What does excellence in education consist of for Cudd, if it is not excellence in the arts and sciences that universities currently teach?

Cudd's paper does not draw out these implications or answer these questions, but rests content with claiming that the entrance criteria considerations the paper has touched on should not be used "as the ultimate measure of merit" (Cudd, in this volume, p. 194). The paper's conclusion is that universities which seek to identify merit as their admissions criterion are engaged in a failed endeavor, which is an obstacle to social mobility on a society-wide scale, benefits the affluent and majority white students disproportionately, is psychologically damaging, and creates unjust social inequalities. The solution which the paper supplies is a reimagining of the purpose of the university, of the notion of merit and excellence, and of the criteria for college entrance.

The paper is correct in citing the deficiencies of all the criteria currently used, which are well documented, well known, and widely admitted. Yet more progress has been made than Cudd's paper would lead us to expect. Many universities have stopped using or requiring the SATs and other similar exams. There is hardly any large university that doesn't have an office of discrimination and inclusion (or something similar). Despite the paper's disparagement of the knowledge it generates, universities are still sought for the knowledge one can learn there and the many advances in science, the social sciences and the humanities that emanate from faculty and graduate student research. The paper ignores the fact that U.-S. colleges have long been seen and have in fact been used by many poor people as the best ticket for their children to get out of poverty, and for immigrant children to advance in society beyond what their parents could achieve. Statistics show that racial minorities are doing better than whites. The National Center for Education Statistics reports that "At the bachelor's degree level, the number of degrees awarded to Hispanic students more than tripled between academic years 2000–2001 and 2015–2016 .... the number of bachelor's degrees awarded also increased by 75 percent for both Asian/Pacific Islander students ... and Black students ..., and by 29 percent for White students.... [T]he share of bachelor's degrees earned by White students decreased by 12 percentage points over this period. American universities are a magnet for foreign students who want to come here to study. They can't be all bad.

As to fair admissions, various proposals have been made, which the paper does not consider. Open admission to state supported institutions for all students who graduate from high school is one that does away with entrance qualifications. If the best criterion of success in college is whether students actually do well in college, then let them all try. Many universities have tried their own affirmative action plans and have made serious attempts to be more diverse and inclusive. They find no place in Cudd's paper.

The admissions processes of the college and universities are far from perfect. But there is a continuing attempt to make them better, fairer and more transparent. Most people are not about to throw them over in favor of something unknown, untested, and possibly with more unfavorable than favorable consequences.

3 The Purpose of the University

Cudd's proposed solution to the problem of fair university admission digs deeply and finds the problem not on the level at which it appears—where, if she is right, it seems intractable—but at the level of re-envisioning the university and its purpose. Cudd's paper starts with the traditional purpose of the university: "Universities exist primarily to create new knowledge, educate individuals, and serve society through related activities and products. . . ." (Cudd, in this volume, p. 191). But it later states, that although universities have different specialties and emphases, "we should see the university admissions as aiming to convene groups of students with faculty and facilities to optimally educate and inspire creative, innovative research in an equitable and democratic environment, with special focus on the areas of education, research and civic engagement that the particular university's mission emphasizes" (Cudd, in this volume, p. 198). While the traditional university puts the individual and his or her education first, the new focus is the good of the university. Hence, the students aren't admitted on the basis of how they can profit from the university, but students are admitted on the basis of what they can contribute to the university and help it fulfill its social mission. The consequence is that the task an admissions committee faces is not choosing the most meritorious students. The proper role of the admissions committee is to choose the best mix of students to fulfill the institution's mission. Since no student has a right to entrance to any particular university, the claim any applicant might make that they were denied admission while less meritorious students were admitted has no traction because merit is not a criterion used.

The key to the new approach to admissions, on Cudd's view, is "to improve its ability to admit a diverse set of students. Diversity serves both the economic productivity and the equality goals of universities" (Cudd, in this volume, p. 199). Diversity now becomes the driver of the new mission of the university and hence of its admissions policy. How these square with the goal of elite institutions bringing together "the most motivated, interested, and accomplished students" seems puzzling until we learn the hitherto hidden benefits of diversity. We are told that "diversity can, when properly nourished, demonstrably improve creativity, innovation, and productivity," and this, presumably is the product of the most motivated, interested, and accomplished students. I wish the demonstration were more persuasive than simply the claims made in the paper, such that "we do our best work collaboratively", "complex problems require groups with multiple tools and perspectives" and the like. All that might be correct to some degree in some contexts (I have never seen a great poem written by a committee), but they do not show that any or all diversity yields these results, or that by gathering a diverse group it will solve problems better than a less diverse group. The elite universities did not become elite because they were diverse.

The aim of the new admissions procedure is to "improve its ability to admit a diverse set of students." This seems to presuppose that a diverse set of students will create new knowledge and educate individuals better than present procedures. "Diversity brings different ideas, ways of thinking and analyzing problems together" (Cudd, in this volume, p. 199). But, of course, it must be the right kind of diversity, the right kind of problem, and the right people. And there's the rub. What kind of diversity is desired, for what purposes, to what extent, who decides and how? For some problems in science, it is helpful to have someone with chemical expertise, a physicist, a mathematician and a computer scientist. Their gender, age, religious or political beliefs, race or country of origin or sexual preferences don't matter. Where diversity helps, do we want it with respect to gender, race, religion (Jewish, Buddhist, Muslim, Catholics, Protestants, and any other?), national origin (from which countries?), politics (liberal, conservative, anarchist, libertarian, other?), rich poor and in between, and any other group I have not mentioned that someone demands, or do we just rely on the categories currently listed by the U.S. Department of Education? According to the U.S. Department of Education today 56% of U.S. college students are women, 44% are men. Does that make men a minority group? If one aim is preparation to engage in the political system, shouldn't we aim to have the various political parties all represented in both the faculty and student body? Is diversity to be achieved through quotas? If there aren't enough motivated, interested and accomplished people (however that is decided) in some approved group, should the admissions committee lower that bar or give up on getting diversity from that group? These are questions the paper does not address. It assumes we all know and agree on what diversity means, and there is reason to doubt that.

Cudd cites Scott Page's interesting model (Page (2018)) and his discussion of "diversity bonuses" (Cudd, in this volume, p. 200). Although his model makes sense when discussing many groups, I think the paper misapplies it in discussing college admissions. In his model "there are only certain kinds of problems where diversity bonuses are possible" (Cudd, in this volume, p. 200). These are open-ended or complex problems, which the paper says are the kinds of issues that universities tackle. But for the most part, the complex problems in a university are not tackled by undergraduates and so they are not applicable in deciding undergraduate admission. Page rightly refers to "a toolbox full of tools that we use to solve problems." But the pertinent toolbox of the beginning freshman, according to the paper, is not represented by grades or performance but is primarily the tools gained by experience, race and cultural background. These are useful in adding diversity of view for some problems. But they are irrelevant for a great many problems. Having students brought up in a different culture or suffering as a minority doesn't automatically make the group of college freshmen better. Even if the claim is that each discipline would be better and more productive if it included more minority members, a greater variety of nationalities, people of different gender preferences, different religions, and so on—an empirical claim that the paper seems to make—it doesn't follow that in all classes with diverse students the students learn more than do students in classes in the same subject with less diversity. It might help in some classes, but it is not clear that it does in beginning Latin, in algebra, in logic or in many other subjects.

Page envisions each individual bringing a toolbox full of tools, and each tool yields a different perspective on the problem. If they are pertinent to the problem at hand, someone who has this tool provides a diversity bonus. The quality of one's tool is also pertinent.

Two points are important. Page's notion of tools makes most sense when a group is faced with a certain specific problem, say, the quick production of a vaccine to fight the Covid-19 virus. For that, we obviously need chemists, pharmaceutical experts, and other specialists. Would the group produce a better vaccine more quickly if pharmaceutical companies hired not only the best people they could, but made sure they had cultural diversity? There seems no reason to think that is the case. If universities tackle complex problems, the same holds true. For each problem certain people with certain skills will be needed. We choose the people because of the skills they bring with them. Not all physicists are equal. Some are better than others. In a word, we look for individual merit. To think and act as if there is no such thing flies in the face of reality. Some people are also better than others at social skills. Part of the purpose of any school, including universities, is to teach students skills they don't have, to enlarge their toolbox. The new approach to university admission seems to deny that students have learned skills in high school which we can test, experiences we can evaluate and which can be used in deciding the likelihood of their both contributing to and profiting from a university education. If they didn't in high school, the paper gives no reason to view what students learn in college any differently.

The second point is that Page's model works well if we have a specific problem that needs solving and we choose the people with the appropriate skills to solve the problem. But the college admissions officers aren't given a specific set of problems that the college or university wants to solve. So, it cannot be the job of the admissions officers to come up with a set of teams that will best solve the problems. Page's model is simply not applicable to university admissions.

It seems that the real aim of the admissions approach Cudd's paper proposes is to make sure that that minorities, immigrants, those typically discriminated against because of gender or race, those from poor areas and schools, and the others in any protected category in the government's list are included in greater numbers than at present, and in sufficiently large numbers that as a group they do not feel that they have been disrespected. That in itself helps the university's mission because the need for such students is built into its new mission.

Given a choice between the traditional statement of the purpose of the university, which puts students and knowledge creation and transmission at its core, and Cudd's proposed alternative, the paper does not convince me that hers is preferable or that it benefits society better.

4   Collective Merit, the University and Fairness

We now come to crux of the new proposed admissions policy. How will it work and will it be fair? Trying to determine individual merit, according to the paper has been a failure and has led to unfairness and so will be replaced. The bearer of merit is now the group and in admissions the group is the freshman class. The admissions team has to decide on the appropriate criteria it wishes to use to select individuals from among the applicant pool. What diverse tools will be required? If the admissions department can answer these questions, the next question is: how will they know which applicants have the appropriate tools, since grades, etc., are not appropriate? Finally, what does it mean to speak of the merits of the group, how does one determine this, and are those merits automatically held by and represented by all the individuals in the group? If the merits are the merits of a group, what happens when one leaves the group?

Cudd's paper suggests one approach is to "ask ourselves what constitutes the ideal university student body as a collective" (Cudd, in this volume, p. 202). The paper says, "Selecting students in this holistic way is a hard problem to solve in itself, but the solution is clearly not a method that results in a group of mainly white, affluent students." According to the U.S. Census Bureau, white people make up 76.5% of the U.S. population; in some states, including Maine, Vermont, New Hampshire and Idaho, the percentage of whites is between 92 and 95%. Given those figures how can Cudd be so sure that, if the system is fair, it will not produce a majority of white students? If we know in advance that it will not, what criterion of fairness is being used? If we think a priori that race should be represented in our ideal university in proportion to the percentage of each group in the population, the ideal numbers should be easy to determine. The ideal number according to racial percentage would vary from state to state. If some other method is used, as it must to make sure there is appropriate diversity according to the paper, how is it determined? The paper says to consider the ideal university student body as a collective. But we can't know what the ideal is unless we are told what problems the collective is being assembled to solve.

Whatever method the university admissions people aim for as the ideal make-up of the university body, they will have to be able to justify it as being fair. From the perspective of the graduating senior in high school, a now stressful situation will become a nightmare. They will be judged not on any merit or excellence they may have (unless perhaps they excel in sports). Their grades will not count, nor will any test, or essay or anything which should demonstrate what their toolbox looks like because what will be judged is how they fulfill the needs of the student body being selected. The criteria used may well vary from university to university. It will certainly sound like a random selection process with certain pre-determined outcomes, which are not revealed, being used to determine their future. Why is this blind (as far as the applicant goes) process fairer than the current method of selection? It certainly appears to consist of a host of subjective judgments made with little or no objective data. One must simply take the word of the admissions officer that some particular individuals were not chosen because they would not have made the whole better than the applicants chosen. How fairness can be determined and demonstrated is not made clear in the paper, nor is it clear how students can prepare for college.

5 Excellence

Cudd's paper defends the possible social role for elite, publicly supported, higher education in a democracy. Excellence, we are told "advances innovation and discovery, leading to economic benefits" (Cudd, in this volume, p. 202), among other benefits. But "... if we do not aim for excellence in university admissions, then we will fall back on some other way of distributing scarce education, such as what we are actually doing now, which is according to economic and white skin privilege" (Cudd, in this volume, p. 203). Under a scheme that does not recognize individual merit, what does collective merit look like and where does it come from if not from excellent students? Even more difficult, how is the admissions committee supposed to determine the motivation and interest necessary for excellence except by looking at individuals and their history?

Now consider that the place we are to look for excellence is in the collective student body. How are we to determine excellence there? It cannot be through the individual merit of the members because they have no individual merit. If the collective we are to look at is the freshman class, the problem remains. We cannot simply assume that because the student population is diverse that ensures that all classes are better, whether or not the classes themselves are properly diverse. How can a university ensure that? Let us try to think through what a student is expected to do in each year. At present students decide their path through a four-year period. They are guided to some extent by requirements. They are not assigned a task which is part of the joint effort in the school's attempt to solve the problem it has been assigned or chosen. It is not clear how the new model is to work unless all decisions are made by the administration for the student. Unless students are assigned courses and majors to ensure proper diversity how can we guarantee that all classes and majors have the required diversity to produce excellence? How many engineering students have to be women for women not to feel less than full members? If all women want to major only in women's studies, will they be allowed to do that, even if no men enroll as students? Since in the U.S. the majority of the people are white, will the university be allowed to be majority white? If students continue to be free to choose their courses and majors, having the "proper mix" of diversity does not seem to make any difference from what we presently have, except that some preordained kind and measure of diversity has been ensured up front. Why that is fairer than the present system is not clear.

Consider further the students who graduate. All the problems involved with individual merit are replicated in dealing with collective merit. What standards are used to measure collective merit, who sets the standards, and how are they applied? Students cannot be judged on individual merit because that doesn't exist. So prospective employers and professional schools will fall back on the merit of the collective from which they graduated. Although the criteria used is unclear, it is most likely the elite schools will be found to have the best teams or groups. Job applicants from elite schools will obviously have the edge, because they come from an elite collective, and they will be chosen in the same proportion as they are now. The applicants can claim no individual merit but only point to the merit of the collectives of which they were a part. But because they were successful in filling out the group in college says nothing about their ability to fit into a particular group on the job. Under the new plan, there is no individual merit to consider. As for professional schools, there will probably be just as many applicants trying to get into the elite schools as there are now. How those schools will justify choosing students if not on their accomplishments will be interesting to see. In any event, it is difficult to imagine that the selected individuals will not think they are special because they were chosen to be on elite teams at elite institutions. Employers will be all the more likely to choose graduates from the elite schools and then go down the pecking order of schools. Those who succeed are still going to have more opportunities upon graduation, are still going to be perceived as an elite, and are going to perpetuate hierarchy in society. It will be harder for the very talented individuals to be recognized despite the school they went to because only collectives will be evaluated, not individuals. The resulting disadvantaged group may be different from what it is now but the same sort of injustice seems likely to remain.

6 Conclusion

In sum, Cudd's proposal, insofar as I understand it, has more difficulties in being implemented than the present system. The paper offers it as the solution to a moral problem of injustice. The moral argument has not been sufficiently discussed or made out for all schools to jettison the devil they know for the devil they don't know. Full disclosure and informed consent are parts of fairness. Institutions using the new approach must make clear to all possibly interested applicants what its admission criteria are, how applicants will be chosen, and how students will be evaluated, if at all. One kind of injustice should not be replaced by another without stronger justification than the paper provides.

I wish Cudd's paper gave us the solution to fair admissions; but so far as I can see, the proposal it provides has as many problems as the policies it hopes to replace, except that we don't have the empirical data to back up or to dispute its claims. Given that, I conclude that there is still room for many kinds of universities and for many different admissions criteria, none of which is perfect; that our moral obligation is to do the best we can to ensure fairness; and that the nature and mission of the university should remain what they been for a long time.

References

Department of Education. National Center for Education Statistics. FAST FACTS: Degrees conferred by race and sex. Https://nces.ed.gov/fastfacts/display.asp?id=72

Index Mundi. United States - White Population Percentage by State. Https://www.indexmundi.com/facts/united-states/quick-facts/all-states/white-population-percentage#map

Page SE (2018) The diversity bonus. Princeton University Press, Princeton

University Admissions, Non-Ideal Justice, and Merit: Comments on Ann Cudd

Leslie Francis and John Francis

Abstract Ann Cudd reconceptualizes merit in university admissions as a property of the student body collectively rather than individual students. Her aim is to preserve selectivity while addressing inequality. Reconceptualizing "merit" as "collective" merit, Cudd thinks, can justify differential admissions standards in light of the goals of higher education. This comment raises concerns about Cudd's positive account of "merit" as a group-based characteristic. Our argument is that her claims about the relationship between diversity and merit are conceptual and rooted in ideal theory, rather than in the functioning of actual universities in the not-very-just circumstances of the United States today.

1 Cudd's Account of Merit

In "'Merit' in university admissions" Ann Cudd explores the interface between inequality of access to higher education and "merit" as a criterion for admission. Her aim is to reconceptualize merit in a way that preserves selectivity while addressing inequality. Reconceptualizing "merit" as "collective" merit, she thinks, can justify differential admissions standards in light of the goals of higher education. We agree with Cudd that there are many problems with how "merit" is understood in current admissions priorities and the measurements used to try to implement these priorities. In this comment, however, we raise concerns about her positive account of "merit" as a group-based characteristic. Our argument is that her claims about the relationship between diversity and merit are conceptual and rooted in ideal theory,

L. Francis (✉)
University of Utah, Department of Philosophy, Salt Lake City, UT, USA

S.J. Quinney College of Law, Salt Lake City, UT, USA
e-mail: francisl@law.utah.edu

J. Francis
University of Utah, Department of Political Science, Salt Lake City, UT, USA
e-mail: john.francis@utah.edu

© The Author(s), under exclusive license to Springer Nature Switzerland AG 2022
J. McGregor, M. C. Navin (eds.), *Education, Inclusion, and Justice*, Amintaphil:
The Philosophical Foundations of Law and Justice 11,
https://doi.org/10.1007/978-3-031-04013-9_16

rather than in the functioning of actual universities in the not-very-just circumstances of the United States today.

Cudd's positive account of "merit" relies on these three claims:

1. University admissions should aim to assemble a student body that will best achieve the mission of the university at issue.
2. "Merit" should be understood in light of the mission of the university at issue.
3. Different universities have different missions, but all that are publicly subsidized must include social purposes as part of their missions. These social purposes include innovative research for sustainable economic growth, social justice, and democratic equality. These social purposes are at least as important as the contribution of education to flourishing lives for the students attending the university in question.

These claims tie merit to mission, and, for public universities, mission to social purpose. To be fair to Cudd, it is important to note that the links she draws between merit, mission, and social purpose are flexible and admit of significant variation. Cudd does not argue for a univocal view of social purposes: her view is that these purposes include innovative research for economic growth, social justice, and democratic equality. Other social purposes might be compatible with these purposes, such as furthering the arts, preserving languages or cultures, or fostering community. Moreover, universities may pursue social purposes in different ways; some might further economic productivity through science, while others might emphasize social justice through internships or community service.

In addition, the tie Cudd draws between mission and social purpose is not exclusive, even for public universities. Cudd leaves open whether a public university's purpose could include goals other than the social purposes she mentions. So, a public university might both have a social mission and have a mission of helping students live flourishing lives or perhaps even providing a social context in which they may form life-long friendships or find mates. As we read Cudd, these other missions may exist but must be compatible with the public university's social purpose.

Despite this flexibility, on Cudd's view one common thread is essential for a public university: the link from merit, to mission, to social purpose. This is the connection through which diversity enters: it is necessary to the social purpose of the University, however that social purpose is conceived. Because diversity is necessary to the social purpose of the University, without diversity there can be no merit. Admissions thus should focus on creating a meritorious collective, a good student body. Cudd writes, "We should ask ourselves what constitutes the ideal university student body as a collective and this precludes looking at each individual in isolation from the whole."[1] Admissions criteria then may be structured to yield a meritorious group, rather than a group made up of meritorious individuals. These criteria may

---

[1] Cudd, this volume, p. 202.

differentiate for diversity. So, Cudd contends, "merit" must be a property of the collective.

But how does Cudd reach the conclusion that merit is a characteristic of the student body, rather than of individual students? According to Cudd, diversity is necessary to achieving the goals of innovative research and democratic equality. It is not fully clear, however, whether her claims about diversity are empirical or conceptual. On the one hand, she seems to assert only that research is far more likely to be innovative, because diversity "can, when properly nurtured, demonstrably improve creativity, innovation, and productivity." Moreover, diverse individuals will ask different questions and bring different ways of thinking. On the other hand, Cudd also seems to say that a practice cannot count as democratically equal unless it is diverse. She writes: "demonstrating diversity symbolizes and communicates respect across diversity, whereas a lack of diversity, particularly in a group that has high status, projects a lack of respect for minoritized or excluded groups." This is not the empirical claim that a non-diverse group will actually behave in a manner that is exclusionary or disrespectful. Rather, it appears to be the claim that lack of diversity is per se a failure of the respect requisite for excluded groups.

Cudd concludes that "merit" must be viewed "holistically." As we understand her, the conclusion she wishes to draw here is that groups, rather than the individuals who make them up, are the bearers of merit. She argues for this group-based conception of merit based on the contributions made by diversity to innovation. However, it does not follow from the idea that innovative research requires diverse perspectives and the tools this diversity brings that merit must be understood as a characteristic of groups. Whether Cudd can draw the conclusion she wishes depends on whether her claims here are empirical or conceptual.

1.1   Diversity's Contribution as an Empirical Claim

Suppose we take Cudd as maintaining empirical claims about how diversity contributes to the social purposes of the university. That is, in order to assess the significance of a particular feature of an individual, we need to see how that feature fits with the features of other individuals, as well as the circumstances around the individual. A skill of one individual may be more valuable when it supplements or enhances the skills of others than when it duplicates them. Skills that are useful in one context may not be useful in another. Additional skills of a given type are less useful when tools of that type are in oversupply than when they are scarce.

From these empirical claims, however, all that follows is at most is that merit is a relational characteristic, a characteristic of individuals in relation to one another in a given context. Admissions criteria should then measure the contribution of the individuals to the group, not a characteristic of the group itself. The facts are highly likely to be that differences among individuals matter, so diversity matters. How this plays out will depend on how the university defines its social purposes, the mix of individuals in its applicant pool, and the needs of the university in the context in which it operates. In any given context, it is possible to consider the kinds of tools that are predictably likely to be useful. Universities have some general ideas of the needs of the day, the kinds of technologies that are currently available, the likely backgrounds and interests of potential applicants, and the problems to be solved. In admissions, they can seek to select for a reasonable distribution of the tools students have or might develop, along with the interests students might have in deploying and developing them. But this falls short of viewing merit as a collective property. Rather, it supports seeing merit as involving how individuals fit into the more general situation of a public university's conception of its social purposes.

A background problem for university admissions in the United States today is that many decisions must be made in a defined time frame. This poses particular difficulties for public universities that receive many more applications than they have room for entering students. For example, the University of Texas-Austin received 57,241 applications for admission in 2020, admitted 18,290 of these, and actually enrolled 8459 entering students.[2] The University of Michigan received 10,606 applications from in state students, admitted 47.5% of these, and actually enrolled 3542 in state first-year students. Michigan received 54,415 out of state applications and admitted 21.9% of these, of whom 28% actually enrolled.[3] In such situations, there will need to be some kind of decision procedure for sorting students to generate an approximate distribution of the required tools.

Different sorting procedures are possible. At present, Texas uses an automatic rule for 75% of its entering class: students in the top 6% of their high school graduating class qualify. The extent to which this rule yields a diverse set of admitted students is contested. The Texas rule appears to have had limited impact on the numbers of high schools sending students to UT-Austin, absent additional scholarship or recruitment efforts.[4] Texas is one of the states with the greatest gap between the percent of Latino/a admissions to the state flagship university and the percent of Latino/a high school graduates in the state.[5] On the other hand, the students qualifying automatically for admissions to Texas are significantly more diverse than the 25% of students admitted through holistic scrutiny of their individual qualifications.[6]

---

[2] Texas Admissions (2021). https://admissions.utexas.edu/explore/freshman-profile.

[3] Michigan News (2020), University of Michigan undergraduate enrollment steady for fall 2020. https://news.umich.edu/university-of-michigan-undergraduate-enrollment-steady-for-fall-2020/#:~:text=Among%20in%2Dstate%20students%2C%2047.5,and%20international%20students%20who%20applied.

[4] Jill Barshay (2019), Texas 10% policy didn't expand number of high schools feeding students to top universities. The Hechinger Report. (July 18). https://hechingerreport.org/texas-top-10-policy-didnt-expand-number-of-high-schools-feeding-students-to-top-universities/.

[5] Meredith Kolodner (2018), Many state flagship universities leave black and Latino students behind. The Hechinger Report (Jan. 29). https://hechingerreport.org/many-state-flagship-universi ties-leave-black-latino-students-behind/.

[6] Matthew Watkins (2017). UT-Austin changes automatic admissions threshold from 7 to 6 percent. The Texas Tribune (Sept. 15). https://www.texastribune.org/2017/09/15/ut-austin-raises-automatic-

Michigan "look(s) at each student as a whole package, a combination of talents, interests, passions, and skills."[7] The result of this process is a student body that is significantly less diverse than the population of the state.[8]

Other proxies for a diverse tool set are also possible. For example, a university looking for aesthetic intelligence as a tool can consider whether the student has played a musical instrument, acted in a school play, or created an art portfolio. Holistic admissions may also take into account a student's likely major or stated academic interests. The strategy looks remarkably like admissions practices at many universities today, including both Texas and Michigan. As an empirical matter, different choices about the interests to select for may yield different diversity mixes at a university. It cannot simply be assumed that diversity of interests or talents will map onto diversity of socio-economic status, ethnicity, or race, or the reverse.

1.2   Diversity's Contribution as a Conceptual or Normative Claim

The strategies of universities such as Texas or Michigan do not try to curate an ideal group. Rather, the strategies look at most for a variety of individual skills, interests, and backgrounds in hopes that the result will be significant diversity. Or, like the Texas top 6% rule, they aim to yield a class that will admit students from a wide variety of high schools throughout the state, possibly thereby yielding diversity.

To reach the conclusion that merit is a characteristic of the group, present only when the group is diverse, requires more. Perhaps the claim is simply that a diverse student body is a more meritorious one. But this is to state the conclusion Cudd wants, rather than to argue for it.

Cudd does seem to believe that further reasons support the link between collective merit and diversity. The most likely link is that without diversity of the group, the university will fail in its social purpose. This claim cannot be only that the university will in fact be less likely to be innovative; innovation can be achieved through selection mechanisms that assure that the individuals making up the university have different interests, talents, backgrounds, and experiences. Instead, the view would need to be that the social purposes of the university must include diversity of

---

admissions-threshold-6-percent/#:~:text=Texas%20students%20who%20graduate%20in,Texas%20at%20Austin%20in%202019.&text=The%20change%20is%20the%20result,each%20year%2C%20school%20officials%20said.

[7] Michigan Admissions (2021). Selection Process. https://admissions.umich.edu/apply/first-year-applicants/selection-process.

[8] Id. The entering freshman class at Michigan was 3.99% Black, in comparison to a state population that is 14.1% Black, U.S. Census (2019). https://www.census.gov/quickfacts/MI.

the group, along the lines of Cudd's claims that diversity is needed to signal respect or democratic equality.

Cudd might further defend this claim by writing as an ideal theorist—that is, as a theorist of a university within an ideal of a just society. Universities are important institutions in societies and should surely play a role in what it is for a society to be just. A society would not be ideally just if its public universities did not evidence respect for democratic equality.

The contemporary distinction between ideal and non-ideal theories of justice originated with John Rawls's determination in *A Theory of Justice* to set aside non-ideal theory and focus instead on ideal theory as a starting place.[9] In the intervening fifty years since *A Theory* was first published, discussions of non-ideal theory have taken many different forms, including theorizing about what justice might require in a society that is in important respects unjust and theorizing about what should be expected of individuals when others around them are behaving unjustly.[10]

While Cudd does not state specifically whether she is thinking as an ideal theorist or as a partial compliance theorist, much of what she says suggests that she is thinking in ideal theory terms. She writes, for example, "In pursuing the admissions goal of crafting the class, we should ask ourselves what constitutes the ideal university student body as a collective and this precludes looking at each individual in isolation from the whole."

We question the advantages of this approach for university admissions. In the first place, it is unclear what an ideal university might be in a just society.[11] To say that it would be a university that mirrors the justice of the society is vacuous, unless we know what the just society looks like. Likely it would be a university that honors values associated with justice, such as freedom of thought or inclusion of difference. Honoring these values, however, does not require attributing merit to the group or recognizing any particular mix as the desired kind of diversity.

Moreover, universities operate in today's world, confronting the structural injustices that shape their applicant pool and the characteristics of those making up that pool. Public universities confront additional problems, such continuing declines in public funding and questions about the levels of public support in their states. These factors suggest that in assembling the mix of students making up an entering class, public universities may be faced with conflicting pressures for spaces in their entering class.

Approaches to justice in partial compliance contexts differ in important ways. Some argue that we should measure justice in non-ideal contexts in terms of linear progress towards justice. Others argue that we should instead consider multiple factors that contribute to improving the justice of current circumstances. The latter view suggests that university admissions are a complex balancing act, involving both

---

[9] Rawls (1971).

[10] For an overview of approaches to non-ideal or partial compliance theory, see Valentini (2012).

[11] See Sen (2009), for more general questions about ideal theories of justice.

efforts to enhance inclusion and caution about using criteria that risk compounding existing structural injustice.

A compounding problem is that universities need money and support to survive. Public funding cannot be assumed. Financial support from alumni and from the community and the state matters. A clear problem with giving these factors too much weight is that they may simply compound injustice, further entrenching privilege. Some data suggest, however, that elite schools do more in augmenting the intergenerational income mobility of people of color who are admitted than white students who are admitted.[12]

In today's world, the balancing admissions of a university like Texas may be the best we can do to encourage innovation. Texas attempts to respond to the diversity of the state by guaranteeing admission to students reaching a high rank in their high school class. Texas also reserves 25% of its admissions spaces for a more holistic evaluation process, taking into account a variety of features of individual students in their applicant pool. This kind of balancing process may be the best that can be done for contemporary public universities responding to the pressures that they face. It recognizes that "merit" can take many forms. But it does not require reconceptualizing merit as a property of the group rather than of the individuals within the group.

References

Rawls J (1971) A theory of justice. Harvard University Press, Cambridge

Sen A (2009) The idea of justice. Oxford University Press, Oxford

Valentini L (2012) Ideal vs. non-ideal theory: a conceptual map. Philosophy Compass 7(9): 654–664

---

[12] Chetty et al. (2017) Mobility Report Cards: The Role of Colleges in Intergenerational Mobility. The Equality of Opportunity Project, https://opportunityinsights.org/wp-content/uploads/2018/03/coll_mrc_summary.pdf.

Collective Merit as an Alternative to Individual Merit in University Admissions? Some Comments on Ann Cudd's "Merit in University Admissions"

Alistair M. Macleod

Abstract Ann Cudd provides a persuasive critique of university admissions policies that are grounded in the so-called "merit system", (a) where this is a system that calls for applicants to be admitted on the basis of their "individual merit" and (b) where their performance in test-scores of various sorts is treated as a reliable proxy for individual merit ((b) is an important qualification here. Cudd's critique of a "test-score-based" approach to university admissions could in principle be accepted by a defender of "individual merit" as a crucial criterion for admission **if**—extremely implausible though the possibility is—some "test-score-**independent**" proxy for "individual merit" could be devised.). She also assembles a compelling list of the many ways in which applicants for admission under this system suffer serious psychological harms whether admission is secured or denied.

However, her argument has a number of intriguingly puzzling features. (1) How is her claim that "unequal access" to institutions of "higher education" is an ineliminable feature of defensible admissions policies to be squared with her recognition that the social goals universities must pursue include the provision of the kinds of *general* education needed—and needed equally—by *all* the members of a society? (2) Again, why does she think that cultivation of (what she calls) a "growth mindset" in all the members of a society would be desirable? (3) Finally, what is the rationale for her attempt to link a university's pursuit of the goal of "inclusive diversity" with endorsement of (a collective version of) a *merit*-based admissions policy?

A. M. Macleod (✉)
Philosophy Department, Queen's University, Kingston, ON, Canada
e-mail: macleoda@queensu.ca

1 General Education as Part of the Mission of the University?

The first question raised by Ann Cudd's paper[1] concerns a tension between (a) what the (agenda-setting) introductory passages identify as her most general claim about "higher education"—viz. that it inevitably contributes to "inequality" in society because higher education admissions policies are necessarily access-restricting[2]—and (b) her recognition (in the body of the paper) of the multiple "social goals" universities (as prototypical institutions of "higher education") ought to serve.[3]

It's true that the educational services universities provide in medical and engineering schools and, more generally, in programs geared to the development of the skills and competences needed in certain other expertise-requiring occupations[4] can be provided to **only some** (often rather small) sub-classes of the members of society. But no such access restrictions are either needed or appropriate when universities are pursuing several of the other "social goals" Cudd lists with approval.

One of the social goals Cudd mentions with approval is the goal of facilitating the living of "flourishing lives" by the members of a society. She writes[5] that "a university education **contributes to flourishing lives for those who consume it.**" (Emphasis supplied.) This is of course true. But its truth doesn't mean that provision of an education that contributes to the living of a flourishing life is **exclusive** to such institutions of higher education as universities. No such restriction can be ascribed to Cudd. It is **not** an implication of her recognition that universities can contribute to the living of a life of flourishing that this sort of education should be available **only** to those members of a society who are fortunate enough to go to a university.

Later in the same paragraph,[6] after noting that the goal of "improv(ing) the productivity of the members of society" is "furthered greatly by mass education," Cudd goes on to identify, as yet another goal that universities justifiably pursue, the goal of "nurtur(ing) democratic habits and values that promote democratic equality." Here too Cudd's claim is obviously correct. But it doesn't mean—nor does Cudd

---

[1] Cudd, in this volume, pp. 191–204.

[2] Cudd, in this volume ("Because not everyone can attain a higher education and because of the stratification of institutions and their unequal benefits, higher education is a source of inequality in society.")

[3] Cudd, in this volume, pp. 197–198 (The "social purposes" in question are set out in the section on "**University admissions to achieve social purposes.**").

[4] Examples might include programs provided by Schools of Public (or Business) Administration or by Schools of Architecture. It's important, however, to recognize that universities, as institutions of "higher" education, do not—and arguably **could not**—have a mandate to provide training programs for **all** skill- or expertise-demanding occupations. Even if no notice is taken of the crucial role played in the development of specialized skills by "on-the-job" training, universities can't be expected to mount programs, for example, for the training of firefighters, carpenters or long-distance truck drivers.

[5] Cudd, in this volume, p. 198.

[6] Cudd, in this volume, pp. 198–199.

take it to mean—that this is one of the **distinctive** functions of a university education. Any such narrow reading of the goal of "nurturing democratic habits and the
values that promote democratic equality" would be self-defeating. For democracy to
be promoted in any society, democratic attitudes must be fostered in **all** its members,
not just in those who receive a university education.

The upshot is that since Cudd would reject any suggestion that the kinds of
education that "contribute to flourishing lives" or that "nurture democratic habits and
values that promote democratic equality" should be available only to selectively
determined groups within a society (only, perhaps, to those who go to universities or
colleges), it's puzzling why she seems to claim (at the beginning of the paper) that
institutions of "higher education" are unavoidably committed to admissions policies
that contribute to "inequality in society".

One more point that Cudd rightly notes is that selective admissions policies must
be consistent with the ideal of "fair equality of opportunity." However, this ideal
must be satisfied by educational programs to which universal access should be
provided no less than by restricted-access programs. It's consequently important
for recognition to be given to an often unnoticed (and certainly under-emphasized)
distinction between two conceptions of "fair equality of opportunity" in educational
contexts. For the first of these versions of the ideal of fair equality of opportunity,
educational opportunities must be made available to **all** the members of a society
without exception: a primary education, for example, must be provided to all
children. But for the second version, universal provision is neither necessary nor
feasible. For example, opportunities for admission to training programs for skill-
demanding occupations need not—indeed cannot in principle—be provided, strictly,
to absolutely all the members of any society, both for "division of labor" reasons[7]
and because not all members have the relevant talents and ambitions. But whenever
access to educational services can be made available to only certain (typically quite
small) sub-classes of the members of a society, the second version of the ideal of
equality of educational opportunity cannot be satisfied unless the criteria for
restricted access are appropriately identified and applied. Preferred access shouldn't
be provided, for example, on the basis of such considerations as race, color, creed, or
socio-economic status.

---

[7]In a "division of labor" society, there can be no single occupational group to which all members
belong.

2   Is Fostering a "Growth Mind-Set" in the Members of a Society a Desideratum?

A second possible criticism of Cudd's argument arises out of a suggestion she makes when discussing Carol Dweck's book on the psychology of success.[8] Cudd notes that admissions policies based on the "merit system" tend to generate, in student applicants, a sense that "innate intelligence" or "innate intellectual talent" is what's crucial to securing admission to university. Both students whose applications are successful and applicants who fail to secure admission often internalize this attitude. In Dweck's language, a highly undesirable "mindset" is then "fixed"—a mindset that encourages successful applicants to see themselves as possessing "innate intellectual talent" and that induces unsuccessful applicants to see themselves as simply not having, unavoidably, what it takes to secure admission. Understandably, Cudd follows Dweck in finding this sort of "fixed mindset" deeply disturbing. She finds it objectionable for two reasons. The first is that it mistakenly identifies possession of "innate intellectual talent" as the key to success in university admissions contests. The second, relatedly, is that it seems to imply that there's hardly anything applicants themselves have in their power to do to secure admission. The truth, as Cudd sees it, is that such things as "motivation, interest, encouragement, and practice"—things that are largely within the control of individual applicants—are important determinants of success. "For almost any university-level skill or topic," she writes, "these are the attributes needed to succeed, not some specific innate talent," and she adds (borrowing the expression "growth mindset" from Carol Dweck) (a) that the belief "that almost anyone can succeed in almost any skill given dedication, practice, and good coaching is the idea of *the growth mindset*," and (b) that "if we want to build a society of educated self-directed people, then we want to encourage *a growth mindset* in everyone."[9] (Emphasis supplied.)

But would it be desirable to "encourage a *growth mindset* in everyone"?

Part of what Cudd wants to encourage under this head is of course incontestably desirable: potential applicants should recognize the various ways in which things that are subject to their control can contribute to success in university admissions. However, a "growth mindset" **as defined** is open to objection for overstating the degree to which applicants have it in their power to secure a university place. Even when applicants make every effort to do the things that Cudd's list represents as crucial to success—and even when, for good measure, "innate intellectual talent" is abandoned as a putative key to gaining admission—considerations that are entirely beyond the control of individual applicants sometimes play a decisive role in the securing of a university place. For example, applicants are powerless to determine how many acceptances a university is in a position to offer. Again, applicants cannot

---

[8] Dweck (2006).
[9] Cudd, in this volume, p. 197.

know either how many other applicants there are or how strong their applications are.

There is consequently a downside to a "growth mindset" both for successful and for unsuccessful applicants. In successful applicants, it can generate the sort of *hubris* that Michael Sandel reports he finds in many of the students in his classes—a false sense that they have secured a university place entirely because of the effort they have expended and the hard work they have done.[10] On the other hand, internalization of the sort of "growth mindset" Cudd describes can induce unsuccessful applicants to believe that they have only themselves to blame for failing to win a place—a belief that can have a (sometimes lasting) impact on the confidence with which they approach the challenges of life.[11]

3   Promoting Inclusive Diversity and "Collective" Merit?

A third question Cudd's paper raises has to do with her suggestion that when universities give an important place in their admissions policies to the goal of promoting "inclusive diversity," these policies can continue to be characterized as "merit"-based provided a collective version of the notion of merit is adopted. How is this to be understood?

Part of what Cudd has in mind is clear—viz. that once the "merit" system (with its emphasis on "individual merit") has been rejected, one of the fundamental goals a university should pursue when it is making decisions about whom to admit is the goal of "inclusive diversity." She provides examples of what she takes this goal to encompass and also offers several arguments in support of its adoption. Thus, in spelling out the "economic productivity" argument for this goal, she claims that "inclusively diverse groups are more innovative, productive and responsive to a wider range of social issues."[12] Again, she argues that "inclusive diversity" is required by "democratic equality" because, as she puts it, "demonstrating diversity symbolizes and communicates respect across diversity whereas a lack of diversity, particularly in a group that has high status, projects a lack of respect for minoritized and excluded groups."[13]

---

[10] Sandel (2020), p. 60. "Beginning in the 1990s and continuing to the present, more and more of my students seem drawn to the conviction that their success is their own doing, a product of their effort, something they have earned. ... most voice the conviction that they worked hard to qualify for admission to Harvard and therefore merited their place. The suggestion that they were admitted due to luck or other factors beyond their control provokes strong resistance."

[11] It is particularly regrettable when unsuccessful applicants for admission to a university or college internalize the belief that they have only themselves to blame for not getting the place for which they had applied when the belief itself is often more likely to be false than true. After all, many of the determinants of success are beyond the control of applicants.

[12] Cudd, in this volume, p. 199.

[13] Cudd, in this volume, p. 199.

However, even if "economic productivity" and "democratic equality" arguments for the goal of inclusive diversity are accepted, it's puzzling why Cudd goes on to try to represent "inclusive-diversity-promoting" admissions policies as **merit**-based policies.

She recognizes, of course that inclusive-diversity-promoting policies can't be merit-based in the way required by the "merit system" with its insistence on the importance of **individual** merit. But she claims they can still be characterized as merit-based if "merit" is conceived as **collective** merit.

But how is the collective version of the merit criterion to be understood?

The possibility of a "collective" version cannot be rejected on the ground that the notion of merit can only be applied intelligibly to individuals. The commonest application of the notion of merit in most contexts is indeed to **individuals**—and this is the use that's at issue when, under the "merit system," university admissions officials try to admit applicants "on merit." However, there's no conceptual barrier to characterizing **groups** as satisfying a merit standard. For example, merit can be the criterion for awarding the top prize in a juried musical competition to the **group** the judges deem to be the best, and in sports contests, a hockey **team** may secure the right to represent a country in the Olympics on "merit" because it is deemed to be the best of all the teams competing for the honor.

However, it's not at all clear that Cudd's argument for making "collective merit" the centerpiece of a defensible university admissions policy calls for attention to focus on the sort of "merit" that groups, as distinct from individuals, can exhibit. It's not the case, for example, that universities have to decide whether or not to grant admission to a **group** of some sort—that is, a group that is seeking admission **as a group.** Even when all the members of an identifiable group—the graduating class at a particular school, say—happen to be seeking admission to a specific university, and even when (in the event) all of them are successful in gaining admission, it would be a mistake to suppose that the university had granted admission to that school's graduating **class**. On the contrary, while it would have granted admission to the individual members of that class—to **all** the members, as it happens—it would still **not** be the **class** as such that had been admitted.

Moreover, there's an interesting feature of merit-based judgments that seems not to be met in the sort of case Cudd presents, the case where a university's admission policies reflect its pursuit of the goal of "inclusive diversity." The reason is that whether the notion of "merit" is being applied to individuals or to groups, the basis on which the application is made must be some action or quality (or some set of actions or qualities) ascribable to the individuals or groups in question. Thus, when the individual merit criterion, as understood by university admissions officials who are operating under the aegis of the "merit system", is represented as satisfied by a given applicant, it is that individual applicant's actions (for example, that applicant's performance in whatever test-scores are deemed to be merit-conferring) that provide the basis for the university's decision to grant admission. Similarly, when the notion of merit is applied to a group of some sort (a hockey team, or a music quartet, say), it's some group feature—something the group as a group can do—that contributes to its being selected "on merit." Thus, a hockey team may be selected on "merit" to represent a country at the Olympic Games, and "merit" may be the basis on which a music quartet is selected as the star attraction in an upcoming musical festival.

However, when it comes to Cudd's invocation of her "collective" version of the merit criterion for the fashioning of a university's admissions policy, it's neither the case that those who are admitted form an antecedently identifiable **group** nor (*a fortiori*) that any action attributable to that **group** provides the basis or ground for representing the group as satisfying the university's "collective merit" standard.

How, then, are we to identify the group that might be thought to meet this standard?

It seems to be an implication of the general description Cudd provides of the "collective" version of the merit standard (as well as of the examples she gives) that the members of the "inclusive-diversity-exhibiting" group that the university hopes to form by the admissions policies it adopts are **not** some identifiable subset of those who are **applying** for admission. Rather, most of the members of the group she has in mind are an identifiable subset of the **existing** student body (the student body constituted by those who **have already been admitted**) and the applicants whom the admissions committee have an opportunity, under Cudd's "inclusive-diversity-promoting" admissions policy, to add to this group will have to qualify for admission **as individuals**!

If this is correct, it seems to follow that "collective merit" **cannot** serve as an alternative criterion to "individual merit" for determining which of the applicants **should be granted admission**, for two reasons. First, the individuals who are granted admission under this policy do not belong to any identifiable **group of applicants**: they still qualify for admission because of the qualities they have as individuals. Second, the qualities that make them successful applicants are qualities that happen to be in short supply in the parts of the existing student body within which they will be pursuing group projects after they are admitted—which means that the qualities in question get their salience from considerations over which the applicants have no control. The qualities in question consequently don't qualify as merit-conferring qualities in any sense of "merit."

The conclusion to be drawn about Cudd's discussion of "inclusive diversity" is that, while she presents interestingly powerful arguments for regarding it as one of the goals universities ought to pursue, and while pursuit of this goal can be a partial determinant of the shape of a university's admissions policies, her representation of the rationale for "inclusive-diversity-promoting" admissions policies as merit-based—as satisfying a putative "collective merit" principle—is mysteriously problematic. For one thing, successful applicants under such policies are still granted admission **as individuals**—individuals who happen to have qualities a university needs to promote its own goal of enhancing inclusive diversity within the student body—rather than qualities they have **as members of some identifiable group of applicants**. Moreover, the qualities that bring success don't even qualify as merit-conferring qualities, because their salience is indebted to the assessment by admissions committees of the contribution the qualities in question can make to the university's achievement of the goal of inclusive diversity. Successful applicants may be pleased that they have been granted admission and pleased too, perhaps, that their admission will help the university achieve the goal of inclusive diversity, but if they can take no personal credit for the fact that they happened to have the qualities that provided (at least a crucial part of) the basis for admission, there's a conceptual barrier to their being regarded as having been granted a place "on **merit**."

References

Dweck C (2006) Mindset: the new psychology of success. Ballantyne Books, New York
Sandel M (2020) The Tyranny of Merit. Farrar, Straus & Giroux, New York

The Merits and Demerits of Collective Merit: Replies to Commentaries on "Merit in University Admissions"

Ann E. Cudd

Abstract The commentaries to "Merit in University Admissions" raise several important objections to the notion of collective merit and how it could be used in university admissions processes. This opportunity to provide a reply allows me to clarify my critique of the way individual merit is currently used in university admissions and my idea of collective merit. I am grateful to Amintaphil for a conference format that encourages the writing of multiple commentary papers, and to the editors of this volume for capturing the benefits of the format by publishing this symposium.

I will respond to the commentators by grouping together in four sections similar critiques. First, I respond to what I take to be points where the commentators and I deeply disagree, such that no reconciliation or clarification can resolve the matter. The second section attempts to clarify my views about university missions and the role of diversity in fulfilling them. The third section replies to objections from the commentators that "collective merit" is incoherent or misguided as an approach to university admissions. The fourth section responds to commentators' views about how university admissions should or should not be conducted.

1 Deep Disagreements

One type of disagreement I would characterize as the commentators holding that there is no problem with the current system of university admissions that relies on individual merit; the status quo is fine. Both Richard DeGeorge and Alistair Macleod argue this in their commentaries. I emphatically reject these claims. The most significant problem is that universities, at least in the US and similar competitive admissions systems of higher education, compound privilege on the affluent and majority racial and ethnic groups, contributing to the rise in social inequality. I

A. E. Cudd (✉)
University of Pittsburgh, Department of Philosophy, Pittsburgh, PA, USA
e-mail: acudd@pitt.edu

© The Author(s), under exclusive license to Springer Nature Switzerland AG 2022
J. McGregor, M. C. Navin (eds.), *Education, Inclusion, and Justice*, Amintaphil:
The Philosophical Foundations of Law and Justice 11,
https://doi.org/10.1007/978-3-031-04013-9_18

maintain that the concept of merit as it is currently employed in admissions contributes significantly to this problem.

Further, I argue that the concept of merit as it is used in university admissions is confused and counterproductive. The concept is confused in the case of "merit scholarships," which are more of a marketing ploy than a real indicator of individual excellence (e.g., the most elite institutions do not give "merit" scholarships). They are typically used to price discriminate to bring in students who fit a certain test score range that the university wants to compete to enroll, and who can pay the balance of the cost of attendance. Merit scholarships lead to greater economic and social inequality because they artificially inflate the sticker prices of institutions, creating a situation that more affluent students can game in a variety of ways. The current understanding of merit and measures of merit limit diversity in the student body and are thus counterproductive to maximizing innovation and dynamic learning environments and to bringing about greater equity and inclusion in society.

Macleod argues that competitive university admissions do not create social inequality by limiting access to credentials and experiences because there are other ways that people can find happiness. But clearly many people who are excluded from it value higher education and the higher incomes that come with the credentials that one can only earn through higher education. Therefore, it is a problem of justice if these goods are not fairly distributed.

DeGeorge writes that the lack of diversity in universities is not a problem. He argues that affirmative action has improved diversity enough. He writes, "statistics show that racial minorities are doing better than whites." (p. 66) But his evidence for this is that the percentages of underrepresented minorities have increased over the past 20 years, not that equity has been achieved. In fact, the percentage of Black (36.3%), Hispanic (38.3%), Native American (18.8%), and Hawaiian and Pacific Islander (20.4%) students between the ages of 18–24 who are enrolled in college lag significantly behind White (42.2%) students. (ACE 2017, p. 40) This inequity is much more pronounced if only four-year, not-for-profit institutions are included. (ACE 2017, p. 49)

DeGeorge further maintains that more cultural diversity is not necessary to make groups better, that diversity cannot help in certain kinds of classes, that there is no evidence for the existence of diversity bonuses, and that affirmative action has improved diversity enough—equity is being achieved already. He says that cultural diversity is not important for many kinds of technical professions: "would the group produce a better vaccine more quickly if pharmaceutical companies hired not only the best people they could, but made sure they had cultural diversity? There seems no reason to think that is the case." (p. 213) Perhaps cultural diversity did not make a difference in creating the new MRNA vaccines, but we have clearly seen that cultural diversity plays a critical role in persuading people to take the vaccine, which therefore can play a role in creating and manufacturing it. For example, there is a large group of people who refuse to take vaccines that are connected to fetal tissue research because of its connection with abortion, which they object to on religious grounds.

DeGeorge raises doubts about the existence of a diversity bonus. I cannot offer an original argument for this, but I respond with citations from a large body of existing research (see Levine 2020; Page 2017; Phillips 2014), and point out that firms seem to believe in the importance of diversity and inclusion (Green 2021). DeGeorge also doubts that even if there are diversity bonuses, there is no need for diversity bonuses for the kinds of courses or research experiences that undergraduates take. For one thing, courses like algebra or logic involve basic skills that do not involve group work that requires diversity. But modern pedagogies do suggest that group work and active learning is useful even to learn basic skills. Working in groups allows individuals to view problems from a different perspective and forces group members to articulate their approach to thinking about problems. Diversity enables these different perspectives and viewpoints that facilitate these educationally beneficial aspects of group work. DeGeorge also intimates that the problems or questions that undergraduates take up as well as the methods they are able to employ to solve them, are not original research, and therefore it is not necessary to seek diversity bonuses, if they exist. But again, modern pedagogical techniques emphasize active learning with real world problems, such as experiential learning, engaged and laboratory research, and collaborative research, which undergraduates do take on these days. DeGeorge further thinks that cultural identity diversity is not automatically important. "Having students brought up in a different culture or suffering as a minority doesn't automatically make the group of college freshmen better." (p. 213) I agree that it doesn't *automatically* make them better, but this is the kind of diversity of experience and perspective that is likely to bring about diversity bonuses in many kinds of problem-solving, research, and community service situations we want our students to experience. For example, an important learning experience for our pharmacy students in the pandemic has been to provide vaccine clinics for the public. One of the main problems to solve in this endeavor is vaccine hesitancy, and one valuable solution has been for people from similar cultural backgrounds to understand and address obstacles, beliefs, and fears specific to the culture. Having students with diverse cultural backgrounds has been helpful in raising the vaccination rate and thereby accomplishing their goals in the experiential learning situation.

Macleod says that it is not good for society to cultivate a growth mindset in everyone because those who are not admitted to universities will blame themselves for their situation, while those who are admitted will see themselves as inherently better than others. Macleod attributes to me the view that a growth mindset is the belief that one can gain admission to a university if one puts forward enough effort. My view is rather that a growth mindset is the belief that almost anyone can succeed in learning almost any skill given dedication, practice, and good coaching. Having a growth mindset does not concern what one can achieve in a competition for socially determined rewards that are subject to biases and gaming, such as university admissions. My aim with the focus on collective merit is to lower the emphasis on individual innate ability and desert in university admissions so that students neither give up because they believe that they cannot learn as well nor put forth less effort because they believe that they need not try as hard. Having a growth mindset, like having an optimistic outlook more generally, motivates people to learn more, which I maintain is a good thing for everyone.

2 Clarifying My View: Mission, Diversity Bonuses, and the Collective in "Collective Merit"

DeGeorge charges that the way I describe their missions is university-centric rather than student-centric: "While the traditional university puts the individual and his or her education first, the new focus is the good of the university." (p. 238) This confuses the mission of the university and the purpose of the admissions process with the operational tactics that achieve the mission. While universities educate students as one of their three main traditional aims (education, inquiry, and outreach), they do so within a context and constraints defined by their mission. The mission defines the special areas of emphases, the degree to which the university emphasizes research and community outreach as compared with teaching, whether and in what fields graduate or professional education is offered, and so forth. Defining this mission does not make a university less student-centric in its operations, but it does contextualize the admissions selection process (and the faculty hiring process). Not every individual will want to attend or benefit from attending every university. Different universities have different missions. I argue that at least publicly supported ones, including traditional (e.g., land grant) universities, have commonalities in their missions. Namely, to support research and innovation to create sustainable economic growth, social justice, and democratic equality, in addition to educating students who can benefit from their educational offerings (a mission which all universities share).

John Francis and Leslie Francis point out that innovative research can arise without diversity, which is obviously true, but not problematic for my view. I only need to claim that diversity brings out more innovation in order to argue that university admissions should aim for diversity in the student body. They argue that "admissions criteria should then measure the contribution of the individuals to the group, not a characteristic of the group itself." (p. 221) I agree with this clarification. My point is that the goal in admissions is to assemble a group that can optimally learn, discover, and innovate together, an attribute of the group which I call collective merit, and they should choose individuals so as to achieve that goal. But Francis and Francis are correct to say that they should choose individuals according to the contribution they expect those individuals to make to that potential collective excellence, and that does not contradict my view. I am arguing that the way we have assessed individual merit in university admissions as contextless and absolute is mistaken and warrants stepping away from the term in a radical way so as not to continue the same way of thinking.

3 Replying to Objections to Collective Merit as Incoherent or Misguided to Use in Admissions

Macleod argues that "collective merit" cannot refer to either an attribute of a group or of an individual. First, he argues that there is no identifiable group or collective that is admitted but rather a set of individuals, each of whom is admitted. While it is true that we admit each individual one by one, that does not preclude us from speaking of the "class" that has been admitted as a group. Admissions officers and other administrators regularly report about the class that has been admitted: their aggregate qualities, median scores, and average or median gpa. Just as a team of ballplayers is composed of players recruited one by one does not preclude us from speaking of the team and characterizing its collective merits, so we can speak of a class of students and characterize its collective merits.

Second, Macleod argues that the term merit does not apply since the qualities that make the admitted students successful applicants are "qualities that happen to be in short supply in the parts of the existing student body." And this "means that the qualities in question get their salience from considerations over which the applicants have no control. The qualities in question consequently don't qualify as merit-conferring qualities in any sense of 'merit.'" (p. 233) I have two responses to this point. First, just because a quality is one over which one has no control does not mean that it cannot qualify as a "merit" if by that term we mean something like a good-making quality. Even setting aside determinism, there are many good-making qualities for students that one does not have control over if one believes, as I argue, that identity or cultural diversity can be a good-making quality. Second, the concept of collective merit is designed (by me) to be an attribute of the collective, to which the successful applicant is judged to contribute. The fact that the value of the contribution of the individual is relative to the existing group does not take away from the idea that it is a good-making, i.e., meritorious, contribution that the individual brings.

4 Admissions Standards That Take Into Account the Collective Merit of the Student Body Is Unfair to Students, Will Cause Students More Stress, Impractical, or Politically Unwise

DeGeorge argues that my solution will make things worse: more stressful and less fair. He writes:

> Their grades will not count, nor will any test, or essay or anything which should demonstrate what their toolbox looks like because what will be judged is how they fulfill the needs of the student body being selected. The criteria used may well vary from university to university. It will certainly sound like a random selection process with certain pre-determined outcomes, which are not revealed, being used to determine their future. (p. 215)

First, I do think grades, test scores, essays *and other indications of the applicants' toolboxes* should be considered in an admissions system that looks to create collective merit in the class. Second, the criteria will assuredly vary from university to university, but in this way the new system would not be different from the current system. Third, while it will be difficult for applicants to know why they have been admitted or not to a particular school, that is also currently the case.

The difference with the collective merit approach is that one cannot blame one's individual efforts, failings, abilities or other attributes for one's admission or failure to be admitted to a particular school. While DeGeorge concludes that "from the perspective of the graduating senior in high school, a now stressful situation will become a nightmare. They will be judged not on any merit or excellence they may have," (p. 215) I maintain that the entire admissions process will create less stress because it is less tied to some supposed, objective, absolute, fixed individual merit or excellence. My goal in moving away from the (unfairly rigged and biased) individual merit system is to make it clear that one's fate in the admissions process is not due to one's individual attributes alone, but rather to the way in which one can be seen to contribute to the student body as a whole, given the attributes of the other students and the mission of the university. An important goal of my approach is to deflate the sense of both individual accomplishment and individual failure, so that university admissions is not seen as a competition for status and hoarded by elites.

Francis and Francis argue that the admissions process that they infer from my view would be impractical, and emphasize that admissions decisions have to be made at scale on a tight timeline. First, I didn't actually offer any details of an admissions process. I agree that in designing one we need to take into account the feasibility of the process under the actual constraints in the real world. In fact, I have been closely involved with operating and changing the admissions process of a large public university and I am very familiar with the kind of investments needed to make less reliance on test scores and create a more diverse class in the legal context in which racial preferences are highly contested. I also agree that the University of Texas top n% rule is a good one as a starting point, given the racial, ethnic, and socio-economic segregation that currently exists in Texas high schools. But as Francis and Francis point out, it has not yet resulted in the diversity that would be hoped for and needs to be supplemented by outreach to the primarily non-white high schools that do not send students to UT. I am not prepared to offer an alternative admissions process in detail here, but there are two important points I want to make based on my experiences. First, making test scores optional in applications is likely to result in a more diverse class than either ruling out any scores (and thereby disallowing students with poor gpa's for whatever reason to show that they have academic abilities in some important areas) or using test scores as the primary means of selecting applicants for admissions or scholarships. Second, reallocating scholarship monies from so-called merit to need-based financial aid also results in a more diverse class socio-economically and racially and meets other equality goals.

Francis and Francis further caution that the admissions procedures that take collective merit into account might make matters worse from the perspective of justice. They state that we do not live in an ideal world, but rather a non-ideal state of partial compliance with the rules of justice. In a partial compliance world, they argue, "university admissions are a complex balancing act, involving both efforts to enhance inclusion and caution about using criteria that risk compounding existing structural injustice." (p. 224) The compounding problem they allude to is that even public universities cannot rely on the state to support them, and so they need to appeal to donors and alumni, as well as legislators and governing board members. In appealing to these powerful stakeholders, universities risk reinforcing the status quo or losing funding that is necessary for subvening the cost of offering high quality education regardless of need. I see this as a serious balancing problem, but not a special problem for admissions procedures that take collective merit of the student body to be the aim of admissions. We could take that to be the goal but keep that in the background and employ rhetorical tactics that appeal to the particular audience. This is why I emphasize the "business case" that rests on the bonuses that diversity brings, rather than the moral imperative to increase diversity, as Scott Page also recommends. (Page 2017)

Finally, Richard Parker also argues that using collective merit for an admissions process would be impractical. He proposes a lottery system that allows any valedictorian or salutatorian of any high school in America to enter multiple times up until age 30. Then this is to be supplemented with any other criteria that the university wishes, including legacy, donations, staff benefits, or specific, narrow, but prodigious talent—provided that these students can be shown to be able to benefit from the education. Parker justifies this system on the grounds that:

- it eliminates individual merit as the criterion for admissions; admitted students could only say "I was just lucky";
- it is easy to implement;
- it guarantees diversity because of the diversity of high schools;
- the additional students would be small in number, so not undermine the aforementioned benefits.

This suggestion has some merit because it guarantees ethnic/racial/socio-economic/geographic diversity, like the University of Texas guaranteed admissions system. Also, I grant that at least the lottery aspect of his admissions system is relatively easy from the university's point of view to administer, though I would point out that it may be difficult for high schools to designate the lucky individuals, since there are often either many valedictorian/salutatorians, because of ties, or none, as some high schools that do not rank students at all. In any case, high schools would be forced to make the choices.

I object to his solution, though, because it relies on individual merit and brings the same problems that I have discussed. First, these students will not say "I was just lucky". They will believe that they deserve admission because of their individual merit (they are valedictorians or salutatorians, after all), so it does little to deflate the sense of accomplishment or failure, except in the few students who are valedictorians/salutatorians who do not gain admission to their favorite university. Second, these students eligible for admission will be the ones who can please high school teachers, not the innovators, the talented, the peer leaders. This will put pressure on the second part of the admissions system to bring those in, if we want collective excellence. Finally, legacy and donor admissions run counter to either collective merit or individual merit based admissions systems, and they compound advantage and inequality. They should be eliminated.

In conclusion, I maintain that individual merit as it is currently used in the university admissions context leads to social inequality and compounds advantage on the affluent. It should be replaced by allowing collective merit, a measure of the educational and creative potential of a group of students, to be the goal for university admissions. Collective merit can best be achieved by assessing how students contribute to the potential, given the composition of the group as a whole.

References

American Council on Education (ACE) (2017) Race and Ethnicity in Higher Education: A Status Report. https://www.equityinhighered.org/indicators/enrollment-in-undergraduate-education/race-and-ethnicity-of-u-s-undergraduates/

Green J (2021) Companies scramble to hire diversity officers, but progress is slow. Los Angeles Times. https://www.latimes.com/business/story/2021-03-12/companies-are-scrambling-to-hire-diversity-officers

Levine S (2020) Diversity Confirmed to Boost Innovation and Financial Results. Forbes. https://www.forbes.com/sites/forbesinsights/2020/01/15/diversity-confirmed-to-boost-innovation-and-financial-results/?sh=1f249b10c4a6

Page SE (2017) The diversity bonus: how great teams pay off in the knowledge economy. Princeton University Press, Princeton

Phillips KW (2014) How diversity makes us smarter. Scientific American. https://www.scientificamerican.com/article/how-diversity-makes-us-smarter/